THE EASTLAND TRADE AND
THE COMMON WEAL IN THE
SEVENTEENTH CENTURY

THE EASTLAND TRADE
AND THE COMMON WEAL
IN THE SEVENTEENTH CENTURY

BY

R. W. K. HINTON

ARCHON BOOKS
1975

Library of Congress Cataloging in Publication Data

Hinton, Raymond William King.
    The Eastland trade and the common weal in the seven-
teenth century.

    Reprint of the 1959 ed. published by Cambridge Uni-
versity Press; Cambridge.
    Includes bibliographical references.
    1. Eastland Company.   2. Great Britain—Commercial
policy.   I. Title.
HF486.E75H5 1975   382'.0942'048   74-18125   ·
ISBN 0-208-01483-7

Printed in the United States of America

CONTENTS

PREFACE

In the seventeenth century Englishmen had a lively idea of common weal and national interest. This book is a study of the application of that idea in a single sphere, namely, in the trade of English merchants with the Eastland.

The word 'Eastland' here stands for the area of the Baltic Sea and Scandinavia, which was the area reserved for the Eastland company by their charter of 1579. It was not a very exact word in contemporary usage. A more precise term was 'East country', which, however, denoted only the ports or lands on the eastern side of the Baltic Sea about Danzig, Elbing and Königsberg, perhaps as far as Riga. These countries were the 'eastern parts'. Scandinavia was more correctly 'northern'. A seventeenth-century man speaking about the 'Eastland' trade always meant the 'East country' trade but did not necessarily mean to include the Eastland company's other trades. When the Eastland company was founded there were only two branches of the Eastland trade, the East-country trade and the Norway trade. During the seventeenth century a Stockholm trade developed. These are the trades discussed in this book.

Common weal and national interest was a less nebulous idea than it sounds and gave rise to precise questions of policy. Was it for the common good to favour the Eastland merchants at the expense of the clothiers? Was it in the national interest during the Thirty Years War to encourage Gustavus Adolphus at the expense of the Eastland merchants? An important question for this study recurs in instructions to councils of trade through the century—'Whether it be necessary to give way to a more open and free trade than that of companies and societies?' History is commonly more familiar with the answers to questions like this than with the questions themselves. It is possible sometimes to forget that the questions were ever asked, so easily do the answers fall into patterns and cloak themselves with an air of inevitability. Familiar landmarks in the history of the Eastland company are:

> 1579, a charter of privileges for the Eastland company;
> 1622, a proclamation giving a further privilege;
> 1630, a proclamation giving yet another privilege;
> 1673, an Act of Parliament taking some privileges away.

But on what grounds were these answers arrived at?

We begin with an introductory chapter on the Eastland trade up to 1620. Detailed examination starts in Chapter II with a study of the great depression of 1620 from which emerged the proclamation of 1622. The book ends about 1700, which is roughly the date of the end of the Eastland company.

Even in a purely economic study the Eastland company would remain the principal character. A fictitious person, it is the author of documents and cannot escape prominence. The people who matter, its members, have not, so far as is known, left records that survive. One feels the lack of them. The acts and ordinances of the company between 1618 and 1688, as they were copied into a book belonging to the residence at York, were edited, together with extracts from the York court book from 1650 to 1697, by Miss Maud Sellers in 1906. Some studies of the formation of the Eastland company and of the trade before 1620, which make it possible to move rapidly over the early years, will be cited in Chapter I, but the only general accounts either of the trade or of the company appear to be Miss Sellers's introduction and a few pages in the economic histories of Cunningham and Lipson.[1]

A source of great value (which was not available to Cunningham or Miss Sellers) is the six-volume Danish Sound Tables, the *Tabeller over Skibsfart og Varetransport gennem Øresund* by Miss Nina Bang and Knud Korst, the first volume of which was published in 1906. These are tables of ships and goods compiled from the Sound toll registers, which were kept to assist the collection of the King of Denmark's duties on trade through the Danish Sound. These records are unique. They are supposed to be more accurate after 1618 than before. The Eastland trade cannot usefully be studied without them, and with them we may have of the Eastland trade probably a more exact knowledge than of any other English trade of the seventeenth century.

The reasons for beginning this study in 1620 are, then, that work has already been done on the earlier period and that the Sound Tables are of doubtful reliability before 1618; but it is hoped that the introductory chapter will be found useful. The depression of 1620, which has long deserved a study in its own right, is the subject of Chapter II. It introduces, with its proclamation of 1622, a period of high privilege. This period is examined in Chapters III–VI. The suggestion is sometimes found that privileges of monopoly in the Elizabethan and early Stuart period owed their origin to a 'spirit of monopoly' or 'principle of restriction'. If this implies that the privileges were useless, the history of the Eastland trade

---

[1] *The Acts and Ordinances of the Eastland Company*, ed. M. Sellers (Royal Historical Society, London, 1906); W. Cunningham, *Growth of English Industry and Commerce in Modern Times* (Cambridge, 5th ed. 1912), 234 ff.; E. Lipson, *The Economic History of England* (London, 3rd ed. 1934), II, 315 ff.

does not support it. The privileges of the Eastland company were *ad hoc* solutions to particular problems. They were a form of government. It cannot be said that they were an entirely satisfactory form of government, but they were granted for the general good of the common weal. In this respect the study of the Eastland trade seems to throw a reflected light on other trades and to tell us something about the mercantile system as a whole. In the chapter on the crucial depression of 1620 it therefore seemed justifiable to range more widely than a study of the Eastland trade would strictly require. Again, where the history of the Eastland trade involves the Navigation Act of 1651 the Sound Tables with their precise evidence about the Eastland trade in particular invite one to reconsider the position of English foreign trade in general. The treatment of the Navigation Act (Chapter VII) is new in some points and two contemporary pamphlets are printed in the appendix to support it. The Navigation Act was a turning-point. It did what privileges had done, and so made privileges less useful. From that date the Eastland company begins to decline. The history of the decline of the Eastland company is the history of the growth of the state (from Chapters VIII to the end), and on this theme the book finishes. The second part of the book is therefore a study in what Cunningham called 'parliamentary Colbertism'; the first part is about unparliamentary Colbertism: the difference appears to be that parliamentary Colbertism employs a higher degree of direct state control.

The Eastland trade has become generally known as a trade that was important in the scheme of English commerce by virtue of its imports of naval stores. This proposition is only partly true and may lead to mistaken inferences. The question of the importance of the Eastland trade is discussed in Chapters IV and VIII, for the periods respectively before and after about 1650.

The chief movements and landmarks in the Eastland trade are: in the sixteenth century, expansion; in 1597, a peak year followed by contraction; in 1620 and 1649, crises; and in 1675, a boom, largely sustained. These can be seen in the tables at Appendix D and the figure at the end of the book. Chapter III is an account of the trade between the crises of 1620 and 1649, based on the Sound Tables and the English port books. Chapter XI is an account of the trade from the crisis of 1649 to the end of the century, for which the main sources are the Sound Tables and the ledgers of the Inspector-General of Imports and Exports. But a complete description of the Eastland trade would require a better knowledge than we now possess of the economic history of western Europe and especially of Holland, which was the centre of European commerce. From the economic point of view the Eastland was a primary producer. Its economy was intimately linked, through Amsterdam, with the economies of France and Spain. The link with England was subordinate. Many questions that suggest themselves in the history of Anglo-Eastland trade therefore remain unanswered.

One of the minor uses of the Sound Tables is as a check on the literary forms of evidence, petitions and so forth, which would otherwise be the major part of the evidence. The result is interesting. Petitions generally contain some numerical statements; rare and conspicuous, these are much used by historians; they turn out to be literally correct but sometimes highly misleading; for example, when the Eastland company give a figure for their 'former' cloth exports, it may be a true figure for the exports of one highly exceptional year. Yet this does not mean that the tenor of the petition is unjustified. Figures in documents of those days were intended more as illustrations than as numerical proof, and the proposition that they illustrate may be true even when the illustration appears to be exceptional. In this sense all the Eastland company's petitions state the position correctly. Literary evidence is in such disrepute that it is pleasant to say this word in its defence.

An illuminating new source has been the treasurer's book of the Eastland company from 1661. Mr N. C. Hunt drew my attention to it and the Russia Company have kindly allowed me to consult it. It contains among other things the names of persons taking their freedom, which I have thought worth collecting in an appendix. One hopes that other books will come to light.

The bulk of the manuscript material is in the Public Record Office, but I have also used by permission manuscripts in the Bodleian Library and in the Pepys Library of Magdalene College, Cambridge.

It is a pleasure to acknowledge my gratitude to the late Professor Eli Heckscher for an invigorating conversation when this work was in its first stages; to Professor Astrid Friis and to Professor Aksel Christensen for advice about the Sound toll registers; to Dr H. S. K. Kent for some help with the Norway trade. The list should be longer. I must acknowledge with special gratitude, however, the criticism and constructive suggestions of Mr C. H. Wilson. Mr E. A. Wrigley was kind enough to comment on some of the chapters to my advantage. Mrs A. M. Millard and Mr B. E. Supple have allowed me to use some of their material.

A version of the present book was awarded a Prince Consort Prize in 1950 and this book could not be published without the help of the Prince Consort Prize Fund.   R. W. K. H.

PETERHOUSE
CAMBRIDGE
January 1957

ABBREVIATIONS

A.P.C.	*Acts of the Privy Council of England* (has reached 1628)
B.M.	British Museum
Cal.S.P.Dom.	*Calendar of State Papers Domestic*
D.N.B.	*Dictionary of National Biography*
E.H.R.	*English Historical Review*
Ec.H.R.	*Economic History Review*
H.M.C.	Historical Manuscripts Commission
Trans.R.Hist.Soc.	*Transactions of the Royal Historical Society*

In the Public Record Office:

E 190	Exchequer, King's Remembrancer, Port Books
P C2	Privy Council Register (in course of publication as *A.P.C.*)
SP 14*	State Papers Domestic, James I
SP 16*	State Papers Domestic, Charles I
SP 18*	State Papers Domestic, Interregnum
SP 29*	State Papers Domestic, Charles II
SP 75	State Papers Foreign, Denmark
SP 88	State Papers Foreign, Poland
SP 95	State Papers Foreign, Sweden
SP 105	State Papers Foreign, Archives of British Legations (including books and papers of the Levant Company)

★ These series have been calendared in *Cal.S.P.Dom.*

Chapter I

INTRODUCTORY: THE EXPANSION OF THE EASTLAND TRADE IN THE SIXTEENTH CENTURY

In the sixteenth century there was a great increase in sea-borne trade through the Danish Sound. The major part of this trade was handled by Hanseatics and Dutch, and the most important single commodity was rye. Rye, the product of Poland, was shipped from Danzig and a few neighbouring ports, and found its way to the countries of western and southern Europe from Norway to the Mediterranean. Much of it went through the Dutch entrepôt at Amsterdam. As the corn trade expanded, Dutch merchants became the most powerful group in the Baltic. For corn, they exchanged salt, wine and fish.

English merchants and English ships began to go to the Baltic at the same time. They had traded there in the fourteenth century but had retreated from it in the fifteenth. In 1497 the Sound Tables show no English ships passing through the Sound, but in 1504 they show a few and in the 1530's they show enough to denote a regular trade, while in the 1560's and 1570's they show numbers that stand comparison with the numbers for most of the seventeenth century. Still it was a small number compared with the total of all nations' ships. In round numbers we may say that a hundred English voyages was normal at the end of the sixteenth century (though there were large fluctuations from year to year), when the total figure approached three thousand, and the Dutch figure alone was about fifteen hundred. The English ships brought to England corn and other Baltic commodities, and took to the Baltic English cloth, including, as the staple export, expensive dyed and dressed cloth made in Suffolk and Essex. The Sound Tables first record ships' cargoes in 1562; from that date for many years the only cloth exported to the Baltic was English cloth in English ships.

The return of the English to the Baltic was part of what we commonly know as the Elizabethan expansion of trade, though, as in some other trades, it had its beginning a little earlier. There was also a revival of trade with Norway, whence English merchants had withdrawn at about the same time as they had turned their backs on the Baltic; so that the whole of our Eastland trade was expanding at the same time. In the same period English ships and merchants began to make voyages to the Mediterranean, to Africa, to Hamburg, to Russia.

HET

This Elizabethan expansion was properly a geographical one, a redistribution into wider channels of the trade that had formerly been largely concentrated on the Low Countries. An increase in volume of exports had taken place somewhat earlier, culminating under Henry VIII, when English trade was still in the main tied to Antwerp, and in a sense, therefore, the opening of the Eastland trade was only the removal of one strand of the old trade to a more distant market. But it was not unimportant. For one thing, the exports probably earned more in the new market, because they were carried further, because they were predominantly finished cloth whereas the Antwerp market absorbed largely unfinished cloth, and because, while the big expansion in cloth exports took place under Henry VIII, some even higher points were sometimes reached subsequently. Mainly, however, it was important because it gave employment to fair-sized ships, carried the name of England farther afield, and reduced the galling and dangerous (if profitable) dependence on the Low Countries.[1]

The movement into the Eastland was therefore a victory. To explain it one may speak of the troubles in the Low Countries and the sack of Antwerp, but the voyages to the Baltic preceded these. Queen Elizabeth harried the Hanseatic merchants in England, but English merchants could hardly have penetrated to the Hanseatic homeland on 'policy' alone. The vital factor was probably that they had a commodity to sell there on favourable terms and one for which there was an increasing demand. This was cloth—*finished* cloth, which they could afford to offer better cheap than cloth either made and finished in the Low Countries or made in England and finished in the Low Countries; for, as is well known, the sixteenth-century price rise came to the Low Countries earlier than it came to England. The Eastland bought this cloth, as it bought wine, salt and all the other western goods of which it stood in need, with corn. Through the sixteenth century, as we have seen, the volume of Baltic corn exports increased, and their value increased too because they were sold to countries where prices were rising fast. Thus, the more corn that passed to these rewarding markets, the more English cloth was bought in the Baltic and the more it yielded. Likewise when Baltic naval stores were in demand in Spain to fit out an Armada or a fleet for the Indies, doubtless

[1] On Tudor trade: P. Ramsey, 'Overseas trade in the reign of Henry VII', *Ec.H.R.* 2nd series, VI (1953), 173 ff.; F. J. Fisher, 'Commercial trends and policy in sixteenth-century England', *Ec.H.R.* X (1940), 95 ff.; L. Stone, 'Elizabethan overseas trade', *Ec.H.R.* 2nd series, II (1949), 30 ff.; N. J. Williams, 'The maritime trade of the East Anglian ports, 1550–1590' (unpublished dissertation, 1952, Bodleian Library), 109 ff. It is difficult to link up the early story of the Eastland trade with the story of sixteenth-century trade as a whole because the main evidence for the latter, being based on consolidated customs returns, is by nature general, whereas the Eastland trade was only a very small part of it.

the English cloth exporter felt the benefit. Furthermore, in England too the demand for Baltic products was increasing. Eastland naval stores were needed not only to resist the Armada but to build ships for the ordinary course of the expanded Elizabethan commerce, including the Eastland trade itself. And as the price of domestic English corn rose—and it rose very steeply from about 1530—so we must imagine a growing demand, especially in years of scarcity, for the cheaper imported Baltic rye. This trade by itself could well have been handled by Hanseatics or Dutchmen, but since Englishmen had penetrated to the Baltic on the strength of their cloth they were the better able to handle their own imports.

In this light the English expansion to the Eastland appears as a subsidiary venture in the general expansion of Baltic trade of which the Dutch were the chief agents and beneficiaries, resting on the ability of England to supply cloth at competitive prices. No new thing, probably. In the distant past, when there had been English factories at Danzig and Bergen similar to those now being re-established, dyed and dressed cloth was the English export; when the English gave up those outposts the Dutch were trading there more and more; and when the English confined their exports to the Low Countries these consisted of white cloth, unfinished. It is therefore possible to imagine English commerce swinging to and fro over the centuries between the distant markets and the nearby one, according as the English gained or lost control of the finishing processes; and to read back into the Middle Ages the same cross-Channel rivalry that is the main feature of the seventeenth century.[1]

We have an interesting account of Poland, with sidelights on Polish trade, from the English traveller Fynes Moryson, who journeyed there in 1593. From Elbing, where the English merchants were then living, he visited Danzig. He describes the granaries. 'The garners for laying up of corn...are very fair, and very many lying together, in which the citizens lay up corn brought out of Poland, and according to the wants of Europe, carry it into many kingdoms, and many times relieve fruitful provinces in time of casual dearth.' Moryson gives an impression of Poland in these words:

The revenues of the king and gentlemen are moderate, scarce sufficient to maintain a plentiful table, and to exchange with merchants for wines and spices (which they much use, especially in dressing of fish) and for foreign stuffs and cloths of silk and wool.... [Poland] hath some, but very few mines of gold and silver....It abounds with honey.... It yields great quantity of wax, flax, linen cloths made thereof, hemp, pitch of both

[1] On medieval trade, see *The Cambridge Economic History of Europe*, II, ed. M. Postan and E. E. Rich (Cambridge, 1952), 232–56.

kinds, masts for ships, boards and timber, rich furs, salt digged out of pits, amber, soap-ashes, and all kind of grain, especially rye, which hath made Danzig famous, for relieving all nations therewith in time of dearth.

No marvel then if merchants bring unto them silks of Italy, cloth of England, wine of Spain, and the very spices of India, with most remote commodities, since they not only sell them at what price they list, but also bring from thence such precious foresaid commodities. Poland is all far within land, excepting Borussia (vulgarly Prussia)...and the very inhabitants of Borussia have but few ships, using strangers to export their commodities. Poland aboundeth with the foresaid most necessary commodities, and the people live content with their own; yet are they not rich, because they want the foresaid foreign commodities far brought, and so dear. And they have so little gold and silver, as despising all in respect of it, they sell all commodities at a most low rate, especially those which are for daily food, and unfit to be exported.[1]

Nothing struck Fynes Moryson more forcibly than this general cheapness. The observation was based on his own experience of the cost of meals and horsemeat and of the ordinary expenses of the traveller, which he hardly ever failed to note down, and is a true reflection of the general level of prices. That is to say that the domestic price level in Poland, though it rose during the sixteenth century as it did in other countries, remained lower than elsewhere; and it was this important fact that encouraged the export of Polish corn. Secondly, Moryson was struck by a fact which he probably learnt from the English merchants at Elbing, that in spite of this low price level there was a good demand in certain quarters for expensive goods from the west.

Under these circumstances English trade could not have failed to expand and English merchants to prosper. They had a firm hand on the cloth trade, and sold more cloth as the Poles sold more rye. The corn trade was principally in the hands of the Dutch, who took it to Amsterdam, stored it, and re-exported it. The state of harvests in western Europe influenced the price of corn at Amsterdam, and the price at Amsterdam governed the price in the Baltic; the rising prices in the west allowed rising prices in the Baltic. Rising prices in the Baltic allowed English cloth prices to be raised (as we know they were), while at the same time the quantity of cloth exports increased as the volume of the corn trade increased. From any vicissitude of the harvest in western Europe the English merchant stood to gain. Since England too imported corn, if by chance a bad harvest in England coincided with lower than usual corn prices in the Baltic (which would occur when the harvest in other western countries

[1] Fynes Moryson's *Itinerary* was first published in 1617. See remarks on Poland (Glasgow ed., 1907–8), I, 131; IV, 69–70.

was good), the English merchant expanded his import trade. If a good harvest in England coincided with higher corn prices in the Baltic (which would occur when the harvest in other western countries was bad), he expanded his export trade. If the harvest was bad in England and all over western Europe as well, he had the opportunity of a good trade in both directions. We know that 1556 and 1596 were years when crops were bad over very wide areas and in which we should therefore expect both his exports and his imports to have been unusually high, and, though the evidence does not permit us to check this in 1556, a striking boom in exports and imports is in fact clearly visible in 1596. Indeed, 1596 turned out to be the end of the period of expansion, and we shall discuss in a moment the decline that succeeded it.[1]

The English made their way into the Baltic as free traders. Fynes Moryson found them as a regulated company. They had received a charter of incorporation from Queen Elizabeth in 1579. There were sixty-five charter members. Their area was Norway, Sweden and the Baltic, except Narva (reserved to the Russia Company, whose charter was earlier; but the Eastland company traded there in our period). There is no need to describe their boundary with the Merchant Adventurers in detail: both companies had rights in Denmark and in the part of Germany bordering on the Baltic Sea, but Copenhagen and Elsinore—the Sound—belonged to the Eastland company only; the Eastland company could pass their goods through Hamburg if they wished (as, for example, when the Sound trade was stopped), although the Hamburg trade itself belonged to the Merchant Adventurers. In their area the Eastland company regulated the trade of all Englishmen; this meant for practical purposes that only members could trade. The charter has been published in part by Miss Sellers in her *Acts and Ordinances*. The foundation of the company has been well described by Miss Deardorff. She sees three contributory occasions. First, piracy: a Danish subject had been pillaged by an English privateer and if not indemnified would have induced his king to take reprisals on English ships at the Sound. The merchants were therefore to advance a sum of money towards the indemnity, and found that they could not levy it equitably without a certain measure of organisation under an authorised government. However, temporary measures could have met this case. Secondly, the same organisation and government were required for

---

[1] On east-west trade through the Sound, see A. E. Christensen, *Dutch Trade to the Baltic about 1600* (Copenhagen and the Hague, 1941); and Astrid Friis, 'The two crises in the Netherlands in 1557', *Scandinavian Economic History Review*, I (1953), 193 ff. For 1596 see Appendix D.

levying money to contribute to the cost of a royal ambassador to the King of Denmark, in order to negotiate among other things about the tolls that were being imposed at the Sound. A more permanent organisation was indicated here, inasmuch as the necessity for embassies might recur. Thirdly, the English merchants or some of them wanted to move from Danzig to Elbing, where they had been offered better conditions. This involved intense diplomacy in which again the crown took part. The English sought privileges at Elbing without giving way to the condition desired by Elbing, namely, to trade at Elbing only. Danzig wanted the English to stay at Danzig, but without the privileges they wished for. The King of Poland favoured Elbing over Danzig (an over-powerful and insubordinate town) but was unwilling for any one town to monopolise English trade. He also required a custom on English goods, which was a matter for negotiation with both towns equally. As the strength of the parties was nicely balanced, so the negotiations were long and arduous, and required the English to speak with a single voice. By the same token they were expensive and required them to contribute to a common purse. They were not in fact concluded before the foundation of the Eastland Company. In the end the company established a residence at Elbing with very full rights, analogous to those of the Hanseatic Stillyard in its heyday. In return the company undertook to confine their export trade to Elbing alone. The performance of this condition absolutely required a permanent company.[1]

The convenience of the arrangements at Elbing can easily be appreciated. Elbing recognised the company as an autonomous corporation with its own court and its own law; the company even had a share in choosing the town's customs officers; the members could keep warehouses, were exempt from municipal taxes, and could freely trade (this was the point chiefly objected to by Danzig, as infringing what Danzig alleged to be the laws of Prussia)—though only at wholesale—with strangers as well as with burghers. Great importance attaches to the warehouses, in which unsold cloth could be carried over from year to year and without which the cloth trade could hardly have been accommodated to the fluctuating demand of the Polish market; for, since the Polish demand for English cloth rose and fell according as the Poles sold more or less corn, it would happen that in some years the English sold less cloth than England could

[1] N. R. Deardorff, 'English trade in the Baltic during the reign of Elizabeth', in *Studies in the History of English Commerce in the Tudor Period* (New York, 1912); also A. Szelagowski and N. S. B. Gras, 'The Eastland company in Prussia, 1579–1585', *Trans. R. Hist. Soc.* 3rd series, VI (1912), 163 ff. For accounts of Anglo-Danish diplomacy in the reign of Elizabeth, see E. P. Cheyney and W. Kirchner in *The Journal of Modern History*, I (1929), 9 ff. and XVII (1945), 1 ff.

produce in a year, and in other years more. Again, we shall see when we come to examine the Eastland company's internal organisation that they used to sell cloth on credit, so that a right to sue in the town's courts was indispensable; the agreement granted it. The agreement also accorded necessary legal protections sufficient to cover more permanent forms of property. It did not envisage that Englishmen would hold real property unless by inheritance or dowry, but it did envisage, by implication, that they would hold goods or money, and it secured to the English community their native laws of inheritance and placed in their own hands the administration of dead members' estates. These estates may have been large, for it is likely that there were plenty of opportunities for profitable local investments, for example by loans at interest and shares in ships. At a much later date, about 1650,[1] the Eastland company claimed it as a major stroke to have been able to bring dead members' estates home to England intact, in defiance of a Polish law that a proportion of the property of deceased foreigners was forfeit to the crown.

During this phase of expansion the value of exports must sometimes (and may generally) have exceeded the value of imports, and there was probably a more or less continuous remittance of money from Danzig to England. In 1620 there will be talk of 'the many thousands of dollars in former times brought by the Merchants Adventurers from Hamburg and by the Eastland merchants from Danzig and other parts of Prussia into England'—not the sort of statement that could be made without some foundation of truth. We gather from the context that this money was silver coin; it was not remitted by bills of exchange.[2]

Fynes Moryson described his arrival at Elbing in 1593.

From Kettell we passed ten miles, and came to the port of Melvin [Elbing]....We saw Danzig seated not far from the sea shore, where it hath a haven, but not so safe as this: and towards the north-east in the same place a channel runneth up to Königsberg, the court of the Duke of Prussia. The port of Melvin is scarce ten foot deep, but our ship passed through the mud, like a plough upon land....Melvin is a little and fair city, lately compassed with new walls, and at this time grown rich by the English merchants, having their staple in the same....The English merchants at Melvin had no preacher, though the citizens gave them free exercise of religion: so that howsoever they excused it, by reason that learned preachers could hardly be drawn to come so far for means to live, yet I thought them not free of blame on this point.[3]

At the time of Fynes Moryson's visit the Eastland company were approaching the high tide of their prosperity. Seven years of extra-

---

[1] Appendix A9.   [2] Appendix A2 (*b*).   [3] *Itinerary* (Glasgow ed.), I, 129–30.

ordinarily high exports from 1595 to 1601 lay before them. That over, their exports declined. According to the Sound Tables, in 1597 they exported 22,000 broadcloths. At the end of the seventeenth century they were exporting about 2000. The downward trend is clearly visible, through interruptions and fluctuations, in the figure at Appendix D. It is one of the symptoms of the seventeenth-century malady known as the decay of the old draperies.

In 1600, according to the Sound Tables, Dutch cloth was beginning to make its way to the Baltic. Competition was also felt from locally made cloth. In cloth a small difference in price made a great difference to demand. Demand was elastic. Thomas Mun observed about 1622 that 'twenty-five in the hundred less in the price...may raise above fifty upon the hundred in the quantity vented'. When they had a monopoly of supply, he wrote, they might charge as much as they could, 'so far forth as the high price cause not a less vent in the quantity'. But when they had no monopoly,

we must in this case strive to sell as cheap as possible we can, rather than to lose the utterance of such wares. For we have found of late years by good experience, that being able to sell our cloth cheap in Turkey, we have greatly increased the vent thereof, and the Venetians have lost as much in the utterance of theirs in those countries, because it is dearer. And on the other side a few years past, when by the excessive price of wools our cloth was exceeding dear, we lost at the least half our clothing for foreign parts. ...For when cloth is dear, other nations do presently practise clothing, and we know they want neither art nor materials to this performance.

It may be relevant to notice that the average price of an English broadcloth shipped through the Sound rose through 1595, 1605 and 1615, whereas some Baltic prices in Polish price histories show a tendency to fall. Since Baltic prices were controlled from Amsterdam, it is possible that there too they were turning downward. We need not speculate in terms of the ending of the price revolution. The demand for English cloth could be affected by price differences imperceptible in constructed price series and with little relation to general price levels.[1]

Professor Friis has written of the difficulties of the English cloth exporter to the Baltic in the first twenty years of the seventeenth century. The volume of their exports declined at the same time as the volume of Dutch exports increased. The Dutch cloth was English-made but dyed

---

[1] Mun, *England's Treasure by Foreign Trade*, ch. 3. Most of this was written as early as 1622 or 1623; B. E. Supple, *Bull. of Inst. of Hist. Research*, XXVII (1954), 91 ff. Polish price histories will be cited in the next chapter. Some average prices of goods shipped through the Sound are given below, pp. 36, 42.

and dressed in the Netherlands. Professor Friis suggests that the scheme known as Cockayne's project was intended to put a stop to this practice. Cockayne's project was to prohibit the export of unfinished cloth to the Netherlands. Cockayne and the chief movers were Eastland merchants. The scheme failed and had no observable effect on the trade to the Baltic.[1]

In this situation the English cloth exporter might gain some relief from his import trade. If English cloth was becoming too dear in the Baltic, it is possible that Baltic goods were becoming cheaper in England. The extra profit thus made possible was transferable, so to speak, in the form of a subsidy to the export trade. This was certainly done later. But, however favourably the terms of trade shifted in favour of the importer, it could no more than palliate the disadvantage of the exporter; for the demand for Baltic goods was inelastic. The demand for all Baltic goods, especially for unpalatable rye, depended more on need than on price. There could be no expansion of the import trade sufficient to counterbalance the shrinkage of the export trade. English cloth exports marched strikingly in step with English corn prices, high and low points together. Yet while corn prices tended on the whole upwards, cloth exports tended downwards.

In any case the time soon came when the English felt Dutch competition in imports. When Antwerp had lost its supreme place in the European economy there was perhaps a chance for London, but it was lost. Amsterdam had long been a shipping centre and corn entrepôt, and by 1609, when the Dutch war of independence ended, its commercial supremacy was well established. Even while the war was in progress Dutch merchants had traded with profit, and the years of peace are full of signs of expansion. Dunkirk privateers ceased to trouble them—Dunkirkers, as we shall see during the Thirty Years War, could double freight charges—and the unarmed economical *fluitschip* came into its own. The States-General promoted their merchants' interests in diplomacy with the Scandinavian kingdoms, with the Hanseatic towns, with Russia. Sooner or later in every field their expansion led to friction with the English. In some places there was fighting. Meetings of Dutch and English commissioners could achieve no lasting settlement of the many deep differences. Meanwhile, a more insidious form of competition was added to the rivalry in foreign markets: the Dutch began to encroach on English merchants' trade in

[1] Astrid Friis, *Alderman Cockayne's Project and the Cloth Trade* (Copenhagen and London, 1927). This is probably the best account of trade and trading policy under James I. It is specially good on the Eastland trade and contains names of Eastland merchants. It accepts, however, the then traditional view of the effects of Cockayne's project, namely that it led to the depression of 1620, an opinion that is now under revision.

England itself. They began to sell foreign goods in England alongside English merchants.

At the small port of Boston the Dutch import trade is conspicuous from about 1615. In French wine, Norway deals and Baltic rye, the Boston port books show the onset of an entrepôt trade from Amsterdam. In three years, 1615–17, there were heavy imports of rye: over 1000 lasts came from the Netherlands, less than fifty from the Baltic. The Dutch invasion must have been as obvious to anyone watching the port then as it is to anyone looking at the port books today. At first arrives a single ship of Amsterdam. It returns, makes repeated visits, plies as fast as it can sail to and fro across the North Sea. One sees the shipmaster building up his business. He becomes a familiar figure in the port books, as he must have been at the quayside among the merchants of Boston.[1]

It is reasonable to suppose that in this respect the port of Boston is typical. In 1615 the Levant company of London complained to the crown that the Dutch were engrossing the import trade in Mediterranean goods. The reason was their cheap freights. The crown gave the Levant company a proclamation which had the effect of making them sole importers of Mediterranean goods. Hitherto the Levant company had controlled trade *in* the Mediterranean, but it was lawful to import Mediterranean goods from elsewhere. The proclamation, by placing the import of Mediterranean goods solely in the hands of the Levant company, ensured that in future they would be imported only from the Mediterranean.[2]

This proclamation was an obvious forerunner of the Navigation Act of 1651. The Dutch entrepôt trade was perhaps the most important single factor in shaping English economic policy in the seventeenth century. It is to be wished that we knew enough about it to assess accurately its effects. Port books are still a relatively untapped source, but in any case they survive inadequately for the two crises of 1620 and 1649, when the entrepôt trade was said to be at its height. The Eastland merchants alleged that when Eastland goods were imported from Amsterdam the export of cloth to the Baltic necessarily and proportionately declined. This raises questions about the structure of European commerce, to what extent it was multi-lateral or bilateral, which are probably better attacked in Dutch records than in English. Here contemporary economic theory can be called in question. It is difficult to see the truth. We are on firmer ground when we notice the effect of the Dutch entrepôt on English shipping: it tended

[1] Hinton, 'Dutch entrepôt trade at Boston, Lincs., 1600–40', *Ec.H.R.* 2nd series, IX (1957), 467 ff. This is based on my *Port Books of Boston 1601–1640* (Lincoln Record Society, 1956).

[2] *A.P.C. 1615–1616*, 98. The proclamation is printed below in Appendix A4.

to ruin it. English importers in competition with Dutch turned naturally to Dutch ships; Dutch freight rates were lower than English; had they not been lower the entrepôt trade would not have been possible. However, an Englishman using Dutch ships was little or no better off than a Hollander using Dutch ships. If events were allowed to take their course it must have seemed possible for the whole trade to fall into Dutch hands. As the maintenance of shipping was a prime object of all English governments, they were highly sensitive to Dutch entrepôt trade.

It is easy to exaggerate the merchants' difficulties. Exports to the Baltic declined, but gradually. (Imports we cannot measure before 1620.) Professor Friis observes that the number of English cloth exporters to the Baltic declined from about 1600. We hear of bankruptcies of merchant houses at Elbing and Danzig in 1618.[1] In 1618 the Eastland company said their trade was decayed, but this was in order to be assessed at a low rate for their contribution towards an expedition against pirates.[2] Suddenly, in 1620, the Eastland trade and other trades were plunged into the worst crisis in living memory.

[1] *Letters from George Lord Carew* (Camden Society, 1860), 63–4.
[2] SP 14/105/42, 44.

Chapter II

THE DEPRESSION OF 1620 AND THE EASTLAND COMPANY'S PROCLAMATION OF 1622

The crisis in the Eastland trade

One of the most memorable depressions in the annals of the English textile industries began in 1620, and lasted four to five years. The export trade declined by one-third; the price of wool fell; clothiers, even those reputed the wealthiest, were brought to the verge of bankruptcy; and unemployment was widespread.[1]

This depression used to be attributed to Cockayne's project. W. R. Scott, for example, believed that Cockayne's stoppage of cloth exports to the Netherlands only succeeded in encouraging the Dutch manufacture, and held that their cloth competed with English cloth even more strongly afterwards than before—strongly enough, by 1620, to throw the English cloth trade completely out of gear. But this explanation does not cover all the facts. We must distinguish between Dutch cloth-*making* and Dutch cloth-*finishing*. Cockayne's project was designed to stop the latter. Now in 1620 English exports to the Netherlands did not fall, it was exports to Hamburg and the Baltic that fell. Thus it looks as though the competition (if any) was from finished cloth. Cockayne's project had failed to stop the Dutch finishing, but there is no material evidence that it had significantly promoted Dutch making. It possibly had little effect on what happened in 1620. Contemporaries explained the depression of 1620 on other grounds and recent investigations tend to support the contemporary analysis. The Eastland merchants' explanation for the depression in their own trade was very detailed, can to a large extent be checked against independent evidence, and applies equally to the Hamburg trade and even perhaps to other trades as well.[2]

[1] Lipson, *Economic History*, III (1943), 305.

[2] J. D. Gould, 'The trade depression of the early 1620's, *Ec.H.R.* 2nd series, VII (1954), 81 ff. An unpublished dissertation by Dr B. E. Supple, University Library, Cambridge, 1955, covers the same subject. F. J. Fisher, 'London's export trade in the early seventeenth century', *Ec.H.R.* 2nd series, III (1950), 151 ff., gives figures of London cloth exports. Friis, *Cockayne's Project*, 78, 98, 129, 382–3, 428, gives London cloth exports to particular markets as follows:

		Low Countries	Hamburg	Eastland
Before Cockayne's	1606	38,000	56,000	?
project	1614	35,000	46,000	8,000
During Cockayne's project	1616		52,000	9,000
After Cockayne's	1618	32,000	35,000	8,000
project	1620	32,000	21,000	3,000

In Appendix A are printed four contemporary papers giving reasons for the decay of the Eastland trade and proposing a variety of remedies. The first is a petition by the Eastland company to the king, undated, but written in 1620 not later than June. This is one of the earliest evidences of the depression. It is not known to have gone before the Privy Council, as would have been normal; it was referred under Buckingham's signature to five referees 'to report to his Majesty their opinions therein'. The referees were Sir Thomas Smith, among the greatest of the London merchants, Sir John Wolstenholme (commissioner of the navy and farmer of the customs), Sir William Russell (treasurer of the navy), Nicholas Leatt and Thomas Stile. Leatt and Stile were probably members of the Eastland company, and Leatt also belonged to the Levant company whose petition he had presented to the Privy Council in 1615. Thus the referees represented two departments of government as well as the world of business. They were experts. There was no representative of industry; this was truly a mercantile era. They reported favourably, enlarging on some of the merchants' points and introducing others, having either called fresh evidence or invoked their own experience, which they were well qualified to do.[1]

By this time the depression was general. There was unemployment and distress in the clothing industry. Ships and mariners were idle. 'Shortage of money' was a common complaint. But in spite of the referees' recommendations the crown did nothing in 1620. It waited perhaps on the parliament.

The parliament of 1621, the first since 1614, debated the decay of trade and took the Eastland trade into serious consideration. In April, Maurice Abbot (member for Hull, the Eastland company's most important outport in the north) and an old associate of his, Sir Dudley Digges (member for the clothing town, Tewkesbury) presented to a committee on trade and money the case of the Eastland company in the same form as in their petition and the referees' report. Shortly afterwards new material was presented, probably by the company, giving rise to a pair of papers which look like summaries made by a committee. One is entitled 'Reasons of the Eastland merchants showing the decay of their trade', the other is entitled 'Collections deduced from the said [merchants trading] into the eastern countries showing in part the cause of the great scarcity of silver in England, and some remedy for the same'. These represent the second stage of the depression.[2]

[1] All the referees except Stile are the subject of articles in *D.N.B.* For members of the Eastland company, see Appendix C.

[2] Internal evidence dates them before the company's main sailing. For Abbot's and Digges's speeches, see *Commons Debates 1621*, ed. W. Notestein *et al.* (Yale University Press, 1935), III, 46–8.

The four papers embody a full description of the Eastland merchants' troubles as seen by themselves. They are printed not only for the facts they contain but as an example of the contemporary mode of economic analysis. They are more technical than at first sight they appear.

The merchants adduced two reasons for their crisis. One reason was Dutch competition. The other, which we shall consider first, was 'the rising of the moneys' in eastern Europe.

In Poland prices were reckoned in gilders and groschen, at thirty groschen to the gilder. This was money of account. There was no gilder coin. The common currency was small silver coins representing various multiples and divisions of the groschen as, say, two-, four-, six-groschen pieces. There was also a much more valuable silver coin, the rixdollar, which was not used in everyday transactions (and a gold equivalent, the ducat). The small coins were tied by their denomination to the groschen but the rixdollar was independent; its value was given in groschen and altered according to the equivalence of silver in it and in the groschen pieces. Rixdollars were transportable silver and were what interested the merchants. In the sixteenth century the rixdollar rose very slowly, from 30 groschen in 1540 to 37 groschen in 1600. In the seventeenth century it began to rise faster and by 1615 it was worth 42 groschen. Then it jumped suddenly and steeply until by 1630 it was worth 90 groschen. The biggest leap was in the years 1618–21 when it went up from 45 to 75 groschen. This is what was meant by the rising of the moneys. It was brought about by progressively debasing (reducing the silver content of) the groschen pieces while maintaining the silver content of the rixdollar. Whenever new groschen pieces were issued from the mints the value of the rixdollar was raised correspondingly by proclamation. It was as if an English government, on reducing the amount of silver in 2s. and 6d. pieces, had ordered the sovereign to be accepted for 30s. instead of 20s.

It is said that the Polish mints embarked on this process in reply to the German mints. In Germany at the beginning of the Thirty Years War there was large-scale debasement which developed into *Kipper- und Wipperzeit*, and·it was necessary to debase the Polish coins in order to prevent their being driven out of circulation by bad German ones. The process was widespread. Scandinavian money moved similarly.[1]

In Germany the reichsthaler stood at 1·1 florins in 1582 and in 1607 had reached only 1·3 florins. (The florin was money of account equivalent to the gilder.) In 1615 it stood at 1·5 florins. In 1619 it stood at

[1] On Polish money, see J. Rutkowski, *Histoire économique de la Pologne avant les partages* (Paris, 1927), 201 ff. The above is somewhat simplified. There were other coins and systems of accounting and the terminology can be confusing.

2·1 florins, in 1620 at 2·3 florins, in 1621 at 3 and 4 florins, in 1622 at 4 and 6 florins. This was the well-known period of German monetary chaos.[1]

Table 1 shows what happened at Danzig. Danzig minted its own money, but the course of other Polish mints' money was similar (actually slightly in advance). The steep rise of the rixdollar beginning in 1615 and ending in 1622 is clearly visible. After a slight pause a more moderate rise began in 1626 and was completed by 1630. Thereafter it was steady.

TABLE 1.*   *The rising of the money at Danzig: the value of the rixdollar in groschen*

1602	37	1623	77
1615	42	1624	75
1616	43	1625	75
1617	44	1626	78
1618	45	1627	86
1619	49	1628	88
1620	59	1629	91
1621	75	1630	90
1622	78		

* J. Pelc, *Ceny w Gdańsku w XVI i XVII Wieku* (Lwow, 1937). Also see similar books by W. Adamczyk for Warsaw and Lublin (1935, 1938), S. Hoszowski for Lwow (1928), and E. Tomaszewski for Cracow (1934).

Our four papers on the Eastland trade describe the process exactly. 'Of late years', said the referees in 1620, 'all moneys are raised to...an exorbitant value beyond the ancient standard and the true worth thereof through all Germany, Prussia, and Muscovia.' In 1621 one of the parliamentary papers said that moneys had 'risen upwards of 50 per cent within less than two years last past'. The other said that in the space of the last four years the common Polish currency had been so debased that good coin had disappeared from circulation and 'base coin by 40, 50, 60 and 70 per cent made thereof'. 'By which means the rixdollar which eighteen months last was worth but 50 Polish groschen are now current at 75, and Spanish royals and silver money óf England and other nations are also enhanced ratably.'

An immediate effect of the rising of the money was to appear to benefit debtors, because debts expressed in gilders were now worth less in rixdollars, less in silver. English merchants who had made loans at interest (if any had), now received a lower return, in silver, than they had bargained for. If they had sold cloth on credit, the price they actually received was

[1] W. A. Shaw, *The History of Currency 1252 to 1894* (London, 1st ed. 1895), 102–5; 'The monetary movements of 1600–1621 in Holland and Germany', *Trans. R. Hist. Soc.* new series, IX (1895), 207–13. Shaw was familiar with the contemporary documents and favoured a monetary interpretation of the crisis.

less, in silver, than they had expected. Of this aspect, however, they did not complain—though to sell cloth on credit was evidently a usual practice, as we shall see in a later chapter. The reason is, probably, that the price of goods remained for some time unaffected by the movement of money. If the price of goods expressed in gilders and groschen does not rise—that is to say if the price expressed in silver falls, if the 'real' price falls—the debts will continue to buy the same amount of goods as they bought before. The Englishman cannot bring his dollars home, but he can invest them in Polish goods.

The petition and the referees' report do not speak about prices, but the parliamentary papers correctly link them with the statements on money. 'Although moneys of late are excessively risen in the Eastland parts and in Germany, yet the cloth and other native commodities of those countries rise not proportionably to the moneys.' 'Those base coins [are] current in payment at the same rates the former were.' The burden of the complaint was that prices had *not* risen and that this made English cloth very difficult to sell. 'The English are enforced to endeavour the sale of their cloth ratable to the true value of their [i.e. the Polish] moneys, which far exceeding the rates of former times (before the rising of the moneys) and the prices of cloth now made in those countries, there is by this means far less quantities of English cloth vented then otherwise would be.' This means simply that while the real price of Polish goods, the price in silver, had fallen, the real price of English cloth, being based on the costs of production in England in which there had been no alteration, had necessarily risen. The Poles could not afford it and the English could not sell it.

The price histories confirm these statements. They show that the debased coin retained its purchasing power and even bought more of some commodities than hitherto. The real price of rye at Danzig was lower in 1621 than for many years past and must have influenced other goods. From 1621 to 1624 the real price of wine at Danzig and of cloth at Warsaw was exceptionally low. In the quinquennium 1621–25 the average real price of all goods at Danzig was lower than it had been. Not till about 1625 did real prices adjust themselves to the rising of the money and allow a commodity to be sold for the same amount of silver—to yield the same quantity of rixdollars—as it had before the rising of the moneys in 1618. We may take it that prices went similarly in Germany.[1] If this seems a longer time lag than one would normally expect it is probably attributable to good harvests in western Europe; in England at any rate harvests were exceptionally good in all three years 1619, 1620 and 1621.

---

[1] The Polish price histories just cited give retail prices. Some of the series are rather bad. There is no good series for an imported commodity.

These facts and their importance were widely known. They informed the writings of Misselden and Malynes and directed them towards discussing money in a fashion which some readers have found obscurantist. John Keymer's tract, published in 1653 as *Sir Walter Raleigh's Observations touching Trade and Commerce*, gives particulars about the rising of the rixdollar which seem to date it not later than 1619. The Privy Council learnt in May 1620 that 'our shilling is in Danzig and further throughout Poland worth 16 pence and there recoined for 18 pence, which gain hath caused much of the weightiest thereof to be secretly carried over into those parts'.[1] An exceptionally detailed statement is that of John Ramsden, an Eastland merchant, on behalf of the port of Hull in 1621 or 1622:

Our trade is the exportation of northern kerseys, northern cloths and northern dozens into the Eastland [and some other places]...all which at present we find much to be decayed in all places; both as to the vent, much less than in former years, and as to the prices, much abated in all the parts beyond the sea.

First, in the Eastland, which hath been our greatest vent for our sorts of cloth and kerseys, [it is] decayed by the great store of cloth now made in Danzig and other places of Prussia, and kerseys made in Silesia, which doth serve the markets where our cloths were formerly vented into Poland; we paying great charges and customs of our coarse cloth, both at home and abroad, before that our goods come to the market, as unto the King of Denmark, Duke of Prussia and King of Poland, and at home the pretermitted custom; being much to pay 12*d.* of a kersey under 30*s.* price, we paying in all in customs and charges for every kersey 7*s.* sterling and so for the rate of other cloths and dozens; that the last two years bypast they have not yielded at the market above seven rixdollars and a half apiece, which is but worth, [at] 4*s.* 6*d.* per dollar into the mint, 33*s.* 9*d.*, out of which 7*s.* deducted for charges there rests but 26*s.* 9*d.*; by which we lose, and cannot be able to help it, by not being able to raise the price there, by reason of the extraordinary rising of their money, and other store of clothing in the country; so that either overcheap pennyworths must cause our said cloth to vent there, or else they will not vent at all; the decay thereof will appear in his Majesty's custom-house books, and we find that this trade grows daily worse and worse. For kerseys are cheaper sold in the Eastland at present by three rixdollars apiece, and dozens by four rixdollars, than they were a few years ago, and yet not half sold.

As for Germany our trade is but small thither, and their money much exhausted, so that we have much ado to sell our kerseys and dozens for any profit.[2]

---

[1] *A.P.C. 1619–1621*, 191.
[2] Printed in George Hadley's *History of Kingston-upon-Hull* (Hull, 1788), 113 ff.

HET

This is to say that Ramsden pays about 30*s*. for a kersey in England, that it costs him 7*s*. to get it to the market in Poland, and that the money he receives for it is worth no more than 33*s*. 9*d*. in England. 'A few years ago' he received 47*s*. 3*d*.

Ramsden does not explain the situation in terms of exchange rates nor does he even mention gilders or groschen, the money of account. He is interested entirely in the good silver coin, the rixdollar—or more exactly in the silver it contains. When he says that in the past a kersey fetched 10½ rixdollars he means us to infer that it was possible to have brought back to England sufficient silver coin to have exchanged it for English money at the mint at a profit of 10*s*., and perhaps to this time belong the 'many thousands of dollars' that were said by the Eastland merchants in 1621 to have been 'brought by the Merchants Adventurers from Hamburg and by the Eastland merchants from Danzig and other parts of Prussia'. But clearly it was not possible in 1620. Ramsden could continue to trade only by bringing back goods on which, when sold in England, the profit would outweigh the loss on exports. In this sense the Eastland merchants stated in 1620 that the proceed of their exports 'was wholly returned in the commodities of the eastern countries'. They called their trade a 'barter' trade.

The second reason given by the Eastland merchants for the crisis in their trade was the intrusion of the Dutch. They complained entirely of the competition of the Dutch in the *import* trade, not in the export trade where W. R. Scott seems to have placed it when he linked the decline in exports with Cockayne's project. About Dutch cloth they were quite silent; we have seen that the Dutch *were* exporting cloth to the Baltic and that it did compete, but it was not (according to the Eastland merchants) one of the causes of the present crisis; they instanced local cloth, not Dutch cloth, as that which competed significantly at this particular time. And this was probably correct, because such figures as are available (see Appendix D) make Dutch cloth exports to the Baltic in 1620 and 1621 lower than they had been in 1618 and 1619, while their westward traffic was exceptionally high from 1618 to 1621. The Eastland merchants must necessarily have experienced some contraction of their import trade as a result of exceptionally good English harvests in 1619 and 1620, but their argument suggests that even had corn been scarce the Dutch, not themselves, would have supplied it.

The second reason, then, was the Dutch import trade:

By means of the Hollanders trading and importing [into England] the foreign commodities as aforesaid, as also in regard divers shopkeepers of London send or remit over their moneys to buy East country commodities in 'Holland, and bring the same into England, the English merchant exporting the manufacry of the land is already in part, and likely to be in short time wholly, discouraged and driven out of trade.

In other words, since the proceeds of the Eastland merchants' exports were wholly returned in imports, if the import trade was reduced the export trade must shrink proportionately.

The advantage of the Dutch was said to lie in three factors. One was their 'practice'. By this the English meant sharp practice; they were thinking of commercial treaties, concessions, and what we would now-adays call economic infiltration, which included farming the King of Poland's mint at Bromberg. Another factor was their cheap freights. We have already spoken of this. The Eastland merchants did not cite figures, but there is no question that Dutch freights were much lower than English.[1] The third factor was their 'merchandising with money', that is to say, their exporting of silver.

The Hollanders, finding the great profit arising by moneys, coined in their own countries certain pieces of coarser silver of 28 and 30 stivers the piece and dollars, by which coins they gained from 30 to 50 per cent according to the rising of moneys in the Eastern parts, and with the said coins bought the commodities of those places, many of them making three returns and more in one year; which made such plenty of Hollands dollars, 30 stiver pieces and 28 stiver pieces, that the most part of payments made by merchants at Danzig, Elbing and Königsberg in the last four years [this was written in 1621] was in the said Holland money, which the Jews, Russes, Poles and Armenians changed up in great abundance and carried into other remote countries.

The Netherlanders do advance upon their moneys 30 in the hundred profit, by which excessive gain upon their moneys they are able to lose 20 in the hundred in their returns of Eastern commodities and be yet great gainers in their adventures, whereby in time it must of necessity follow, that the merchants of this kingdom will be compelled to forsake and give over all those eastern trades.

With this style of trading Eastland goods can have been nowhere cheaper, outside the Eastland, than at Amsterdam.

One would give much for some reliable figures of the Dutch entrepôt trade to England. We have seen that there are signs of entrepôt trade in Eastland goods at the port of Boston from about 1615. Ipswich port books show considerable imports of Eastland goods from the Netherlands in 1617 and 1621. Hull port books show a far greater proportion in 1619 than in 1613. Unfortunately, few port books survive for 1620 and 1621,

[1] V. Barbour, 'Dutch and English merchant shipping', *Ec.H.R.* II (1930), 261 ff.

and we must make do with a book of Englishmen's imports at London
in 1621 and a book for aliens' imports at London in 1622. These show
that there were in fact two entrepôts, Hamburg as well as Holland. In
1621 Englishmen imported more Eastland goods from Hamburg than
from Holland, and Hamburg and Holland together supplied nearly half
as much hemp as Englishmen brought direct from the Eastland, about
a third as much flax, about a tenth as many deals, and much more of pitch
and tar. In 1622 aliens imported hardly any Eastland goods from the
Eastland, but they imported some from Hamburg and a good deal,
including much corn, from the Netherlands. An aliens' book for 1620
or 1621 might be expected to show the entrepôt trades more unmistakably,
for these years were said to be the worst.[1]

As to direct trade by Dutch merchants from the Eastland to England,
there is little sign of it at any time in the seventeenth century. One would
expect such trade to take the form, in the English port books, of shipmaster's trade; but the shipmaster's trade in foreign ships, whether
Eastland or Dutch, was not, so far as can be seen, very great, even at the
worst of times. The question raises difficult problems of interpretation of
the sources, and cannot be regarded as settled. At all events the English
merchants' complaints in 1620 (and again under similar circumstances in
1650) were directed against the entrepôt trade. Although the possibility
of the direct trade may be borne in mind, we are perhaps justified in
ignoring it.

On the foregoing analysis the crisis of 1620 appears as a sudden worsening
of a situation that had been steadily deteriorating for some time. We
suggested in the last chapter that the comparatively low level of prices in
the Eastland had tended since about 1600 to reduce the Eastland merchants'
export trade, and that the competitive advantages of the Dutch had been
a danger to their import trade since, perhaps, 1609. When the rising of
the moneys suddenly depressed Eastland prices still further, and the Dutch
took the opportunity of merchandising with money, their difficulties
were abruptly aggravated.

The consequences were three: lack of employment of English shipping,
stoppage of cloth exports, and a drain of money abroad. The Eastland
merchants, the crown, the parliament, indeed everyone, fastened exclusively on these three points. Nobody suggested that, if English shipping
was expensive, the merchants ought to employ foreign ships. That

[1] E 190/601/2, 13 (Ipswich), 313/5, 314/14 (Hull). The information for London
comes from a preliminary abstract of 24/4 and 26/2 kindly communicated to me by
Mrs Millard.

English ships were employed only by Englishmen and that English merchants ought therefore to employ only English ships, were fundamental assumptions underlying the whole approach to this crisis. Likewise nobody stopped to consider the possible advantages of cheap imports; this point was regarded as irrelevant. The Eastland merchants regarded themselves, and were universally regarded, primarily as exporters, and especially as exporters of cloth. The import side of their trade was seen almost as an expedient to assist exports. Therefore nobody suggested that the Eastland merchants should export money instead of cloth, as the Dutch were doing. The merchants' profit was irrelevant. Even the merchants did not complain about their own ruin, they did not seek help ostensibly on their own account. They alleged that they had been obliged to reduce their trade and that if help were not forthcoming they would be compelled to abandon it, but the people who suffered belonged to the cloth industry, and the merchants' ships were more important than their fortunes.

The Eastland merchants' petition says that they employed in the normal course of trade 'at least 100 sail of English ships beside...at least 100 sail of Netherlanders', and although the import trade fluctuated extremely we can accept this as a fair generalisation. (It refers only to Baltic trade; according to the referees a further 100 Dutch ships were employed in the Norway trade.) For the Sound Tables tell us that in the past thirty years the number of English ships in the Baltic trade had often exceeded one hundred, and that English merchants had freighted (for imports) Dutch ships to the number of eighty as well as a number of Eastland ships. But in 1620 the referees found that the Eastland merchants employed 'little more than one half of the shipping formerly employed'. This again is probably acceptable. In 1620 there were only fifty-four English ships in Baltic trade, and two Eastland ships; the Sound Tables do not tell us the number of Dutch ships freighted by English merchants, but if it was proportional to the number of Eastland ships it was obviously very small. The merchants said that they anticipated the 'utter decay' of their shipping. It may be thought that a reduction by 50 per cent did not warrant such pessimism. But they were referring to a process that had been going on for some years. Compare, for instance, Hull port books of 1613 and 1619; at the first date twenty-four English ships and nine foreign ships arrived from the Baltic, but at the second date the proportion was reversed— eleven English and forty foreign. These forty foreign ships were mainly carrying rye for English merchants, and they evidently represent a deliberate tendency to seek cheaper freight. In 1620 Trinity House, which had no objection to the Eastland merchants' employing foreign ships when English were not available, complained that they were employing them from choice. If the compulsion to seek cheap freights continued, 'utter decay' was not beyond the bounds of possibility.[1]

None of the Eastland company's numerical statements are quite free of ambiguity. For example, does the 'little more than one-half' refer to 1619 or to 1620, and when was 'formerly'? We must remember that the Eastland company had no reason to keep accurate records of its import trade. They were able to be both exact and up-to-date only about the cloth exports of London and Ipswich. Knowing that their information was incomplete, we must not expect their statements to be absolutely precise, and even on the subject of cloth they preserved an element of vagueness about the past.

'Heretofore', says the petition of 1620, 'the English merchants have vented in the eastern parts yearly 25,000 cloths worth £250,000, whereas now they vent not above 7000 or 8000 cloths.' At that price the statement clearly refers to broadcloth. Though precise, it looks incorrect until we realise that a petition made early in 1620 must embody figures collected not later than 1619, and that the 7000 or 8000 cloths consequently do not refer to 1620 at all. In 1597, 22,000 broadcloths were entered at the Sound, and during the decade ending 1619 the figure was generally slightly over 7000. The statement now appears to be almost literally true, but misleading, because 1597 was exceptional. Next year there was a different statement. 'Formerly', says one of the parliamentary papers in 1621, they 'vented 8000 cloths yearly from London, and cannot now vent 3000.' In 1620 and 1621, the years of crisis, just over 4000 broadcloths were entered at the Sound. Some would have been shipped at Ipswich. The figure given in 1621 was therefore up-to-date and not seriously misleading. It is really this figure that justifies (almost) the referees' comment in 1620 that 'this last year there hath been transported from London little more than one third part of the cloths of former years'.[2]

It came to be accepted that the loss of exports during the two years of crisis amounted to 5000 broadcloths a year. At £10 a cloth this gave an annual loss of £50,000. It was evidently calculated that this sum was exported from England by the Dutch in gold or silver. 'They return their ships empty', says the Eastland company's petition, 'without employment of their money in any commodities, and heretofore they have for their

---

[1] For ships, see Appendix D. The number of Dutch ships freighted by English merchants is given in the Sound Tables for every tenth year only, i.e. 1595, 1605 and 1615. The distinction between Dutch and Eastland ships is a matter of the ship's home port or master's domicile, and does not refer to ownership. Trinity House, *A.P.C. 1615–1616*, 98; H.M.C. *8th Report*, I, 239, 246.

[2] Appendix D.

goods and freight made their bargain to receive groats, pieces of nine-pence, and such other coins as have best fitted their profit.' The Dutch then shipped this silver to the Eastland. We have a short note of a speech in parliament by Robert Snelling, an Eastland merchant and member of parliament for Ipswich: 'That £50,000 a year transported to Danzig, and there minted. This done by the Dutch. And hinder £50,000 more in cloths transportation. This done, by colour of bills of exchange. Tendereth a bill for help of it'.[1] The figure occurs again in one of the Eastland company's papers to parliament: 'Silver bearing so high a rate [in the Eastland] there hath been brought into those parts by estimation of English coin £50,000 per annum for these four years space.'

In addition, money was lost in payment for freight to foreign ship-masters. Freights could legally be paid in coin. (At the end of the century Danzig shipmasters required it in coin.) The referees estimated that the freight for 200 Dutch ships employed by English merchants to bring goods from Norway and the Baltic amounted to £30,000.

Nobody suggested that the crisis should be left to cure itself. All agreed that urgent remedies were called for. Perhaps the most urgent argument for legislation was the state of shipping. The hundred English ships were a useful national asset, and to replace them with Dutch ships not only made England weaker but made the Dutch stronger. The referees insisted on this point. Two of the referees were officially connected with the navy and a third had been one of the English commissioners in the abortive Anglo-Dutch negotiations before 1620, as had been Maurice Abbot and Sir Dudley Digges who spoke for the company in parliament. All these had been forced to recognise that the Dutch were enemies. The Eastland company's petition appealed directly to that sentiment. 'The Netherlanders by their practice...have much decayed the trade and shipping of this land and will also in course of time bring our shipping into utter decay.' 'The Netherlanders...do not only weaken all other nations in their shipping but so in exceeding manner they increase their own, which makes them so strong at the seas that they neglect the respect they owe to their neighbour princes and make them bold to offer many insolent wrongs.'

A second compelling reason for speedy action was that unemployment was dangerous. During the depression of 1620 the Privy Council wrote to the justices of the clothing counties that they would 'not endure that the clothiers in that or any other county should at their pleasure, and without giving knowledge thereof unto this Board, dismiss their work-folks, who, being many in number and most of them of the poorer sort,

---

[1] *Commons Journals*, I, 615.

are in such cases likely by their clamours to disturb the quiet and government of those parts wherein they live'.[1] The Eastland trade was reponsible for only a small proportion of the total export of English cloth, but it was made in certain well-defined clothing areas where unemployment would be conspicuous. The broadcloth consisted of short Suffolks dyed and dressed, which were made and finished in a few villages in Suffolk and Essex. Nearly all the short Suffolks that were exported were exported to the Baltic. They were shipped through London and Ipswich. The close link between Ipswich and the Baltic is remarkable: its only important export was short Suffolks and, in 1615, 3600 out of 4000 were shipped for Elbing. Its declining prosperity through the seventeenth century is obviously connected with the decline of the Anglo-Baltic cloth trade. Similarly, nearly all the short Suffolks exported from London were shipped for the Baltic. A highly specialised and concentrated export industry was therefore hard hit when the Eastland merchants' shipments were reduced by a half or two-thirds. It is the same story in the north. The chief exports of Hull from the Yorkshire clothing industry were kerseys and dozens: in 1614, 32,000 out of 45,000 kerseys and 2000 out of 5000 dozens were shipped for the Eastland. (Most of the rest, it should be noted, were for Hamburg.) At Newcastle, in 1616, 12,000 out of 13,000 kerseys were shipped for the Eastland.[2] The Eastland company also appealed to the government's solicitude about unemployment when it introduced the case of the flax-dressers. The flax-dressers gave the finishing process to imported raw flax and it was therefore a disservice to the commonwealth to import dressed flax. But 'the Netherlanders bring as many commodities as they can, ready wrought', and 300 families of the flax-dressers in London and the suburbs, each employing between six and ten servants, 'now for want of the aforesaid work are fallen into great poverty'.

The making of policy

The Eastland company requested in their petition of 1620 a proclamation like the Levant company's proclamation of 1615: a proclamation—that is to say—which would extend their privileges beyond those granted in the charter of 1579, by excluding non-members not only from trading *to and from* the Eastland but also from trading in any *commodity of* the Eastland.

Their request was literally for a 'proclamation to forbid both English

[1] Bland, Brown and Tawney, *English Economic History: Select Documents* (London, ed. of 1937), 383.
[2] The figures are taken from Friis, *Cockayne's Project*, 61–8.

and others not to bring into this land any...eastern goods except the native commodities of their own several countries but in English ships'. This is not on the face of it a request for privileges, and the petition was submitted by the Eastland *merchants*, not by the Eastland *company*; but when the referees reported in favour of the proclamation they added 'as your Majesty hath already been graciously pleased to grant unto the Levant company whereof there is already good fruits'. The Levant company's charter, like the Eastland company's, excluded non-members only from trading to and from the area of their privileges. Their proclamation, strictly interpreted, did not exclude non-members from trading in goods of the Levant; but if that was not the original intention it was the immediate effect. This came about in the following way. In 1617 the Levant company summoned before them a merchant who, not being a member of the company, had imported currants, a Levant commodity. This man said that, being a Merchant Adventurer, he had the right to import currants from the Merchant Adventurers' privileges. The Levant company appealed to the Privy Council, the Council ordered the two companies to come to an amicable settlement, and the Merchant Adventurers consented in future not to import currants from their privileges. (The Merchant Adventurers said that they consented to this limitation of their trade 'because your Honours who are the competent judges in this case seem to judge that the present estate of the said Levant company standeth in need of some special favour'.) This agreement effectually limited the import of Levant goods to members of the Levant company, for we cannot doubt that the same restraint was to be imposed if necessary on foreigners. A clause of the proclamation which prohibited all import and export save in English ships was, in any case, probably sufficient to exclude Dutch merchants, since it excluded Dutch ships.

As to the Eastland company's phrase 'except the native commodities of their own several countries', this exception was also understood, though not stated, in the proclamation for the Levant company; for while the Levant company after the proclamation objected to Venetian merchants who were importing Levant goods in a Flemish ship, they did not object to them 'for importing into this realm upon their own adventures the commodities of their own growth, so the same were freighted in their own bottoms and those bottoms manned by natural born subjects of that republic'.[1]

When the Eastland company's proclamation was granted, it was, *mutatis mutandis*—in the Privy Council's words—in the same terms as the

[1] *A.P.C. 1615–1616*, 174; *A.P.C. 1619–1621*, 372. M. Epstein, *The Early History of the Levant Company* (London, 1908), 110–12; Epstein prints the charter.

Levant company's. Like theirs, strictly interpreted, it did not exclude non-members from trading in Eastland goods. But the Eastland company said that this was due to 'a defect in the penning of the same'.[1] The Dutch entrepôt trade could not be totally stopped save by a proclamation, the effect of which was to place the importation of Eastland goods wholly in the hands of the Eastland company.

However, the proclamation was not granted until two years had elapsed. Nor was a proclamation the only remedy suggested by the Eastland merchants. In the parliament of 1621 they attempted to secure the removal of the pretermitted custom on exported cloth. They sought for legislation which would have permitted them to develop a re-export trade in corn. One of their members proposed a navigation bill, the gist of which was to prohibit imports from the Dutch entrepôt. None of these proposals was successful. In the proceedings of the parliament we can perhaps see an element of confusion and conflict between the various interests represented there, sufficient to obstruct any clear line of policy.

When the parliament was adjourned in May 1621, the crown took up the inquiry into economic matters on an ever-enlarging scale. In June the Privy Council ordered companies of merchants to choose experienced representatives to confer on the decay of trade; in September it assembled representatives of the outports; in October it appointed a committee to study and consolidate their report; in November it appointed a commission of trade consisting of twenty persons 'of quality and experience', landed men and merchants including many members of parliament. Shortly after this the parliament reassembled but was quickly dissolved. In April 1622 a new commission of inquiry into the cloth trade was set up, and two clothiers from every clothing county were summoned to attend. Thus first the companies of London, then the outports, and lastly the clothiers became involved in the inquiry.[2] The well-known report of the clothing commission gave a perhaps unexpected emphasis to the Eastland trade, and its recommendations included every one of those we have mentioned above.

Meanwhile, the Eastland merchants had been coming under fire from the clothiers of Suffolk and Essex. At first, when the Eastland company had complained to the Privy Council against clothiers and others for shipping cloth to the Baltic, it ordered the customs officers to enforce their charter, and in August 1621 it reproved clothiers of Ipswich for exporting 'contrary to the charters of the merchants and in prejudice of their trade'. In 1622, however, when the clothing commission was sitting, it made an

---

[1] Appendix A 5.
[2] *A.P.C. 1619–1621*, 393; *A.P.C. 1621–1623*, 40, 71, 79, 201, 208.

order that, if the merchants did not buy the clothiers' cloth, the clothiers should have liberty to export it on their own account. The merchants expressed the opinion that the clothiers were unwilling to sell, but in reality the dispute was over prices. The merchants said that the price demanded by the clothiers, £9 to £13 a cloth, was excessive, and that they had raised the price to that height in anticipation of liberty of export.[1]

In February 1622 the Eastland merchants petitioned for permission to transfer their foreign residence from Elbing to Danzig, on the ground that navigation at Elbing was difficult and that tolls had to be paid to the Duke of Prussia as well as to the King of Poland. This the Council granted. The merchants also petitioned for the issue of the proclamation that the referees had recommended in 1620. But the Council was probably waiting for the reports of its commissions of inquiry.[2]

The clothing commission reported in June. Of its many recommendations only one—for sumptuary laws—was purely domestic. Otherwise the commission was wholly concerned with the export market, and, as we said, it was much concerned with the market in the Eastland.[3]

In considering the recommendations that relate to the Eastland trade, let us first notice that there was no suggestion to alter the value of money. Since a principal factor in the crisis was the rising of the money in the Eastland and Germany, it was only natural that some men should have turned to monetary remedies, and Misselden and Malynes put forward two aspects of this view in their famous four pamphlets of argument and counter-argument. They made these suggestions to one of the commissions of trade. But the view did not prevail. The referees on the Eastland merchants' petition had said that to reduce the moneys 'either to their ancient or some equal standard through all Christendom we most humbly refer to your Majesty's great wisdom, being a thing far beyond our capacity'. They were practising merchants, and this tactful comment meant that interference with money was dangerous and difficult. Thomas Mun formally opposed Misselden and Malynes in the commission of trade and published his arguments in *England's Treasure by Foreign Trade*. In one chapter he repeated Malynes's attack on Misselden and in another he displayed in turn the vanity of Malynes's proposals. Mun's twelve practical recommendations have in common an emphasis on commodities. 'The good husbandry or excess [of consumption] in the kingdom...will rule all the rest, and without this all other statutes are no rules either to keep or procure us treasure.'

---

[1] *A.P.C. 1619–1621*, 394; *A.P.C. 1621–1623*, 34; SP 14/131/40. The Council's order giving liberty of export is printed at Appendix A 3.

[2] *A.P.C. 1621–1623*, 134, 168.   [3] SP 14/131/55.

The clothing commission recommended a prohibition of the export of gold and silver. This was not contrary to Mun's teaching. It is true that he favoured the export of silver in course of trade, saying that there was a time to trade in goods and a time to trade in money, 'and so by a continual and orderly change of one into the other grow rich', but this does not mean that he approved of indiscriminate export at the will of the individual. He thought that English merchants ought to export silver in trades where it would benefit the common weal; but nowhere does he suggest that foreigners should be allowed to do so. In this sense the proclamation met his requirements, since it could easily be dispensed with on occasion; in fact, we must regard dispensations—in favour of the East India trade, for example—as an indispensable part of it. The prohibition was not therefore merely an expression of the type of thought called bullionism. It had an obvious direct remedial effect on the crisis in the Eastland trade, for by preventing the export of money to the Netherlands it hindered the entrepôt trade in Eastland goods.

The clothing commission recommended a reduction of the customs duties on the export of cloth. (Or rather they ostentatiously did *not* recommend this, but they reported that high duties were a contributory cause of the depression.) This was one of the points that the Eastland company had raised in the parliament. They said that it was too much on a cloth worth £7 to pay 6s. 8d. for the old custom and 4s. for the newly imposed pretermitted custom, as well as a levy of 1s. 8d. for piratage.[1] And so it was; for at that price the two customs well exceeded the acknowledged proper rate of duty, 5 per cent. However, we saw that they complained elsewhere that clothiers were demanding from £9 to £13 a cloth, and at that price the customs were just. The pretermitted custom made only about 2 per cent difference on board ship, and far less in Poland after the cloth had passed through the customs of the King of Denmark, King of Poland and Duke of Prussia. The case against the pretermitted custom was therefore far from overwhelming, and it remained.

The clothing commission recommended that the Eastland merchants should be granted complete and permanent freedom to re-export Baltic corn. This too was one of the Eastland company's requests to parliament. Their idea was to re-export Baltic corn to Spain, Portugal and Italy, exactly as the Dutch did. They said that this would both enlarge their cloth trade and bring in silver from the places where the corn was sold.[2] In the past their cloth exports had fluctuated in accordance with the state of English harvests—bad harvests and high exports in 1597, 1609, 1614 and 1618, and good harvests and low exports in 1591 and 1602—so they

[1] Appendix A2 (*a*).   [2] Appendix A2 (*b*).

were probably right. But the English corn laws stood in the way. These permitted the export of corn only when the English price was unusually low. Actually, in 1620 and 1621 it was unusually low and a re-export trade was permissible; what the merchants desired was legislation to make it possible permanently. But could they really expect this in a parliament where the agricultural interest was feeling the pinch of low prices and had even introduced a bill to prohibit the *import* of corn? Arguments against the bill included the plight of the Eastland merchants and of the cloth manufacturers, and there was so much opposition that it failed, but on the other hand the agricultural interest would naturally oppose with equal determination any measure such as the Eastland company desired which was likely to increase the supply from abroad.[1] The harvest of 1621 was bad, prices rose, the export of corn was forbidden; the Eastland merchants thus recovered their domestic market (if only they could preserve it from the Dutch) but the question of re-export remained in abeyance. Thomas Mun was one of those who supported the proposal for re-export:

For I suppose that £100,000 being sent in our shipping to the East Countries, will buy there 100,000 quarters of wheat clear aboard the ships, which after being brought into England and housed, to export the same at the best time for vent thereof in Spain or Italy, it cannot yield less in those parts than £200,000 to make the merchant but a saver, yet by this reckoning we see the kingdom hath doubled that treasure.[2]

With this in mind one looks with sympathy at the ingenious scheme which the crown proposed after the report of the clothing commission. The problem was to distinguish between corn imported for re-export and corn imported for the home market. The new scheme was for 'increase of tillage, better venting of our native commodities, strength to our shipping, and breeding of many mariners, by erecting magazines of corn which in times of scarcity may serve to keep down the price of foreign corn, and in times of plenty may keep up the price of our home corn at such reasonable rates as will well maintain the husbandman's labour and hold up the gentleman's rents'. All imported corn was to pass through the magazines. It could be taken out of the magazines for sale in England only when the price in England was above a certain figure (32s. a quarter), and it could be taken out for re-export only when the price in England was below a somewhat higher figure (40s. a quarter). This admirable scheme might well have kept corn prices fairly steady between these two figures, while at the same time encouraging re-export; but it would have required

[1] (Sir Edward Nicholas), *Proceedings and Debates of the House of Commons in 1620 and 1621* (Oxford, 1766), I, 287, II, 87; Notestein (ed.), *Commons debates 1621*, II, 378–9, III, 280–3, IV, 357–9, V, 171–2, VI, 163–4.   [2] *England's Treasure*, ch. 4.

very exact administration, was therefore perhaps utopian, and came to nothing. An Act of the next parliament (1624) simply prohibited export when the price exceeded 32*s.*, below which figure it subsequently hardly ever fell. The Eastland merchants thus lost their hope of a re-export trade unless the crown was willing continually to grant them licences.[1]

The clothing commission recommended 'some course' to confine imports to English ships; except that foreign ships should be permitted to bring goods of their own country. This was the gist of a navigation bill which had been introduced in the parliament by Robert Snelling of Ipswich, an Eastland merchant. But there is no evidence that the Eastland company supported it. Sir Dudley Digges, who had promoted the Eastland company's case on other points, spoke against it. The bill would not have prevented the Merchant Adventurers from importing Eastland goods from the Netherlands so long as they used English ships. Perhaps this did not go far enough for the Eastland company. Had the bill passed, the proclamation could not have been granted. At the second reading Snelling spoke but apologetically, and it was lost. The crown also opposed the bill, probably for reasons of state. A common objection was that it would provoke hostility in the Netherlands, and 1621 was not the year to lose a powerful Protestant ally without whose help it was impossible to save the Palatinate. Economic retaliation was also to be expected: 'if we bar the Low Countrymen to bring in any other merchandise than such as is there grown (they having none grown in that state), they will also bar our merchandise to be brought thither'. This underlines a basic English dilemma. To cut free of the Dutch entrepôt by bold legislation required a willingness to give up friendly relations altogether, which was inconceivable in the European scene as it then was.[2]

Tacked on to the navigation bill was a clause for the free re-export of corn. There was also a clause reviving the Statute of Employment, which compelled foreign importers to employ the proceeds of their imports in the purchase of English goods. Another clause prohibited the import of dressed flax. Another clause debarred clothiers, shopkeepers and retailers from engaging in foreign trade; none to trade but mere merchants. All these disappeared with the failure of the bill. All, save (in one detail) the last, were in line with the report of the clothing commission.

[1] Rymer's *Foedera*, xvii, 526; N. S. B. Gras, *The Evolution of the English Corn Market* (Harvard University Press, 1915), 244–50. Subsequently the price was often below 40*s.*, so that re-export from the magazines would have been possible. See Thorold Rogers's wheat prices, Appendix D.

[2] *Commons Journals*, i, 615, 642; Nicholas, *Proceedings*, ii, 192. Notestein (ed.), *Commons Debates 1621*, ii, 432, iii, 427–9, iv, 430–1, v, 400. Snelling and his seconder were prominent opponents of the corn bill.

Since parliament had accomplished nothing, the clothing commission was presumably inviting the king to take action under the prerogative. He responded with the scheme for corn magazines, with a proclamation to prohibit the export of gold and silver, and with a proclamation for the Eastland company.

The clothing commission made recommendations for the better regulation of the cloth trade on the manufacturing side and also for some reform of the trading companies: low entrance fines, no stint of export, no joint-stock companies except the East India company, but all trade to be managed by companies and no shopkeepers or retailers to be members. Evidently they thought that clothiers might be members; otherwise little or no criticism of the Eastland company was implied. They made their report in June and the Eastland company's proclamation was issued in July.[1]

The main points can be briefly summarised:

(1) Its purpose was said to be 'to maintain and increase the trade of our merchants and the strength of our navy, the one being as the veins whereby wealth is imported into our estate, and the other as principal sinews for the strength and service of our crown and kingdom'.

(2) It recited that the Eastland company had for forty years (since their foundation) 'had the sole bringing in' of Eastland commodities, 'whereby our kingdom hath been much enriched, our ships and mariners set on work, and the honour and fame of our nation and kingdom spread and enlarged in those parts'. Therefore the king now ratified the Eastland company's privileges, and commanded those in authority at the ports 'that they suffer not any...commodities whatsoever, brought from any the foreign parts or regions wherein the said company have used to trade, to be landed, except only such as shall be brought in by such as are free of the said Eastland company'. The 'defect in the penning' was probably in this clause, in the words 'commodities whatsoever, *brought from* any the foreign parts'; a subsequent proclamation by Charles I substituted 'commodities whatsoever *of* those foreign parts'.

(3) An exception was 'that the importation of corn and grain be left free and without restraint'.

(4) Lastly, the 'good and politic laws, made against the shipping of merchandises in strangers' bottoms, either inward or outward'—'of late years...much neglected'—were to be strictly put in execution.

(5) Two unstated exceptions were understood. First, English merchants might continue to use foreign shipping for imports when English ships were not available. The use of foreign ships when English were not to be

---

[1] *A.P.C. 1621–1623*, 286–7; SP 14/132/30, 31. The proclamation is printed below, in Appendix A4.

had was, according to Trinity House, just, reasonable and agreeable to the practice of the port of London.[1] Secondly, native merchants of the Eastland were permitted to import into England their own goods in their own ships; the most that was required to enable them to pass their goods through the English customs was a certificate of ownership.[2]

These exceptions were taken for granted, but the proclamation was not silent about them merely for this reason; had they been positively stated they would have become established rights. This would have inconveniently limited the field of administrative discretion. Later, we shall find the crown tightening up against the use of Danish ships. In the second half of the century, we shall find the Eastland company attempting to invoke their monopoly of imports even against the native merchants of Danzig. In a subsequent chapter we shall discuss the flexibility (not always recognised) of the legislation that comprises what we call the mercantile system. It was flexibility in administration. It would not have been possible, but that exceptions were on the one hand always expected, and on the other hand not so openly declared that they became rights.

[1] *A.P.C. 1623–1625*, 375–6.   [2] E.g. *A.P.C. 1623–1625*, 277–8.

Chapter III

THE TRADE BETWEEN THE DEPRESSION OF
1620 AND THE DEPRESSION OF 1649

The depression of 1620 ended for the Eastland merchants, perhaps earlier than for others, with a marked recovery in 1623. But the recovery did not last. Henceforth the volume of cloth exports was disappointingly low. Before 1620 it had been the sign of a bad year when broadcloths in the Sound Tables fell below 10,000. After 1624 it was the sign of a good year when they nearly reached 10,000.

Exports to the Baltic

The course of trade from year to year can be followed in the figures reproduced from the Sound Tables at Appendix D. They are not entirely reliable, though probably a fair guide, before 1618; in 1618 the system of toll collection at the Sound was made more efficient; after 1618 it is possible to use them with confidence. Similarly, it is possible for the first time to use with confidence the extra particulars which the editors of the Sound Tables give for every tenth year. These include values of goods. English, Scottish, French and other 'southern' nations (but not Dutch) paid among other tolls an *ad valorem* duty of 1 per cent on all goods, at the price at the port of shipment, as declared by the shipmaster or as expressed in papers accompanying the goods. The King of Denmark maintained a right to buy goods at the declared value, so there is a presumption that they were declared correctly. The English were freed from this duty in 1647. For the tenth years 1625, 1635 and 1646 we have, therefore, a good deal of useful information. They were neither very good years nor very bad (see Appendix D) and they reveal characteristics that may be taken as normal.[1]

[1] The tolls went straight into the King of Denmark's pocket. His window at Kronborg, overlooking the roadstead where ships lay to pay them, reminds us to this day of the close supervision he was able to exercise. Merchants had to trust the shipmaster to pay what was due and were interested in seeing that he did so, because if he were caught in a fraud all the goods might be confiscated. The possibility of detection after 1618 was high. It is not surprising that after 1618 our Eastland merchants' exports were, on the whole, declared correctly. The Sound Tables, which are summaries of the original registers, have the defects of their virtues; every entry in the registers consists of about half a dozen items, but only two or three can be embodied in a single table, and the original entry can never be reassembled.

The best critical works on the Sound Tables are Friis, [*Dansk*] *Historisk Tidsskrift*, 9R. 4Bd. (1925), 109ff.; *Scandia*, 8 Bd. (1935), 129ff.; Christensen, [*Dansk*] *Historisk*

HET

The normal trade into the Baltic, so far as England was concerned, was nine-tenths a cloth trade, and it was shipped in English vessels and by English merchants. Other activities were on the fringe. There were some other exports. There was a constant small shipmaster's trade. There was a small export in foreign ships, sometimes by English merchants, and a small export by foreign merchants, sometimes in English ships. There was also a slight recurrent trade in English ships from places outside England— a little wine and salt perhaps, from France or Spain. But these branches of trade were abnormal. Only when trading conditions were abnormally bad did foreign ships or merchants take a considerable part in the export trade of England, and only when they were abnormally good did English ships or merchants take a considerable part in the Baltic trade of other countries.[1]

The typical state can be seen at a glance in Table 2, which gives the value in Danish rixdollars of all goods in English ships. The value of the goods of English merchants is given as declared, and that of the few goods of foreign merchants has been calculated by analogy. At the bottom of the table is given the declared value of English merchants' goods in foreign ships. This is therefore the complete account of English trade into the Baltic, except for the omission of foreigners' goods in foreign ships—but the value of this was negligible.

Thus the cloth trade accounted for (almost) 95 per cent of the total trade in 1625, 85 per cent in 1635 and 93 per cent in 1646. Table 3 shows the quantities and values of the main types. We have this information only for the cloth of Englishmen, but if we could include the cloth of foreigners it would make little or no difference to the proportions. The proportions alter, revealing trends: kerseys were declining, perpetuanas rising. The broadcloth (*kleide*) consisted almost entirely (we learn from port books) of short Suffolks dyed and dressed. These and the perpetuanas were shipped from London and Ipswich, the dozens were shipped from Hull, the kerseys were shipped from Hull and Newcastle. In 1625, therefore, the cloth exports of north and south were roughly equal in value but in 1646 those of the south were three times as valuable as those of the north.

All this cloth went almost exclusively to the Prussian ports of Danzig,

Tidsskrift, 10 R. 3 Bd. (1934), 112 ff.; *Hansische Geschichtsblätter*, LIX (1935), 28 ff. Professor Friis, on the English cloth trade, is specially relevant.

All references in this chapter are to the first series, N.E. Bang and K. Korst, *Tabeller over Skibsfart og Varetransport gennem Øresund 1497–1660*, I (Copenhagen, 1906), 2 A (1922), 2 B (1933).

[1] These facts emerge from the Sound Tables by comparison of various tables for every year. One table in vol. 2 A gives quantities of goods in English ships, another gives quantities from England. A third, in vol. 2 B, gives quantities from all places separately, subdivided into the ships carrying them. We discover the nationality of the merchant only in the tenth years. Shipmaster's trade is observable only in English port books.

TABLE 2.* *English trade into the Baltic: value of goods in Danish rixdollars*

A = Englishmen's goods in English ships. B = Foreigners' goods in English ships.
C = Englishmen's goods in foreign ships.

		1625	1635	1646
Cloth	A	544,776	480,014	511,610
	B	1,700	12,900	13,754
Salt	A	1,273	16,821	3,150
	B	0	1,682	0
Herrings	A	30	5,736	468
	B	0	0	0
Wine	A, B	1,000	768	4,500
Spices	A	850	9,324	2,616
	B	0	400	0
Hides and skins	A	3,219	12,157	8,706
	B	725	76	66
Leather	A	5,462	2,624	1,366
	B	0	0	0
Tin	A	5,784	15	0
	B	0	840	0
Other goods	A	9,121	19,034	9,951
	B	0	0	0
Total in English	A	571,515	548,493	542,367
ships	B	2,425	15,898	13,820
Englishmen's goods in foreign ships	C	0	13,271	6,904
		573,940	577,662	563,091

* Sound Tables 2A, table 1*b* and notes. Coal was not dutiable and is omitted. 'Other goods' are mainly *kram*—cutlery, haberdashery and small mixed goods. Wine paid a special duty. Of the above, goods from outside England were: in 1635, wine, about half the total quantity of 467 pipes in English ships; in 1646, salt, 180 lasts out of 230 lasts in English ships. Goods from England in foreign ships were so few that they must be mainly accounted for in C, details of which are not given in the Tables.

TABLE 3.* *Englishmen's cloth exports by types*

	1625	1635	1646
Broadcloth	7,474	5,823	6,725
	(269,769 Dr.)	(218,759 Dr.)	(293,472 Dr.)
Kerseys	36,949	17,966	6,069
	(246,392 Dr.)	(146,096 Dr.)	(62,709 Dr.)
Single dozens	2,350	4,972	2,922
	(26,276 Dr.)	(70,320 Dr.)	(69,396 Dr.)
Perpetuanas	30	2,337	6,318
	(344 Dr.)	(31,380 Dr.)	(77,829 Dr.)
Other types	322	1,288	1,205
	(1,995 Dr.)	(13,459 Dr.)	(8,204 Dr.)

* Sound Tables 2A, notes to table 1*b*. The figures for kerseys and perpetuanas in 1646 are slightly inexact.

Elbing and Königsberg. This mainly appears from port books. When the Eastland company's residence was at Elbing most of the entries were for Elbing; when the residence was at Danzig most were for Danzig. In 1641, thirty ships sailed from London for the Baltic, twenty-one for Danzig, two for Königsberg, and seven for 'the Sound'. In 1636, twenty-nine ships sailed from Ipswich for the Baltic, all for Danzig. In 1637, fifteen ships sailed from Hull for the Baltic, twelve for Danzig, two for Königsberg, and one for Elbing. In 1640, nine ships sailed from Hull for the Baltic, seven for Danzig and two for Königsberg.[1]

Danzig and Königsberg are about eighty miles apart; Elbing lies between them. They were gateways to a vast area of central and eastern Europe, the basins of the rivers Vistula and Niemen. English cloth probably penetrated great distances. It was generally understood that the chief market for broadcloth was among the Polish gentry. Thus the English merchant did not pretend to reach the consumer. He dealt with merchants of the Prussian towns, men of his own type.

A few ships carried most of the cloth, perhaps about 80 per cent of the trade by value. Many ships went lightly laden, many sailed in ballast. Return cargoes were cheaper and bulkier than export cargoes.

The price of cloth was rising. Having fallen during the depression, it took ten years or more to recover. On the eve of the depression of 1649 it was higher than it had ever been.[2]

The value of exports remained, on the whole, lower than it had been before the depression of 1620. On the basis of the figures given in Table 2, and at four Danish rixdollars to the £, exports were worth (at first cost) £144,000 in 1625, £145,000 in 1635, and £141,000 in 1646. This remarkable constancy is a coincidence, but the lowness, compared with similar figures for earlier tenth years, is significant.[3]

[1] Respectively E190/44/1, 604/6, 318/1a, 318/7.

[2] Prices derived from the Sound Tables are averages. In reality there was a wide range. For example, in the original registers, in cloth ships from Ipswich in 1624, *kleide* (which must have been short Suffolks) ranges from 26 to 55 dollars the piece. This demonstrates, incidentally, that prices at the Sound were not just a convention. It also means that there is a possibility of alterations in length or quality having created the illusion of price movement; yet the apparent price movement in cloth looks plausible. These are prices in Danish rixdollars, from Sound Tables 2A, going back to 1565:

	1565	1575	1585	1595	1605	1615	1625	1635	1646
Broadcloth	21	22	34	33	38	41	36	38	44
Kerseys	6	7	8	8	8	8	7	8	10
Dozens	8	10	10	10	12	12	11	14	24

The dozens are supposed to be singles, but some doubles have perhaps been included in 1646.

[3] These are the values in Danish rixdollars (thousands), of Englishmen's goods only, going back to 1565, from Sound Tables 2A. It is to be remembered that before

Imports from the Baltic

We cannot speak with the same assurance about the trade out of the Sound, because the customs officers at the Sound recorded only the ports of departure, not destinations.

Yet it is a fair assumption that English trade out of the Baltic was normally a simple homeward trade to England. The merchants habitually spoke of their 'returns', and whenever it was a question of supplying other countries with Baltic goods everyone took for granted that the only method was re-export. The unmistakable impression of a two-way trade, out and home, has some support from the Sound Tables, inasmuch as the English ships *from* other countries were so few that one supposes there can have been but few *to* them. Thus the cargoes of all English ships at the Sound can be taken as English imports.[1]

Of Baltic ships too it is plausible to assume a two-way trade. Therefore Baltic ships returning homeward from England had probably been outward bound, laden, to England. For every tenth year the Sound Tables tell us the goods they had carried outward.

In the period after the 1620 depression, English and Baltic ships carried practically the whole trade. Dutch ships had disappeared from English trade: three were freighted by English merchants from the Baltic in 1625, none in 1635, three in 1646. (The port books confirm this eclipse. Even imports from the Netherlands were brought in English ships.)[2] One Bremen ship was freighted by English merchants out of the Baltic in 1646, and one Scottish ship. These foreign ships of western nations, whose cargoes are not specified in the Sound Tables, were therefore of small importance, and the cargoes of English and Baltic ships constitute— perhaps for the first time—almost the complete tale of English imports.

Nearly all this trade was handled, evidently, by English merchants. Merchants of the Baltic did not as a rule export to England even the products of their own countries in any considerable quantity. This

1618 the quantity of goods (though perhaps not their price) was not declared correctly. According to Professor Friis we must add perhaps a tenth to the broadcloth and as much again to the kerseys; the correct total might therefore be 50 per cent higher:

1565	1575	1585	1595	1605	1615	1625	1635	1646
103	192	426	472	581	562	572	562	549

[1] There is an assumption that the number of English ships *to* other countries was smaller than the number *from*. This was the case after 1669, when destinations began to be recorded.

[2] For a study of port books see O. A. Johnsen, 'The Navigation Act of 9 October 1651', *History*, new series, xxxiv (1949), 89 ff. (or in *Revue d'histoire moderne*, 1934); but Professor Johnsen's main thesis is insecurely based on that evidence. The abrupt disappearance of Dutch ships can be observed in my edition of Boston port books.

emerges from Table 4, in which the Baltic ships returning from England tally closely with those freighted by Englishmen.

TABLE 4.* *Foreign ships in English trade out of the Baltic*

A = Baltic ships that subsequently returned from England. B = Foreign ships freighted by English merchants.

Ships of	1625		1635		1646	
	A	B	A	B	A	B
United Provinces		3		—		3
Bremen		—		—		1
Scotland		—		—		—
Lübeck	4	3	10	9	10	8
Stralsund	—	—	—	—	2	—
Danzig	1	—	2	5	4	8
Denmark	—	3	5	10	2	1

* Sound Tables 2A, table 1 *a*, note B (for column A), table 5 (for column B). This is an example of the difficulty of combining separate items in the Tables. Note that some Danish ships do not count as 'Baltic'.

TABLE 5.* *Probable English trade out of the Baltic*

	1625	1635	1646
English ships, laden only	80	114	85
Their cargoes in dollars	256,000	500,000	436,000
Foreign ships	11	25	27
Their cargoes in dollars	15,000	50,000	85,000
Total shiploads	91	139	112
Total value	271,000	550,000	521,000

* The figures for English ships, are taken from Sound Tables 1. Those for foreign ships are the higher in every pair in Table 4.

The value of English ships' cargoes includes small quantities belonging to foreign merchants, calculated by analogy. (For these goods see Table 6.) English ships were freighted by foreign merchants as follows: 1625, two (Danzig); 1635, one (Danish), three (Swedish); 1646, one (Swedish).

We are therefore in a position to assess the volume and value of the English import trade. The value of the cargoes of the Baltic ships that returned from England (A in Table 4) can be calculated, by analogy with English ships' cargoes, as, respectively, about 9000, 27,000 and 58,000 dollars. The value of English-owned goods in foreign ships (B in Table 4) was declared as, respectively, 10,000, 47,000 and 66,000 dollars. The two categories considerably overlap. In table 5 the value given to foreign ships' cargoes is an approximation in which the probable error is of the order of 2–3 per cent of the value of the goods in English and foreign ships together. But the values must be treated with reserve. All authorities agree that westward cargoes were less correctly declared than eastward

TABLE 6.* *English trade out of the Baltic in Danish rixdollars: goods in English ships and in certain foreign ships*

Rye:	1625	1635	1646
In English ships:			
For Englishmen	41,241	126,494	21,765
For foreigners	0	0	0
In Baltic ships	0	20,454	2,142
Wheat:			
In English ships:			
For Englishmen	2,600	14,210	23,860
For foreigners	0	0	0
In Baltic ships	3,640	0	0
Hemp and flax:			
In English ships:			
For Englishmen	134,603	175,877	247,864
For Foreigners	0	0	0
In Baltic ships	0	895	15,865
Linen and canvas:			
In English ships:			
For Englishmen	6,121	32,364	26,682
For Foreigners	0	0	0
In Baltic ships	0	120	0
Wood:			
In English ships:			
For Englishmen	4,680	8,662	18,702
For foreigners	1,138	150	0
In Baltic ships	656	663	3,300
Pitch and tar:			
In English ships:			
For Englishmen	9,482	8,786	7,029
For foreigners	0	8,281	0
In Baltic ships	2,414	3,828	1,570
Potashes:			
In English ships:			
For Englishmen	39,232	88,403	36,087
For foreigners	864	0	0
In Baltic ships	0	0	1,100
Iron, steel, and iron goods:			
In English ships:			
For Englishmen	4,888	1,142	30,577
For foreigners	0	10,240	190
In Baltic ships	0	0	5,000
Other goods:			
In English ships:			
For Englishmen	9,969	22,718	17,111
For foreigners	829	2,180	0
In Baltic ships	c. 2,000	c. 1,000	c. 29,000
In all:			
In English ships:			
For Englishmen	252,826	478,656	435,793
For foreigners	2,831	20,851	190
In Baltic ships	c. 9,000	c. 27,000	c. 58,000

* Sound Tables 2 A, table 2 and notes, table 4 b. The values of foreigners' goods in English ships and of all goods in Baltic ships are calculated by analogy. The foreign ships are those identified as having subsequently returned from England.

cargoes. The ships were heavily laden, the cargoes heterogeneous; it was easier than in the eastward trade to declare low quantities and to disguise heavily taxed goods as cheaply taxed. In addition, the merchants had less control over the shipmasters. With this warning, Table 6 gives the value of the most important commodities in English ships and in Baltic ships that subsequently returned from England. It therefore falls slightly short of being a complete picture of the trade; but it is sufficiently complete to show the range of commodities and their relative importance.

The most valuable group of imports was hemp and flax—commodities which the registers often fail to distinguish. Linen and canvas were derived products, and a certain quantity of linseed, hempseed, yarn and tow is included under 'other goods'. In 1635 corn came a good second; this was naturally a fluctuating trade. Rye predominated, but the increasing proportion of wheat is probably no accident. Small amounts of other grain are included under 'other goods'. The third group of commodities was wood and wood products. In the table, 'wood' includes wainscot, clapboard, pipestaves, a few planks and deals, some oars, and masts only in 1646. Descriptions of Anglo-Baltic trade sometimes give the impression that masts were an important part of it, but this is only true in the sense that ships cannot be built without them—it is not true in the sense that there were many of them. The same holds good for other naval stores; deals and planks, pitch and tar, were indispensable for building ships, but not very important commercially. The table is a good guide in this respect, so far as one can judge from earlier tenth years and from English ships' cargoes in ordinary years.[1] Potashes, not a naval store, were evidently a new trade, grown up since the beginning of the century; in the table they were worth more than any other product of the forest. A fourth group of growing value was iron and iron goods.

The bulk of these goods came from Danzig, Elbing and Königsberg. Here we have the ports of departure of English ships for the same three years (Table 7). This table shows two movements. First, with the shift of the Eastland company's residence from Danzig to Elbing between 1625 and 1635, Danzig took Elbing's exports, just as it took the imports of cloth. But the position of Königsberg was not affected. Königsberg supplied most of the flax, linen and canvas, while Danzig had the rye, wheat and potash. Elbing had little or no special exports, and as a source of English imports was probably never wholly satisfactory. A second

---

[1] It is true that ships for long timber were predominantly foreign-built, and that in these goods it is especially hard to identify the trade to England; yet I believe the conclusion is justifiable, if only by the smallness of the total Baltic export of these goods.

TABLE 7.* *English ships westward bound*

	1625	1635	1646
Danzig	14	78	34
Elbing	19	0	2
Königsberg	45	31	34
	78	109	70
Other ports	3	8	19
(incl. Riga)	(0)	(2)	(12)
	81	117	89

* Sound Tables 1. Ships in ballast are included. The ships from Danzig in 1646 include one from the nearby port of Putzig.

movement, of greater importance in the long run, was the movement to Riga; about half the hemp came from there in 1646. There was also a movement to Sweden. Most of the tar and iron in English ships in 1635 and 1646 came from Stockholm. Further, most of the tar and iron in 1635 belonged to foreigners, namely, to Swedish merchants. We are observing early signs of a great seventeenth-century expansion of Sweden's foreign trade.

Compared with the export trade, the import trade had a greater diversity of commodities and came from a wider area geographically. A higher proportion of it was carried in foreign ships. In Swedish trade, though not elsewhere, native merchants had a big share. The importance of the Eastland company's residence, always less marked for imports than for exports, was diminishing still further as the trade reached out to Riga and Sweden.

The desire for imports

On the basis of Table 5, imports from the Baltic were worth, at first cost, about £70,000 in 1625, £140,000 in 1635, and £130,000 in 1646. The low value in 1625 is noteworthy. It was only partly due to the low volume of corn imports.

If we separate the violently fluctuating corn trade from the trade in all other goods—which can be done for every tenth year, with some guess-work—we find that the latter is relatively stable, and that the figures appear to show a trend. This trend was upwards through 1575, 1585 and 1595, and downwards through 1605, 1615 and 1625. There was a low point in 1625. The decline was not simply a matter of price; to some extent, therefore, it was a case of low demand.[1]

[1] These are values and prices, in Danish rixdollars, from Sound Tables 2 A. The division between corn and other goods is made on the assumption that the proportion

At the same time the demand for imported rye was probably, on the whole, decreasing as well. Broadly speaking, whereas England imported corn in the first half of the century, in the second half she exported it. The unusual cheapness of wheat about 1620, owing to exceptionally good harvests, is said to have accelerated a change of taste from rye to wheat, and we are told that even poor people began to refuse rye bread. Periodical crises in the clothing industry doubtless tended to increase tillage. In 1631, when wheat was exorbitantly dear, the Eastland merchants could not dispose of all the rye they brought to London.[1]

It is sometimes suggested that the mercantilist era was characterised by 'fear of imports', but this was not the case with the Eastland trade in the first half of the seventeenth century. In the Eastland trade imports were welcome and there was a fear of losing them.

The problem created by a low volume of imports was expressed with the utmost clarity in the years immediately following the depression of 1620. The merchants said firstly that, having 'no exchange from thence', the value of what they exported was necessarily equal to the value of what they imported; and secondly that, money being 'high' in the Eastland, they could not import silver without loss. It followed that the value of commodities exported could not possibly exceed the value of commodities imported. Therefore low imports meant low exports. We must examine this proposition.

In the sixteenth and seventeenth centuries, it is generally held, the in foreign ships was the same as in English ships, and the figures are for Englishmen's goods only. The values are in thousands:

	1565	1575	1585	1595	1605	1615	1625	1635	1646
Value:									
Rye and wheat	0	40	4	169	36	135	46	155	52
Other goods	145	189	286	313	285	203	197	371	449
Total	145	229	290	482	321	338	263	526	501
Prices (lasts):									
Rye	?	20	29	35	23	26	53	35	29
Flax	55	71	98	69	93	79	63	95	94
Hemp	?	40	48	49	63	46	37	79	61

The price of hemp bought by the navy in England, in shillings the cwt., was as follows (Sir William Beveridge and others, *Prices and Wages in England* (London, 1939), 670, 676):

1565	1575	1585	1595	1605	1615	1625	1635	1646
?	?	?	?	27	25	18	37	23

This tends to show that the price of Baltic goods in England followed fairly closely the price in the Baltic.

[1] Sir William Ashley, *The Bread of our Forefathers* (Oxford, 1928), 44–7. For 1631, see below, p. 79.

complete balance of trade in the sea-borne trade through the Sound was heavily in favour of the Baltic. In England's trade, however, we have suggested that in the earlier phases the balance was favourable to England. It would therefore look more natural had this balance been offset by bills of exchange against the Baltic's credit with other western nations, rather than brought back in the form of silver coins, as the merchants said it was.[1] But had this been a false statement it would surely have been questioned during the depression of 1620, when the whole picture would have been radically altered had it been possible to sell English cloth at Danzig in exchange for Baltic goods bought at Amsterdam. The entire discussion assumed that this was not possible; John Ramsden talked as if silver were an ordinary commodity of trade.[2] One should perhaps bear in mind that it is easier to transport silver by ship than by cart, that the convenience of bills of exchange is greater in long overland trades than in sea-borne trade, and that it is not impossible that bilateral trade was commoner in the seventeenth century than it had been in the fifteenth. Other indications that Baltic trade was bilateral are that the merchant Lewes Roberts, in his compendium *The Merchants' Map of Commerce* (1638), had a long section on the European exchanges but nothing about an exchange in the Baltic, while Josiah Child wrote in the second half of the century that there was a settled course of exchange only with Hamburg, Holland, Flanders, France and Italy;[3] and one who must have known the truth said in 1651 that rixdollars were imported from Hamburg for re-export to Denmark and Norway.[4]

As to the 'height' of money in the Eastland, we have seen that between 1618 and 1622 it was raised by no less than 73 per cent, and with this in mind the merchants thereafter referred to it as 'raised', 'high', 'scarce', 'mixed' and 'base'. They meant that the ordinary coin was mixed and base, and that the rixdollar was raised, high and scarce. In another phrase, silver went at a high rate there. These words expressed the belief that goods were cheap in terms of silver, that a piece of English cloth earned no more silver than it had cost to buy and transport, and that the exchange of cloth for silver was therefore out of the question; cloth could only be exchanged for goods. Can this be true? Lewes Roberts wrote in 1638 that 'the Polanders...are noted to have so little gold and silver, as despising all in respect of it, they sell the rich commodities of their country at a low rate';

---

[1] Appendix A 2 (*b*). [2] Above, p. 17.
[3] *A New Discourse of Trade* (London, 1694), 163 (ch. 9). This was written about 1668.
[4] Thomas Violet, *The Advancement of Merchandise* (London, 1651), 47–9. 'Denmark and Norway' does not normally mean the Danzig area, for which 'East country' is the normal phrase.

but his whole account is obviously a plagiarism of Fynes Moryson, whose description was based on a visit made in 1593.[1] In the Polish price histories it cannot be observed that real prices were especially low after they had caught up with the debasement by about 1625, but for cloth prices, which matter most, there is no good series.

Already in 1620 the merchants told the king that their exports were 'wholly returned in the commodities of the eastern countries'. In 1621 they told the parliament that 'thereby raising some benefit [they] were enabled to afford the cloth and other commodities of England at indifferent rates, and consequently in greater quantities'. This referred to an unspecified length of time *before* 1620, namely 'formerly'.[2] After the depression, in their fear of losing imports, they categorically stated the same thing on three separate occasions. Their argument was self-interested, but it was not refuted even by those whose interests were opposite.

Before the depression of 1620 was fairly over, certain projectors broached a scheme for making soap by a new method. The scheme had several apparent advantages, among them that it dispensed with imported potash which was used in the old method. Since the Eastland company imported potash, they raised objections. The chief was, that if they could not import potash they must export less cloth. They said that £30,000 of potash imported yearly was equivalent to 3000 cloths. They also said that their imports maintained shipping. The projectors replied that 'there is a maxim in trade not to be denied, that if our importation exceed our exportation, what pretence soever of employment of shipping and mariners is put upon it, that trade is unprofitable'; they suggested that the merchants import more silver, corn or other commodities.[3] The projectors, with their balance-of-trade thesis, look more 'mercantilist' than the merchants, but the merchants successfully made out that the only alternative to potash was silver coin and that they could not import silver coin without great loss—'the common coin minted in those parts being base and nowhere else current, and dollars and ducats lately risen to more than double their old value'.[4] This the projectors accepted, and agreed to saddle themselves with the burden of paying, as compensation for the loss of potash, 10 per cent on whatever base foreign coin the merchants found necessary to import: 'The merchants may bring bullion instead of ashes but cannot without loss. This loss may be recompensed, and then this work may

[1] *The Merchants' Map of Commerce*, ch. 233; he repeats the statements of Fynes Moryson, above, p. 4.
[2] Appendix A 1 (*a*), 2 (*a*).
[3] SP 14/155/39.
[4] Appendix A 5; January 1624, reflecting the situation as known in 1623.

yearly increase our treasure by about £20,000.' It was calculated that
£20,000 in silver was the equivalent of £30,000 in potash.[1]

In this extreme disparity may be discerned a reflection of the peculiar
circumstances of the debasement. After it had worn off the Eastland
company's argument became less extreme. But the substance remained:
if you reduce our imports, we must reduce our exports.

The soap business was not put into effect at that time but it was revived
some ten years later. Again the Eastland company protested:

> Money being scarce in the East Country, the greatest part mixed and
> base, and no exchange from thence, their returns lie wholly in commodities,
> of which potashes are a principal part. . . .
> In the Eastland trade exportation and importation stand in such relation
> that the one prospers not without the other; if the importation or use of
> potashes (a fourth part of the company's returns) be restrained, the vent
> of a fourth part of the manufactured cloth exported will then be hindered.[2]

Again in 1635 the Eastland company used this argument to stop the
Merchant Adventurers from importing Baltic commodities from Hamburg. They alleged

> that from these parts they have no exchange, nor by reason of the excessive
> rising of moneys can make any return in coin or bullion, so that in what
> proportion any other merchants bring in their returns in the same measure
> they hinder the exportation of dyed and dressed cloth.[3]

If these facts had not been true the well-informed Hamburg merchants
would have denied them, but they did not.

What a change from the prosperity of the sixteenth century is suggested
by these arguments! In those days the English merchant had a virtual
monopoly of the cloth trade in the Eastland, and the demand for his
product was limited only by the extent of the demand for Eastland corn
in the rest of Europe, but in the seventeenth century he competed with
Dutch and local producers and could not hope to recover his great trade
short of out-and-out price-cutting, which was out of the question.
Regarded as a cloth-exporting trade, the Eastland trade held small

---

[1] SP 14/155/41. But in Appendix A 5 the merchants put the probable import of
money at £30,000, presumably making 3000 cloths = £30,000 potash = £30,000.
This reduces the force of their argument but explains (what otherwise is rather odd)
why they accepted compensation at only 10 per cent. The calculation accepted by
the projectors was as given above, namely, that 3000 cloths = £30,000 potash
= £20,000.

[2] Appendix A 8.

[3] PC 2/44/482. The soap business and the case against the Hamburg merchants will
be referred to again, below, pp. 79, 81.

promise. The merchant was slow to acknowledge this publicly, but he had already begun to find his main profit on imports.

These arguments were not used after 1635. There was no need of them. The demand for Eastland goods increased, and the fear of losing imports was removed.[1]

The import boom

Eastland commodities were cheap, and freight made a large part of their final cost. In wartime freight charges were high. This was due to the activity of privateers, which in the seventeenth century were every country's chief weapon against enemy commerce. The most efficient privateers were those in the service of Spain, operating from Dunkirk and Ostend, and both English and Dutch trade in the North Sea and Channel was highly vulnerable to them. When, therefore, in 1621, the King of Spain resumed his struggle with the Dutch, their freight charges naturally rose. In their Norway trade, between 1625 and 1640, their freight charges rose progressively by no less than 100 per cent. And they also imposed a convoy system which necessarily reduced the number of voyages that a ship could make in a year.[2]

For the first few years of the Thirty Years War England remained at peace, but in 1625 came war with Spain and in 1626 war with France. Charles I, however, reverting to the policy of his father, made peace with France in 1629 and with Spain in 1630. It was inglorious, but it was good for trade. Charles made an arrangement with the Spaniards whereby their stream of silver from Spain to the Spanish Netherlands was diverted from the route through Genoa and made to flow through London, where one-third of it was to be sold to the mint. English commerce had always desired Spanish silver, and by this means it was brought to the doorstep. How was it paid for? The mere fact of neutrality opened the way for an expansion of trade with the belligerents, especially of the always profitable Spanish trade.

Such were the advantages of neutrality that English ships were even hired by the Dutch. We find them chartered for the Norway trade,[3] and in 1640 nine sailed from Dutch ports into the Baltic. Thus Charles I's

---

[1] The cases outlined above are evidence that the Eastland merchants were not *exporting* silver, for the soap manufacturers would not have omitted to make so powerful an argument in their favour had there been any possibility of its being substantiated. But there may have been an export of silver to Norway.

The general question of bilateral trade is discussed, with special reference to Baltic trade, by C. H. Wilson and the late Professor Eli Heckscher, in *Ec.H.R.* 2nd series, II–IV (1949–51).

[2] J. Schreiner, *Nederland og Norge 1625–1650* (Oslo, 1933), 49.

[3] *Ibid.* 49–50 and Appendix.

policy directly encouraged navigation. All English trades must have been stimulated by the now relatively low freight charges of English ships. The Eastland trade is a barometer of the state of trade in general. When we see English ships doing well in the Eastland trade itself—where freight charges were a more important factor than in any other trade— we may assume that they were successful elsewhere. The general expansion of shipping will then result in a swelling of the Eastland import trade in naval stores. Lastly, when conditions in French, Spanish and such-like trades are favourable, we shall expect to see Baltic goods re-exported to those places and their goods re-exported (or exported directly) to the Baltic Signs of all these things are observable about 1640.

In 1640, 1641 and 1642 the Sound Tables disclose three or four English ships a year entering the Baltic from north German ports: small numbers, but exceptional. In 1641 there was a ship from Spain, in 1643 a ship from Portugal. More significant, in 1641 and 1642 there were ten ships each year from France, whose cargoes doubled the normal salt trade in English ships. Between 1633 and 1642,. and especially in the three years 1640–42, English ships carried out of the Baltic large quantities of corn which bear no relation to the state of English harvests as evinced by domestic wheat prices, and which, therefore, were presumably, in part, re-exported, or carried to other countries direct.[1] Entrepôt trade is seen most clearly in the success of an interesting device of economic policy, the Dover composition trade. The Sound Tables show that this worked extraordinarily well in Baltic trade from about 1636 to 1643.[2]

Between 1633 and 1642 the cargoes of English ships outward bound from the Baltic included, besides corn, unusually large quantities of hemp and flax. Hemp, perhaps the most vital naval store, implies the presence of others. We may be sure that a great part of them went to English shipyards, to support the expansion of the merchant marine. Not all the

[1] Re-export of corn was permitted in 1635; PC2/45/177.
[2] The following ships of Dover passed through the Sound westward (Sound Tables, 1):

1616	0	1624	0	1632	—	1640	11
1617	0	1625	0	1633	2	1641	31
1618	0	1626	0	1634	—	1642	11
1619	0	1627	0	1635	2	1643	14
1620	1	1628	0	1636	5	1644	7
1621	0	1629	0	1637	9	1645	6
1622	0	1630	0	1638	6	1646	0
1623	1	1631	1	1639	7		

Ships of Sandwich and other southern ports show a like trend. From a short examination of the Sound toll registers I have the impression that they were mainly engaged in the westerly trade.

new ships were foreign-built; we know there was a surge of building at home.[1]

We can hardly speak of an export boom. It is true that cloth exports reached a peak in 1640, but it was a minute peak. Compare it, for example, with the great boom of 1597. In 1641, in the westward traffic, the value of English trade was probably higher than in 1597 by something in the region of one-half. In the eastward traffic, on the other hand, 9000 broad-cloths exported in 1640 contrast with 22,000 exported in 1597. They were a little dearer, and there were more of other kinds of cloth, more salt, more wine, more coal, but their value was almost certainly lower, perhaps a fifth lower. In the boom of 1597 it looks as if exports were worth more than imports, but in the boom about 1640 it looks as if imports were worth more than exports.[2]

The import boom may therefore be thought to have required an export of silver. Accused of this in 1638, the Eastland company replied that they exported silver only for payment of customs dues in places where they did not trade, or where their goods sold slowly; and they received per-mission to export a dollar and a half per ship's ton, 'care being taken they transport not other coin but dollars'.[3] It is certain that some people were

---

[1] A Dutch observer at the Sound reported in 1642 that most English ships passing through the Sound were Dutch-built, having been bought at the prize market at Dunkirk; cited by V. Barbour, 'Dutch and English merchant shipping', *Ec.H.R.* II (1930), 288. But this may be an overstatement. One of the volumes of the Sound toll registers for 1641 (vol. B) records the build of ninety English ships; fifty-eight were built in England, twenty-six in Holland, one in Zealand, one in Flanders, two at Lübeck, one at Danzig, and one in France. (The figures refer to voyages, however, and the same ship may be counted more than once.)

The rate of shipbuilding in England will be discussed below, p. 100.

[2] Rough estimates of quantity and value in 1597 and 1640–1 can be based on the more detailed information available for adjacent tenth years, 1595, 1635 and 1646. For 1597, I estimate eastward trade at 900,000 Danish rixdollars and westward trade at 600,000. For 1640, I estimate eastward trade at between 600,000 and 700,000, and for 1641, I estimate westward trade at nearly 1,000,000.

[3] 'Whereas the Governor, Assistants and Fellowship of the Eastland merchants did by their humble petition this day read at the Board represent that divers of the said company, being questioned in the Star Chamber for exporting dollars, which they took for payment of their foreign customs in places where they either trade not at all or where their commodities vend slowly and uncertainly; but upon examination of their charter and the nature of such foreign customs, paid only in and for passage, and of the sundry hazards and distresses their ships are subject to, in which exigents they shall hardly get any help without money not of a foreign but a known coin; their Lordships were pleased not only to free those particular merchants, but to grant liberty for a future exportation of a limited proportion of dollars; and now they humbly besought their Lordships' warrant and licence that each of their ships according to their burthen and tonnage may carry out a proportionable quantity of dollars for the use above expressed; and they conceive a dollar and a half per ton may suffice, so that a ship of 100 tons shall not carry above 150 dollars, and accordingly one of

exporting not merely silver, but English silver coin to Norway at this time, for in the 1640's it circulated there, and English crowns, shillings and half-shillings were bought by the Norwegian mint in large quantities.[1] The export of foreign coin was permissible under certain circumstances, but the export of English coin was always wholly indefensible. This export to Norway was therefore clandestine, and if it could be concealed in the Norway trade it could perhaps be concealed in the Baltic trade.[2]

The expansion of trade under Charles I was conspicuous. One could actually see the ships, and new types of adventures—our ships with salt from France, for example—could become common gossip. It was the sort of expansion that people could easily exaggerate. On the other hand, it did not solve the problem of the old draperies, and there was a scare about the export of silver. Therefore it was possible for a period of mercantile prosperity to be full of complaints of hardship. At the very time when the Eastland trade was at its height, Sir Thomas Roe, fresh from an embassy to the Baltic, made a speech in parliament about the 'decay of coin and trade'. He thought that riotous consumption had created an adverse balance of trade and that the cloth industry was in a bad way, but he began the speech by saying that 'it is a general opinion that the trade of England was never greater'. So a profound pessimism was not inconsistent with the belief in a great trade. And Sir Thomas Roe had doubts about the great trade itself; he knew about commercial matters and he did not think that it would last:

> I said at first, it was a general opinion, that trade never flourished more than now, and it may be so; but we must consider this be not accidental and changeable, and depending more upon the iniquity or misery of the times, than upon our own foundation and industry; and if that be so, then

300 tons (which is the greatest they employ) not above 450 dollars; their Lordships taking the same into their consideration do recommend the examination thereof [to a committee]....'

A few days later the committee reported in favour of granting the request, 'being for payment of their customs abroad and other occasions set down in the order, which exportation we conceive both necessary and reasonable, care being taken they transport not other coin but dollars' (PC 2/48/502, 620).

[1] J. Wilcke, *Møntvaesenet under Christian IV og Frederik III i Tidsrummet 1625–70* (Copenhagen, 1924), 177, 188. For the history of Danish money before 1625 (which followed the same lines as Polish money) see the same author's *Christian IV's Møntpolitik 1588–1625* (Copenhagen, 1919).

[2] If there was a regular export of silver to the Baltic it is somewhat surprising that the Council of Trade of Charles II, which recommended the free export of foreign coin and bullion, did not cite the Baltic trade as one that required it. It only said that the East India, Turkey and Norway trades could not be managed without it. B.M. Add. MS. 25115, 42 ff.

it is no sure ground for a state to rely upon; for if the causes change, the effects will follow.

Now it is true, that our great trade depends upon the troubles of our neighbours, and we enjoy almost the trade of Christendom; but if a peace happen betwixt France, Spain and the United Provinces, all these will share what we now possess alone, and therefore we must provide for that day; for nothing stands secure but upon his own foundation.[1]

When we come to the crisis of 1649 it will be clear that this was a true prophecy. Roe's solution was to develop and reform native industry; this, however, as we shall see, was little regarded, and trust was mainly placed in the development of an entrepôt. What had chiefly captured the public imagination in the trading expansion under Charles I was, apparently, the expansion of the re-export trade.

A note on war and peace

The Baltic trade was twice interrupted by war. In 1626 Gustavus Adolphus captured Elbing and in 1627 and 1628 he blockaded Danzig. He had already taken Livonia and he wanted to add the mouth of the Vistula to his conquests. The Eastland company, trading with Gustavus's enemies, were in an awkward situation. For some time they had no foreign residence. Some of the company said that

because that the times were troublesome they did and would forbear to venture into the East Country, and...that the company was dissolved because in those times of war in those parts they were driven and put from their place of residence, and protested that they thought there would be no more trading unto those parts for four years after.[2]

Cloth exports were lower than in the 1620 depression, and imports suffered too. The trade was 'at a stand', the merchants standing pat, waiting for better times, either living on past profits or diverting their energy to other trades. There was no universal outcry of ruin and disaster such as there had been during the depression. This sort of interruption must have been regarded in the seventeenth century as part of the normal way of trade. When the war was over the Eastland company moved their residence to Danzig and resumed their trade.

The second interruption was in 1643–4. This coincided with the outbreak of civil war in Yorkshire, when Hull suffered a short siege. But the export of broadcloth was as much reduced as the export of northern

---

[1] *Sir Thomas Roe his Speech in Parliament: wherein he sheweth the cause of the decay of coin and trade* (London, 1641).
[2] Appendix A6.

cloths, although there was no campaign in Suffolk and Essex. It is difficult to gauge the effect of the civil wars on economic activity. The major factor in this stoppage may have been a naval war at the Sound between Denmark on one side and Sweden and the Netherlands on the other, the first of a series of conflicts for the command of the Baltic. English ships had no protection.

These interruptions were the penalty that the English merchant paid for going to trade in places where English warships could not penetrate, and where his government had little or no influence.

The Norway trade

For knowledge about the Norway trade we rely on English port books. The chief import was Norway deals, supplemented by poles, balks, spars and small masts; there was hardly anything not derived from the Norwegian pine forest. Oak grew in Norway but its export was forbidden. These commodities supported a busy trade employing many ships, which are prominent in port books of the east coast. Hull has twenty-seven entries from Norway in 1631, thirty-one entries in 1637, and twenty-nine entries in 1640; and from Gothenburg (a similar trade) three entries, seven entries and four entries; which may be compared with seventeen entries, thirty-six entries and thirty entries from the Baltic.[1] Newcastle relied on Norwegian spars for its coal mines. Boston port books have frequent entries from Norway, and at places as small as Scarborough entries recur almost annually. Grimsby had a specially close link with Norway, with anything up to five shiploads a year. These bulky goods were not easily moved by road and were therefore brought by sea as nearly as possible to the consumer.

Norwegian goods were cheap. Their total value is hard to judge. If one hazards the suggestion that in this period they were worth a little more than one-third of the trade from the Baltic, it is little more than a guess.[2]

Exports to Norway were mainly cheap cloth, kerseys. A high proportion of Newcastle's textile exports went to Norway, some of Hull's, very little of London's. The value was slight.

Most of the imports came from the neighbourhood of Oslofjord. Tønsberg is a prominent name. The ships were about half English and half Norwegian. (That is to say, they had Norwegian home ports; they

[1] E 190/316/12, 318/1A, 318/7.
[2] At London, according to Mrs Millard's preliminary calculations from port books E 190/24/4 and 26/2 (1621–2) and 37/8 and 38/5 (1633–4), imports were respectively £14,000 against £74,000 from the Baltic and £12,000 against £40,000 from the Baltic, at the valuation of the 1604 book of rates.

may have been Dutch built and even Dutch owned.[1]) Most of the imports were entered in the name of an English merchant, but some, especially at the smaller ports, were entered in the name of the foreign shipmaster. Exports were habitually entered in the name of an English merchant.

The Norway trade, like the Baltic trade, was liable to competition from the Dutch entrepôt. In 1621–2, at London, Norwegian imports from the Netherlands were about one-third by value of those imported direct; but in 1633–4 there were no Norwegian goods from the Netherlands.[2] We cannot follow the ups and downs of the Norway trade, but it probably fluctuated in parallel fashion to the Baltic trade without, however, feeling the political interruptions to which the Baltic trade was subject.

In one respect the Norway trade differed from the Baltic trade. It frankly was and always had been an import trade. The ships had to seek their cargoes at a multitude of Norwegian harbours and there could be no question of a staple town. In England the cargoes were distributed to small ports and creeks where the Eastland company had no residence. The Norway trade was therefore a freer trade than the Baltic trade.

[1] For an often quoted remark by Roger Coke to the effect that the English used Dutch ships in the Norway trade before the Navigation Act of 1651, see below, p. 147.
[2] Mrs Millard's abstract of port books.

Chapter IV

THE PURPOSE OF A REGULATED COMPANY

When the Privy Council of Charles I issued on behalf of the Eastland company a second and even fuller proclamation than that issued by James I in 1622, it used these words:

[that it was] careful (as always) to preserve and maintain companies of merchants in their just privileges and immunities...well knowing how much the supporting and encouragement of this company in particular imports the service and benefit of his Majesty and the state.[1]

Then again in 1635, giving judgement against a member of the company who had infringed one of the company's regulations, the council said that it was

careful to preserve and maintain the liberties and privileges of the said company and not to suffer the orderly government of a trade so much importing the good and benefit of the common weal in general to be violated by any particular person out of private respects.[2]

To what extent were these words sincere and this attitude justified? Did the liberties and privileges of the Eastland company really import the good and benefit of the common weal in general?

The Eastland company is to be regarded primarily as an organisation for the export of cloth. This becomes clear as soon as we look at their by-laws. In the records of the company at York we have a set of these, apparently a complete set, as they were 'confirmed and agreed upon' in 1618 after a dispute between London and the outports. Others were added from time to time.[3]

The most detailed and exacting group of rules regulated the shipment of goods from England. The procedure was as follows. A shipmaster who wished to carry goods for the company went first to the treasurer (or the deputy or other officer) and entered bond of £50 (from 1631, £300) (i) to pay truly the tolls of the King of Denmark, King of Poland and Duke of Prussia; (ii) not to carry goods for unfreemen; (iii) to deliver the cargo at Elbing and not elsewhere; and (iv) before sailing from England to hand to the treasurer 'a just and true content' of his cargo. The treasurer then gave to the master a certificate without sight of which merchants were not to lade their goods in his ship; and with it he also

---

[1] Appendix A 7.   [2] PC 2/44/526.
[3] Sellers, *Acts and Ordinances*, 11 ff.

gave to the master 'a sheet of paper or two sheets annexed together if need be, entitled "The content of all such goods as are now laden in such a month and year in such a ship whereof is master *A.B.* and from such a place for the said East parts"'. This is the 'content' referred to above; it was more commonly called a toll-bill. The master had to present the toll-bill to every merchant who shipped goods in his ship, and the merchant had to enter a full description of his shipment 'as the same are to be tolled in the Sound'. When the master had finished lading he returned the completed toll-bill to the treasurer. The treasurer checked the toll-bill against the customs books, sealed it, and addressed it to the Danish customs officers at the Sound. He also made a copy, which he sealed and addressed to the company's deputy in the East parts. He gave both to the shipmaster for delivery. He then issued a note to the English customs officers to let the ship sail, and the voyage could begin. The by-law about the toll-bill is the longest in the whole collection, the procedure is laid down in minute detail, and the penalties are exceptionally severe.

A second prominent group of rules regulated conduct at Elbing. It was forbidden to employ foreigners as factors and brokers. There were rules about giving credit to purchasers. No longer than a year's credit was to be allowed for fine cloths and six months' for other cloths, in two instalments at most. The form of bill to be accepted from purchasers was laid down.[1] The deputy had great authority. He was to receive the toll-bills from shipmasters and had power to search and seize in case of false entries. He collected the company's impositions, he could stop members trading and must send home sons, servants and apprentices in case of misbehaviour. The by-laws are full of references to the necessity of preventing disorderly conduct by factors.

These rules were appropriate only for an export trade to a staple. There are few signs of an intention to regulate imports, even imports from the staple. By the 'act for establishing of trade at Elbing' merchants were strictly forbidden to 'transport convey or deliver or cause to be transported conveyed or delivered any goods wares merchandises whatsoever (being native commodities of this kingdom) directly or indirectly to any other place than the town of Elbing'; but with this proviso:

that it shall and may be lawful to any brother of this company to trade and traffic into and with the kingdoms of Denmark, Norway, Sweden, and the towns of Riga and Reval in Livland, they making their returns directly from thence through the Sound westward to this realm of England or elsewhere.[2]

---

[1] The bill promised payment 'mitt gutten gungbhar geldt'; Sellers, *Acts and Ordinances*, 49, 55–6.   [2] *Ibid.* 22–3.

Thus the company did not profess to regulate re-exports, nor to regulate either export or import trade in places where they had no foreign residence.

The company further regulated the cloth trade to the staple by appointing ships and shipping times. For example, in 1664 they appointed three limited days for London and Ipswich, viz. the 15th of March for stuffs and for Spanish and white cloths only; and the 15th of May and 20th of August for cloth; which are to be the last days of water bearing; and no cloths or stuffs are to be laden from thence for the east, but in the said appointed ships and within the limited time; on penalty of 40 shillings a cloth and ten a piece of stuff.[1]

Evidently the company were responsible for charter parties and had fairly permanent arrangements with shipowners. They were able to make a rule that disorderly shipmasters 'shall be dismissed of the company's service here for 12 months after'. As the shipping dates indicate, exports to the Baltic went in one large and one small block. We normally find in the port books a sailing of perhaps three heavily laden cloth ships from London and perhaps two from Ipswich in April or May; and one or two of the same ships would make a second voyage in August or September.

Thus one group of by-laws regulated shipping *to* the staple and a second group regulated behaviour *at* the staple. The remainder were such as every professional association requires for good order: they refer to the keeping of books and to the auditing of accounts; to penalties for unprofessional conduct, for indecent words, for fighting with weapon blunt or sharp, for disclosing secrets, for interrupting the governor's speech, for attendance at courts, and so forth. Although the body of the company met infrequently, the officers were busy: under-officers 'shall every day as well Sunday as other give their attendance upon the governor or deputy as well before noon as afternoon'.

Let us consider with what success some typical free-trade arguments could be employed against this organisation.[2] The company could withstand them fairly well. The appointing of ships and shipping times, for example, was clearly a service as well as a restriction, for it enabled merchants to spread their cloth over several ships and yet be as sure as

---

[1] Sellers, *Acts and Ordinances*, 82.
[2] What follows is not entirely hypothetical. I have no evidence of a concerted free-trade attack on the Eastland company at any time, but the following points were constantly in the air. Bland, Brown and Tawney, *Select Documents*, 443 ff., give all the possible free-trade arguments that could be mustered in 1604. SP 16/487/50 (probably 1640), which is a company's answer to a free-trade attack, is attributed by the *Calendar* to the Eastland company, but probably belongs to the Merchant Adventurers.

possible that it would arrive at the same time. The company could arrange convoys[1] and could even obtain exemption from impressment for the crews of their ships.[2] The strict rule about the toll-bill prevented ship-masters from defrauding the Danish customs officers, thereby protecting the merchants' goods from confiscation.

Free traders might have accused the Eastland company of oligarchy. The company consisted of residences at London, Ipswich, Hull, York and Newcastle, but the government was vested by charter only in the court at London where the provincial residences had no voice, and at London all power resided in the governor and twenty-four assistants. The assistants themselves elected members to fill vacancies in their number; only they could dismiss an assistant; they elected the governor, and made laws for the whole company. Thus according to the charter a group of less than thirty men ruled the Eastland trade of the whole kingdom. The outports continually protested against this arrangement. In 1616, after a dispute, the Privy Council laid down that laws affecting the whole society were to be made only at an annual court, held on a fixed day, at which representatives from the outports were present as well as the London commonalty. The outports like the commonalty were only observers at this general court, but if they felt aggrieved they had an appeal to the Privy Council, which would have declared invalid any law not in the best interests of the company. The oligarchy of the Eastland company—unless it is better called an aristocracy—could be contrasted unfavourably with the more democratic form of other companies, but was probably not a matter of great importance. The Eastland company did not stint the trade of individuals, as did the Merchant Adventurers.

Free traders would have said that the company's membership was too restricted. The Eastland company, like other regulated companies, was a professional association open only to 'mere merchants'. A mere merchant was 'such a one as hath of some good continuance not less than three years traded at home and abroad beyond the seas merchantlike'.[3] The company were bound to admit any mere merchant who offered to pay the entry fine of £20; so it could be said that there was no serious bar against those who were already merchants. A young man could obtain admission to the Eastland company without payment if he were the son of a member or if he graduated by apprenticeship. Apprentices served eight years (reduced to seven in 1688). No member could make free more than two apprentices in seven years. It is impossible to judge if this rule reduced the number of traders below the number there would have

[1] E.g. *A.P.C. 1625–1626*, 463; SP 16/170/36.
[2] *A.P.C. 1625–1626*, 19.   [3] Sellers, *Acts and Ordinances*, 3.

been under free trade. The justification for admitting only mere merchants was that the art of merchandise required experience and training. An Eastland merchant had to know about relatively few commodities—a few kinds of cloth and a short list of Eastland goods—but he had to be master of a great deal of information about the Eastland. He had to be familiar with several foreign currencies and systems of weights and measures, with the rates of toll and commercial practices in foreign places, with the state of war and peace and the risks and prohibitions incidental to war. (A regulated company performed a useful service for its members by disseminating information about these matters.) If one man's wit was fully employed in one area of trade, it is not surprising that a predominating characteristic of English foreign trade in the first half of the seventeenth century was specialisation by areas rather than specialisation by commodities. If we look at a London port book of 1640, when the Eastland trade was prosperous, we find that 123 Englishmen exported both to the Eastland and to Hamburg, that forty-eight made more than one venture, but that only four exported to both places. Fifty-eight exported to the Eastland, twenty-five made more than one venture, but only three exported to Norway as well as to the Baltic.[1] This degree of specialisation seems normal; one cannot fail to recognise, looking through port books, that names familiar in the Eastland trade do not occur in other trades. And it seems to reflect the difficulties of commerce rather than the exclusiveness of companies.

But free traders would not be content with this answer. They would assert that all who wished to assist in the export trade should be free to do so. They would state dogmatically that the export of cloth could not be in too many hands; their argument was, that a large number of exporters in competition with one another, being compelled to adopt every possible device to reduce costs, would by low prices export more cloth than a regulated company whose members exported in co-operation rather than in competition. This if true was a powerful argument because it was the quantity of cloth that mattered to the commonwealth, rather than the profit of the merchant. And any monopoly probably tends to keep prices high. But the company would have replied that it was not true. They would have pointed to the disadvantages of 'selling off the ship's keel', as the phrase went. A trader with limited capital, having sent a shipload of cloth to the Eastland, would find himself forced to sell at a price set by the purchaser, because otherwise he would be unable to collect his return cargo quickly enough to make the voyage profitable; the purchaser's price would be too low for profitable trading, but in the

[1] E 190/43/1.

meantime merchants who demanded a fair price would have found no buyers. The argument was, briefly, that price-cutting was bad for all traders and would *diminish* the quantity of cloth exported. There is obviously much to be said for the company's point of view, and we cannot dismiss it without knowing much more than we do about the practical difficulties and profit margin of the merchants. The company would have objected further to free trade that the free trader's eagerness to cut costs would drive him to employ foreign ships, and this argument would be hard to answer. The company necessarily insisted on English ships at least for exports, since foreign shipmasters could not have been subject to the necessary penalties.[1]

Free traders would have said that the company's impositions were a burden. On a short Suffolk cloth in 1618, worth perhaps £10, the king took 6s. 8d. and the company 8d. On a northern dozen in 1618 the king took 3s. 4d. and the company 3d. On a kersey in 1618 the king took 2s. and the company about 2½d. On a fother of lead in 1618 the king took 28s. and the company 8d. In 1623 the company took 1s. 6d. on a cloth, and on other goods at the same rate. Even so, the company's impositions seem not excessive.

We see clearly in what circumstances free-trade theory would be likely to prevail, but they had not arrived in the time of James I and Charles I. The Eastland company argued never more strongly than when they showed that they provided practical benefits in the way of privileges and immunities in the foreign market, 'which services were not to be effected by single persons, who are not able to make so vigorous resistance against oppressions, nor can expect that respect abroad which an united company may enjoy'.[2] When the Eastland company alleged that free trade was ruinous, they were implicitly contrasting it not so much with regulated trade as with privileged trade, in which merchants abroad had rights of warehouse, freedom from taxation and security of property. Tangible benefits such as these chiefly justified their discipline and impositions. Thus, when in 1631 they were negotiating for the move to Danzig, in order to

---

[1] Compare *Sir Walter Raleigh's Observations*, 39–40; Some Eastland merchants 'send over an unexperienced youth, unfit for merchandising, which bringeth to the stranger great advantage but to his master and commonweal great hindrance; for they before their goods be landed, go to the stranger and buy such quantities of iron, flax, corn and other commodities, as they are bound to lade their ships withall, which ships they engage themselves to relade within three weeks or a month, and do give the price the merchant stranger asketh, because he gives them credit, and lets them ship away their iron, flax and other commodities, before they have sold their kerseys and other commodities'.

The Eastland company seem to have this sort of situation in mind in their representations given at Appendix A9 and 10.   [2] Appendix A9.

strengthen their hand, they proposed a temporary embargo on exports, and at the same time, doubtless in order to defray the cost, they increased their impositions and also charged them for the first time on Baltic imports.[1] If the company failed to provide these benefits their discipline and impositions became indeed burdens. Likewise if they were provided by other means—let us say by the state—the arguments of free traders against the company would be immeasurably strengthened. Both these things occurred in the second half of the seventeenth century. But in the first half of the century the Eastland company succeeded more or less in providing privileges for the greater part of their trade. They were able to assert that free trade would forfeit them. Those who wanted a greater measure of freedom in the Eastland trade merely proposed that the entrance fine should be reduced and/or that the eligibility should be widened.

Let us now examine the attitude of the crown. There can be little doubt that the crown did really support the Eastland company on grounds of public interest and that these grounds were cloth and ships. As to cloth, it wished to promote the cloth trade chiefly for the sake of employment. Unlike the Merchant Adventurers, the Eastland company exported dyed and dressed cloth—'dyed and dressed cloth fully manufactured and fit for the garment, in which respect their trade concerneth not themselves alone but many thousands of his Majesty's subjects from the wool grower to the poor workman employed in making and finishing of cloth'.[2] We have seen that at the time of the 1620 depression the cloth industry of East Anglia and Yorkshire depended in great part on the Eastland merchants, and it is equally true that about half the cloth exported from Hull in 1633 and nine-tenths of the cloth exported from Ipswich in 1636 was shipped for the Eastland.[3] It is not surprising that the company received their greatest favours at times of depression in the cloth industry. In the seventeenth century the export of the older kinds of cloth was on the whole declining, while the export of the lighter and brighter new draperies was increasing, mainly for southern markets; this is a sign to us of technological change and economic progress, but at the time people were more aware of the distress in the old industry. Highly skilled workers do not readily change their trade, so that there could be too few workers in one place and too little work in another. Unemployment caused riot and endangered the peace. States without police forces are sensitive to this sort of trouble, and states without an adequate system of poor relief must do everything to keep the people employed. Against this background the

---

[1] Sellers, *Acts and Ordinances*, 64–5. Cloth was raised to 1s. 6d. It must therefore have been reduced after 1623.

[2] Appendix A 8.　　　　[3] E 190/317/6 (Hull), 604/6 (Ipswich).

Eastland company naturally emphasised that they provided employment. They also emphasised that they provided employment by their imports. Flax and hemp-dressers, whose raw material came from the Baltic, are unexpectedly prominent in the state papers of this time. But the theme of employment recurs constantly on all hands.

The crown promoted the merchant navy for the sake of sea power. Royal ships were only the nucleus of the navy, and the availability of fit merchant ships and trained seamen was therefore an important consideration. The Eastland company said on one occasion that they employed ships up to 300 tons,[1] which were big enough to fight in the fleet; they called themselves 'a singular nursery of seamen';[2] and their ships made one, two or at most three voyages a year and were therefore constantly available. They could therefore claim to serve the commonwealth better than the Netherlands and French trades, which were said to employ small ships, and better than the East India trade, whose ships were large and stout but often far away. In the Eastland company's proclamation of 1622 the crown declared that its intention was (in part) 'to maintain and increase...the strength of our navy...as principal sinews for the strength and service of our crown and kingdom'.[3] These words recall an instruction to the Council of Trade in the same year:

And because the maintenance of our navy and the shipping of our kingdom, is a principal means to advance the honour, strength, safety and profit thereof, we will and require you, *chiefly and above all things,* seriously to consider by what good ways and means our navy and the shipping of this kingdom may be best maintained and enlarged.[4]

The crown did not support the Eastland company because of the monetary value of the Eastland trade. We have seen that the normal value of the Eastland trade in the first half of the seventeenth century, exports and imports together, with freight, charges and profit, was in the region of £400,000. The total trade of England had been estimated at about £5 million.[5] On this reckoning the Eastland trade accounted for less than one-tenth. The crown bestowed more care on the Eastland trade than this proportion warranted.

The crown did not support the Eastland company in the belief that they would import silver. It is true that the proclamation of 1622 announced that its second purpose was 'to maintain and increase the trade of our merchants...as the veins whereby wealth is imported into our estate',[6]

---

[1] Above, p. 49n.   [2] Appendix A9.
[3] Appendix A4.   [4] Rymer, *Foedera*, XVII, 410ff.
[5] Edward Misselden, *The Circle of Commerce* (London, 1623).
[6] Appendix A4.

and that the company boasted whenever they could that they had *formerly* or *hitherto* imported money. Nevertheless, there was no question of their importing money either when that proclamation was issued or later. The crown did not support the Eastland company because they imported commodities that were vital. Their imports *were* useful. The Eastland company boasted that 'the commodities which we bring out of the East parts are necessary for the use of this land, and as the worthy late Lord Treasurer often said, for the necessariness of their commodities they were to be nourished'.[1] The Eastland trade imported naval stores; after 1650 the importance of naval stores can hardly be exaggerated; but before 1650 there were no shortages of imported naval stores and the crown was little troubled about their supply. In any case, had it been so troubled, this would have been an argument for free trade rather than company trade. The Eastland trade also imported corn. Corn was a vital commodity of which there were sometimes acute shortages, and it was expressly exempted from the provisions of the proclamation of 1622. After 1650, when the supply of naval stores became urgent, it was one of the factors tending to destroy the Eastland company. Meanwhile the crown supported the Eastland company because they *employed* ships, not because they imported materials for building them. Otherwise it would have been absurd to use the same words in the Eastland company's proclamation as in the 1615 proclamation for the Levant company; the Levant company imported no naval stores, and always applied for the crown's favour on the ground that its cheap and bulky imports—like the Eastland company's—employed many ships.

The crown did not support the Eastland company from a mere love of privilege. One of the instructions to the Council of Trade in 1622 was as follows:

And because it is conceived by many, that by reason of the discouragements happened to trade, the number of merchants now applying themselves in course of merchandise are of too small a number to manage the same, and that if the number of traders were enlarged, trade itself would now be enlarged, which is now said by some to be imprisoned, being for the most part confined to companies and societies of merchants, and others excluded which are not members of those companies, we will and require you to take into your consideration, whether it be necessary to give way to a more open and free trade or not?

We must take it that this question was intended seriously. While the Dutch traded successfully under free trade, privilege could never become an obsession in England.

[1] SP 14/118/143, undated.

We said that the Eastland company was an organisation for the export of cloth. After 1622 it was also an organisation for the protection of English trade against the Dutch. The influence of the Dutch on English economic policy in the seventeenth century can hardly be exaggerated. When James I came to the throne one of his first acts was to end the state of war with Spain. It seems that some people foresaw a new era as well as a new reign, and, as the free traders put it,

Under our gracious Salamon, a prince of wisdom and peace, we are like to be in league or amity with all nations; whereby, as there will be greater freedom abroad to trade to all places, so fit to have greater at home for all persons to trade. The alteration of times may make that fit now, which in times of hostility might have seemed unfit.[1]

For some years England was at peace while the Dutch remained at war. The free trade movement broke the Spanish and French companies, and the Levant company was in some danger. The Dutch made peace with Spain in 1609. It is probably no coincidence that the French company was incorporated in 1611. The Levant company, complaining against the Dutch, were granted a proclamation in 1615. The Eastland company's proclamation fits into this pattern.

To speak of Dutch 'competition' in this period is something of a euphemism. It implies that the chief danger from the Dutch was their export of cloth to foreign markets where the English also sold cloth. This was not so. It is true that English cloth exporters complained that Dutch cloth was sold cheaper than their own, but the chief danger arose from the import into England of foreign goods from the Netherlands. Dutch competition in the cloth trade might have led to free trade, since free traders could argue that it was best met by reducing prices. But competition in imports unquestionably required measures of protection. The Dutch could supply everything that England required.

No timber in Holland, and yet they have the staple thereof.
No corn there, and yet they have the staple thereof.
No fish there, yet the staple thereof is in Holland.
No vineyards nor salt in Holland, yet they have the staple thereof.
No wools there, and yet they have the staple of many manufactures.[2]

They traded on a lower margin of profit, paid less for freight, used more efficient commercial techniques, could buy for ready money. These advantages were not ephemeral. They had also shown that they were

[1] Bland, Brown and Tawney, *Select Documents*, 445.
[2] Lewes Roberts, *The Treasure of Traffic* (London, 1641), 58–60. Similar words occur in *Sir Walter Raleigh's Observations*, 25–7.

prepared to carry competition on the fishing grounds and in the East Indies to the point of expelling English traders by force. Thus many commodities were liable to be cheaper in the Netherlands than in England, and some—when Dutch competition was most warlike—were available nowhere else. It is possible that the English thought they might become entirely and permanently dependent on the Dutch entrepôt, as they had been dependent in the past on the entrepôt at Antwerp. If so, the expansion of trade that had taken place in the previous century, and of which the English were proud, would be reversed. If the English import trade fell into Dutch hands, they could please themselves to some extent whether they took money or goods in return, they could take white cloth rather than finished cloth, or even wool instead of cloth. Above all, experience taught that the first consequence would be the laying-up of English ships while the ports were thronged with Dutch ships. It was necessary to protect the import trades if only for the sake of navigation. Protection could be afforded in two ways: either by a navigation act or by privilege. We have seen that a navigation bill in the parliament of 1621 was rejected, probably because it would have antagonised the Dutch. For as well as being commercial enemies they were political allies. The less radical course was slightly to extend the existing privileges of regulated companies whose trades were most affected.

The Eastland company after 1622 protected English trade against Englishmen as well as against the Dutch. There is no reason to suppose that the English trader welcomed restrictions on his freedom or that he gladly shouldered the responsibilities that accompanied privilege, even though the latter protected him in the long run. In his heart he doubtless favoured a situation in which all merchants were subject to good rules except himself. He would wish on occasion to hire Dutch ships and to buy goods in Amsterdam. But if one man gained an advantage over his fellows in this way, they, being also his competitors, would be obliged to follow suit, and so one man's benefit might prove the ruin of all. This perhaps was in Misselden's mind when he wrote that 'those that trade without order and government, are like unto men, that make holes in the bottom of that ship, wherein themselves are passengers. For want of government in trade, openeth a gap and letteth in all sorts of unskilful and disorderly persons. And these...sink themselves and others with them.'[1] The extreme *laissez-faire* economist McCulloch, to whose reprints of seventeenth-century literature we are much indebted, asserted more

---

[1] *Free Trade, or the Means to Make Trade Flourish* (London, 1622, first edition), 84. He wrote truly a few pages earlier that 'the name and nature of monopoly is more talked of than well understood'.

than once 'the absurdity of supposing that any trade advantageous to the merchant can be injurious to the public'. Thomas Mun, however, expressed the typical seventeenth-century view when he said that a merchant 'by his laudable endeavours' might trade 'to good profit, which is the end of his labours, when nevertheless the commonwealth shall decline and grow poor'.[1] That individuals followed their private interests was for the seventeenth century a law of nature. It was the function of government to direct their private interests into channels profitable to the commonwealth. The merchant's work, said Mun, 'ought to be performed with great skill and conscience, that so the private gain may ever accompany the public good'.[2] What conscience lacked, the privileges and regulations that comprised the mercantile system supplied.

One of the curious features of the history of the Eastland trade is that the Eastland company was one of the most popular companies in the first half of the seventeenth century but was one of the first to have its privileges seriously curtailed in the second half. What we have just said may suggest the reason for this. Their privileges at home were reasonable in the first half of the century, on the one hand in order to maintain their privileges abroad and on the other hand to protect their trade against the Dutch. In the second half of the century, first, the Navigation Acts took over their function of protecting trade against the Dutch; secondly, they developed trades in which foreign privileges were unobtainable; and thirdly, the state began to look after the merchants' welfare abroad. Thus, what was reasonable in the first half of the century became unreasonable in the second half. This explanation takes for granted that the question of privileges was judged on practical grounds relating to the good of the commonwealth. There is evidence for this. The parliament of 1624 took a strong line against patents and monopolies, and handled the Merchant Adventurers roughly. But on the Eastland company's privileges Sir Edwin Sandys—no friend of privilege in general—reported as follows:

First, for the Eastland company; who have the sole importation of all necessary commodities for shipping. These, brought in rough, set many subjects on work. [They] export yearly 8,000 cloths dyed and dressed. Their patent 31 Elizabeth never altered since. The suggestions of this patent, four. A grant, [1] to impose on persons of traders, [2] to fine, and [3] imprison; and [4] a prohibition to all others to trade thither.

The Committee conceived it not, for the present, a monopoly.

A proclamation, in July, 20 Jac., restraining the importation of all these commodities, but corn.

This company have shewed themselves very tractable. The company

---

[1] *England's Treasure*, ch. 7.   [2] *Ibid.* ch. 1.

submitteth itself to this House, but tendered four propositions to the Committee. (1) That shopkeepers, and other, might not be admitted into the company, but mere merchants. This the Committee not against. (2) That no merchants should trade thither, but only in English bottoms; which will be a great means to increase the shipping of this land. This received some alteration. The Committee resolved, these commodities should be fetched by our merchants, at those parts, where this company's mart is. (3) That those, which came into their company, might be subject to government. (4) That they might pay a reasonable fine. Some of the Committee thought, five marks to be a reasonable fine to be of this company; but the committees of the outports desired to trade freely, and not be of this company. The Committee left this to the House.[1]

The House decided 'to have a petition to his Majesty, for accommodating these things'. The parliament took the Eastland company's privileges for what they were—a measure of public policy designed to promote and safeguard trade. Their Statute of Monopolies, which declared all monopolies void, made an exception in the case of 'corporations, companies or fellowships of any art, trade, occupation or mystery, or to any companies or societies of merchants within this realm, erected for the maintenance, enlargement or ordering of any trade of merchandise'.

[1] *Commons Journals*, I, 681, 732; 710, 793; 712, 796; two versions, without discrepancy. That given here is a combination of both. Where one version speaks of the proclamation as restraining importation (as here), the other speaks of it as restraining merchant strangers; these were the same thing. The outports who 'desired to trade freely' were probably not the outports where the company had its residences; it is more likely that they were western ports, especially Plymouth. Plymouth claimed such a right later and was able to produce a precedent. If that precedent was this case, it would appear that the petition of the Commons was effective.

HET

Chapter V

DIFFICULTIES ABROAD: THE WEAKNESS OF THE ENGLISH STATE UNDER CHARLES I

In the first half of the seventeenth century, trade did not follow the flag. The flag followed trade. No English warship penetrated the Baltic Sea. There were no consuls at ports in the Eastland, there were no permanent ambassadors. It would be no exaggeration to describe the Eastland company's foreign residence as a seventeenth-century outpost of empire, which the crown controlled, and at the same time was obliged to support. But its support was less effective than its control. In the following statement the crown asserted its power to control:

The act for residency is one of the fundamental laws of the company, without the maintenance of which neither their government nor trade can subsist. We find also that the state hath always had an interest in settling the residence of companies beyond the seas, and did settle the residence of this company at Elbing, and that the payment of customs to foreign princes in amity with his Majesty dependeth thereupon. In which respects (without direction from the State) residency may not be changed by any company.[1]

In the following statement the crown confessed its helplessness. The company having made a formal representation of their difficulties abroad, the Privy Council could only record that

Now as their Lordships upon the hearing of those particulars were very sensible thereof, so, because they of the said company had not propounded any course or means by which they might be holpen, their Lordships could say no more than this, that if they would propound any thing they should be assisted by the Board with all the favour that might be fitly and conveniently afforded.[2]

The Council would only help the Eastland company in ways that it thought fit and convenient, and without that help the company could do nothing. Even with it, what could be achieved was limited.

During the depression of 1620 the company had received permission to move from Elbing to Danzig, but they did not move immediately. We have seen that in 1626 the King of Sweden, Gustavus Adolphus, having conquered Livonia, advanced on Elbing and Danzig; and that the trade

---

[1] *A.P.C. 1626*, 438–9.   [2] PC2/41/456.

of the Eastland merchants was interrupted. Charles I sent Sir Thomas Roe as ambassador with instructions to mediate a peace between Sweden and Poland, which, 'for the opening of the trade of Danzig and other ports adjoining which are shut up by reason of that war, is behoveful both to our own subjects and those of the United Provinces'. But he was instructed to work for this peace only so long as the terms of it did not prevent Gustavus Adolphus from carrying on the war in Germany against the Emperor, 'which he is entered into with so princely a resolution'. 'In this case we, preserving public respects of state before our particular interests of merchandise, do not think it fit your endeavours should tend to the advancement of that peace.' Thus diplomatic considerations arising from the Thirty Years War were held to transcend interests of trade. Further, the crown's interest in the opening of trade arose chiefly from a fear of the 'Baltic design' of the Hapsburgs.

It hath been long and well observed how such as have been instruments of the Austrian greatness with aim to the universal monarchy...have for many years had a design to bring the free town of Danzig...into a total subjection, and to get other seaports upon the Baltic sea, to make equipage of shipping and turn such materials as we and our friends and allies draw for that purpose out of those parts to their own use, and further to intercept the transport of corn from Danzig and those parts adjoining which were wont to serve as a granary to the Low Countries and to our kingdoms likewise in times of scarcity. This great design marvellously to our prejudice...hath been of late days...much advanced....The Austrian princes [have] left nothing in effect unconquered upon that coast but Stralsund...[and] are masters of all Holstein and Jutland except Glückstadt only....The Spaniards do there join in design with the Imperialists, and...seek to make a connection and correspondence betwixt the ports of those provinces and those they have in Flanders, after the same manner of admirantasgoes as they have established of late years betwixt the ports of Flanders and those of Spain, and this with a great and dangerous design of perfecting that dominion at sea which of late years beyond the example of all former times they have advanced at land.

We may say on the evidence of these instructions that England was not so much afraid of being shut out of the Baltic trade as that, being shut out, Baltic goods would be available only to her enemies. This attitude gave little place to the interests of the merchants themselves.[1]

All over Europe Charles I's diplomacy rested on negotiation without strength. His very weakness made it necessary to support the merchants for the sake of the strength which their trade lent to the state; but, weak

[1] Roe's instructions are printed in *Letters relating to the Mission of Sir Thomas Roe to Gustavus Adolphus 1629–30*, ed. S. R. Gardiner (Camden Society, 1875).

as he was, he could not support them effectively. When Sir Thomas Roe arrived in the Eastland, armed only with the voice of reason, he found that a peace (the truce of Altmark between Sweden and Poland) was nearly completed, and that Gustavus was determined to carry on the war in Germany. He was therefore free to follow a subsidiary instruction to assist the merchants. Their situation was difficult. They wished to move to Danzig, but not without good terms. But Danzig, having taken the side of Poland against Gustavus Adolphus, had secured in the Polish diet an act called the 'Danzig seal', whereby all foreign cloth offered for sale in Poland was to bear the seal of Danzig; that is to say, that all foreign cloth for the Polish market was to be imported through Danzig. This would compel the Eastland company to move to Danzig on whatever terms Danzig chose to offer. The Swedes, on the other hand, wished the Eastland company to continue at Elbing; and, having command of the sea, they imposed a toll on goods entering Danzig. Roe's instruction was to establish two residences. He therefore worked for the abrogation of the Danzig seal and the removal of the Swedish toll. With him was the Eastland company's secretary, Richard Jenks. He secured a reduction of the toll, but not the abrogation of the seal. When he returned home, a member of the Eastland company, Theophilus Eaton, holding a commission from the king, continued the negotiation in collaboration with the king's agent in Poland. He returned in 1635 without the abrogation of the seal. Meanwhile the Eastland company had settled their sole residence at Danzig, where they remained henceforth. They obtained at Danzig no formal concession of privileges such as they had obtained at Elbing, yet it appears that they enjoyed in practice some privileges which were not disturbed until 1650; until which time they traded at Danzig with great prosperity. But to this outcome the efforts of Charles I had contributed little.[1]

The merchants were also troubled from time to time by the King of Denmark's habit of raising his tolls at the Sound. These consisted basically of the 'hundredth penny' on the declared value of English and some other nations' cargoes, an additional tax called last-gelt or poundage (the rate varying according to the commodity) and a ship-tax of a rose noble on every ship, all of which together came to about 2 per cent in 1624. In course of time the king levied not only the hundredth penny but a 'new' hundredth penny, and not only last-gelt but an 'additional' last-gelt and also a 'new' additional last-gelt; all of which in 1640 amounted to about 5 per cent. He refused to publish a book of rates. He could also make

---

[1] The negotiations can be followed in the State Papers, especially SP 16/144/81, 180/51, 198/35, 206/38, 229/25, 268/62, 307/80, 533/47, 54; SP 88/6/57, 7/181.

difficulties by refusing to accept an equivalent of silver money for the rose noble, an obsolete gold coin. He could delay the ships of one nation in favour of another and could vary the strictness of search. The English merchants desired to have the tolls reduced whenever they were raised, and to have the book of rates published, the procedure standardised, and the penalties fixed; they also wished to enjoy securely an alleged ancient privilege of paying on the return voyage the tolls incurred on the outward voyage.

Royal ambassadors negotiated on these matters without much success— Sir Thomas Roe in 1629 and 1639 and the Earl of Leicester in 1632. But in 1643 the Swedes made one of their lightning wars against Denmark. The Dutch fleet helped the Swedes, and while the Swedes obtained territory and exemption from the Sound tolls, the Dutch obtained a reduction of tolls. England took no part in the war but was able to profit from the King of Denmark's humiliation and need for allies. Richard Jenks of the Eastland company and Thomas Skinner of the Merchant Adventurers went to Denmark with a commission from parliament. They secured a very favourable commercial treaty. The hundredth penny was abolished, the rate of last-gelt fixed at not more than 1 per cent, the rose noble was to be paid in silver, tolls were to be paid on the return voyage, English ships with a 'court roll' (toll-bill?) were not to be searched; and (perhaps most important of all) 'if the Hollander or any other western nation shall either now or hereafter obtain better conditions the English may equally enjoy the same'. This treaty was also useful to the state in that it involved a Danish recognition of Jenks's and Skinner's masters— 'the Lords and Commons of the Kingdom of England assembled in Parliament at Westminster'.[1]

These negotiations for privilege and immunities—the tangible benefits to which we referred in the last chapter as chiefly justifying regulated trade—were expensive. The company said that they paid Jenks's entire expenses on this embassy,[2] 'not without contracting a great debt'.[3] It is

---

[1] The history of Sound toll diplomacy is complicated. An account exists by Charles E. Hill, *The Danish Sound Dues and the Command of the Baltic*, Durham, North Carolina, 1926. For Leicester's mission in 1632, see James Howell, *Familiar Letters* (ed. Jacobs, London, 1890), 302–5. Some of the papers of Roe's mission in 1629, already mentioned, refer to his negotiations about Sound tolls. The State Papers, Foreign (Denmark), contain material; see also, for 1639, SP 16/463/57, 468/116, 482/74. For Jenks and Skinner, *Cal.S.P.Dom. 1644*, 296, 489, 493; *Cal.S.P.Dom. 1644–1645*, 272, 303, 515; *Cal.S.P.Dom. 1645–1647*, 127, 130, 131. Sellers, *Acts and Ordinances*, 159ff., prints the articles concluded in 1645. They are particularly referred to in Appendix A11 (1660). The examples of the weight of the tolls, given above, are from a brief examination of the registers.

[2] Appendix A9.   [3] Appendix A11.

probable that they had contributed to the embassy of Sir Thomas Roe, and in addition they had been obliged in 1626 to lend Gustavus Adolphus 15,000 rixdollars, about £3500. This gave rise to a quarrel with York. The company obtained the approval of the Privy Council to recover the loan from their members, but York refused to pay, saying that they had not traded at Elbing in the year in question, but had gone to Danzig instead. The Privy Council commanded York to pay. This was the occasion for the Council's remark, quoted above, that the 'act for residency is one of the fundamental laws of the company'.[1] In spite of this levy, in 1631 the company were £800 in debt to the treasurer, and it was for this reason that they raised their existing impositions and set new impositions upon Baltic imports. Expenses of the sort we have mentioned justified these impositions, and therefore justified the existence of the company and its whole system of discipline. For if the merchants banded together for protection in time of trouble (which seems almost an instinctive reaction) they were bound to incur charges, and the privilege of levying money is therefore not merely one of the incidents of incorporation, but a necessity which may in itself make incorporation unavoidable.

[1] *A.P.C. 1626*, 312, 382, 438–9.

Chapter VI

THE EASTLAND COMPANY'S PRIVILEGES AT HOME: AN EXAMPLE OF GOVERNMENT BY PREROGATIVE

The mercantile system in the period we are now discussing had a quality which may be described as flexibility. The uncompromising language of the formal laws and enactments is deceptive. We need only glance at the edicts of the mercantile period—whether acts of parliament, proclamations, letters patent, or orders of the council—to realise that most of them were simply too short to have been capable of rigid enforcement. They were more often intended as declarations of principle *against* some evil practice than as exact instructions for the performance of a correct practice. Threats of extreme penalties took the place of a police force; often they were meant to stand *in terrorem*; the full penalties were rarely exacted; a dispensing power was always understood. It was thought proper in that age to temper justice with mercy, because justice, legal justice, was hard and ruthless. Moreover, real justice could not lie in strict enforcement of written laws, if only for the reason that law-makers had too little information and too short a memory to be aware of all the detailed implications of their laws. It follows that the scope of legislation was relatively narrow in comparison with our own days, and the scope of administration relatively wide. The verbal rigidity and restrictiveness of legislation would have been ridiculous had not flexibility and tolerance in administration been taken for granted.

The crown governed in economic matters largely through the prerogative. It sat at the centre of a web of rights and privileges which were designed to guide the self-interest of individuals into channels profitable to the commonwealth. It was entirely the master. It could abrogate privileges by *quo warranto* at common law, by recalling the patent, or merely by withdrawing the support which was necessary for their enforcement. When two privileges clashed the crown was free to make whatever adjustment it thought fit. Sometimes it simply commanded the parties to compromise. It judged these disputes on the basis of the common good, ignoring rights that it had previously granted. In grants of privilege it freely delegated great power, but it habitually imposed moderation in their exercise.

It may be added that holders of privileges were not entirely happy under this régime, which must have seemed to them temporising and arbitrary. The Eastland company, for example, would have felt more secure had their privileges been embodied, as were the Russia Company's, in an Act of Parliament, and we find them requesting such an Act in 1624 and again in 1660. But to grant privileges by Act of Parliament would have made the mercantile system too rigid. Statutes granting rights, which thereby became a sort of private property at common law, could not be repealed and amended as easily as letters patent. Statutes in favour of corporations would have made them too powerful, whereas privileges granted by patent left the holder at the mercy of the crown. The crown was therefore right, in a sense, to cling to its prerogative in these matters. But, on the other hand, we can see that the mercantile system in the first half of the seventeenth century began to suffer from overcrowding. As the privileges multiplied they more and more frequently collided. The crown was obliged to readjust them more frequently and to control them more and more closely. Its proceedings looked more and more arbitrary. This tendency reached its height in Charles I's policy of *Thorough*, when the weight of the Privy Council was felt on all sides. Its commands were enforced with an unaccustomed severity. The tendency can be observed from time to time in the history of the Eastland company, and perhaps explains why the Eastland company, though highly privileged, can be regarded as hostile to the régime at the beginning of the civil war.

Some evidence for the foregoing remarks has already been adduced. The proclamation against the export of gold and silver referred to in Chapter II was in appearance absolute, but it was understood that the East India Company would be allowed to export. Similarly, the proclamation for the Eastland company was addressed 'unto all persons as well subjects as strangers', but it was not intended to prohibit the trade of native Eastlanders in their own goods. It ordained that the law 'against the shipping of merchandises in strangers' bottoms either inward or outward' was to be strictly enforced, but this was not to be taken literally; for the Eastland trade could not be carried on without the use of foreign shipping when English ships were not available, and especially for imports from Norway since the carriage of timber required a special type of vessel. The town of Newcastle reacted immediately to the proclamation by representing to the Privy Council that strict enforcement would cause a shortage of Norwegian timber necessary for the coal mines, and received permission to import it in foreign ships. The merchants of the West country protested that their shipbuilding would suffer if they were compelled to rely on London merchants for their materials. The Council refused to allow them to supply themselves from Dutch and Scottish merchants as hitherto, saying that they ought to become free of the Eastland company rather than enrich foreigners; but when they did not it placed squarely upon the London company the responsibility of supplying them at reasonable rates. In the parliament of 1624, as we have seen, they objected to this arrangement; and apparently they were left to trade freely.[1]

The charter of the Eastland company granted to the company at London an apparently absolute power, without exception, to make laws for all the Eastland merchants of England. In 1616, however, a dispute between London and the outports was settled by the Privy Council, in such a way that this power was considerably limited. The company was to make laws only at a single annual court at a fixed date to which the outports should send representatives; the laws were not binding 'without the approbation of the Lord Chancellor, Lord Treasurer and the two Chief Justices according to the statute of 19 Henry VII cap. 7'; and the outports were empowered to inspect the company's accounts, 'whereunto if any just exceptions may be taken, then to complain to his Majesty's Privy Council for redress'.[2] To complain to the Privy Council was the easiest thing in the world.

In 1626 the town of Yarmouth petitioned the Council for permission to import Eastland goods for the use of their own shipping. The Eastland company objected to this, but 'were nevertheless contented at the motion of the Board' to make Yarmouth men members of the company. They proposed to charge £20 apiece for admission. This was the correct fine according to the charter, but when the Yarmouth men said that it was too much the Council took their side and ordered the company to admit them more cheaply.[3]

When the Eastland company proposed to levy money to meet the loan to Gustavus Adolphus referred to in the last chapter, they were careful first to obtain the Privy Council's approval. We saw that York objected and that the Privy Council overrode the objection; but the Council took into consideration that 'the company at London have dealt very moderately with their brethren of York in taxing the broke so low, for whereas by the act [for residency] it should have been 13s. 4d. a kersey or thereabouts, they have remitted all but 12d. a kersey, and in that 12d. have also included impositions due to the company'. This was moderation indeed.[4]

In 1623, William Gore, an apprentice of the company at London, was accused of trading contrary to the rules. The company disfranchised him

---

[1] *A.P.C. 1621–1623*, 342, 502–3; *A.P.C. 1623–1625*, 7–8. For 1624, see above, p. 65.
[2] Sellers, *Acts and Ordinances*, 155 ff.   [3] *A.P.C. 1626*, 80.
[4] *A.P.C. 1626*, 438–9.

but he continued to trade. The company brought him before the Privy Council. The Council ordered the company to readmit him at a moderate fine. When Gore then protested that the fine was excessive, the Council ordered the company to reduce it.[1]

After these examples of exceptions and moderation, it is not surprising to discover that the Eastland company enforced on their own members the proclamation of 1622 less absolutely than it appeared to require:

This court by general consent do order and decree, that from henceforth no commodity of the Eastland country growth shall be imported into this kingdom by any brethren of this fellowship, other than from the places of their own privileges, and that in English bottoms only, according to the intent of the said proclamation; upon penalty of forfeiting and paying to the use of the company for a broke one sixth part of all the goods so at any time imported contrary to the tenor of this act.[2]

Whereas the proclamation made an absolute prohibition, the by-law imposed a penalty equal only to one-sixth of the value of the goods improperly imported. This penalty calculated on the first cost of the goods might amount to no more than 10 per cent of the selling price in England. A merchant might on occasion think this worth paying, and indeed, in the 1630's, the port books of Hull contain entries of Eastland goods imported from the Netherlands by men known to belong to the Eastland company. And a by-law of 1631 speaks of lists, to be returned to the treasurer, of all members' imports 'whether they be brought out of the East country or from Amsterdam or any other place'.[3]

When the Eastland company proceeded against certain clothiers in the Court of Exchequer for shipping cloth to the Eastland in violation of their privileges, the case turned not so much on the question of right as on the question of public benefit. More exactly, the question of right depended on the question of public benefit. It will be remembered that in 1622, during the depression, the clothiers had applied to the Privy Council for leave to export cloth, and that the Council had declared that clothiers might export if merchants did not.[4] In 1623 and 1624 the merchants exported much cloth, yet even in this period they complained of clothiers interloping. 'The offenders', they said, 'plead law for themselves, as at present the clothiers do, against whom we have a suit depending in his Majesty's Court of Exchequer.'[5] (It was for this reason that they requested an Act of Parliament: an Act of Parliament would have made their right

---

[1] *A.P.C. 1623–1625*, 45–6, 59; SP 14/148/16, 108 and probably SP 16/408/7. Gore was a great name among London merchants.

[2] Sellers, *Acts and Ordinances*, 59–60.

[3] Sellers, *Acts and Ordinances*, 67.   [4] Above, p. 27.

[5] Appendix A 5.

indefeasible.) When the high exports were not maintained—for in 1627, 1628 and 1629 they were very low, owing to the interruption of trade in the Baltic—the case was resumed, and we have both parties' interrogatories to witnesses with the witnesses' answering depositions, dated 1629. The clothiers freely admitted that they had exported cloth to the Baltic. Their witnesses deposed that for six or seven years past Suffolk had been clogged with unsold cloth despite the fact that it had been offered to the merchants at lower prices than hitherto; that one of the defendants' cloth had got the moth through lying so long on his hands; that the same defendant had once employed one hundred workers and now employed twenty; and that 'the work and livelihood of a multitude of the poor people' in Essex and Suffolk was much decayed. An Ipswich clothier said that he had sailed with his cloth to the Eastland for the past fifteen years and had never failed to sell it; another said that, as factor to one of the defendants in the Eastland in 1622 and 1623, he had sold cloth to the same people as the Eastland merchants sold cloth to; another said that merchants had told him that there could be no trading to the Baltic as a company while the foreign residence was beset with war. The clothiers also alleged that they had sought admission to the Eastland company and had been refused. And they produced the Privy Council's order of 1622—'that if the Eastland merchants did not then forthwith buy all the cloths which were then upon the hands of these defendants and other of the said county of Essex and Suffolk that then these defendants and other the clothiers of Essex and Suffolk should have free liberty to ship forth their cloths into foreign parts and trade there'. They wished to show that the merchants had refused to take their cloth not from necessity but from wilfulness. And the merchants countered this argument in the same terms. The merchants' witnesses deposed that the clothiers of Suffolk and Essex did not depend entirely on the Eastland merchants, and that the defendants had deliberately set higher prices on their cloth than the trade would bear because they wished to export it themselves. They established the fact that the clothiers had returned the proceeds of their cloth in goods of the Eastland, and they brought evidence to show that these goods had not been sold easily; this, of course, tended to justify the merchants in having refused to buy the cloth at the price demanded by the clothiers. The case was heard on the equity side of the exchequer. No judgement is recorded. Indeed, it is hard to see what judgement was possible on the evidence. On the one hand the clothiers had exported cloth and there was no doubt that every cloth exported was for the public benefit. On the other hand, to authorise clothiers to export cloth at will would have overthrown the Eastland company. The Privy Council's order that the clothiers might export if the merchants did not was a typical Jacobean compromise. One may say that it was reasonable. It was certainly well intentioned. But it saddled the Court of Exchequer with a difficult if not impossible task. It was left for Charles I to put matters on a firmer footing with a new proclamation in 1630.[1]

In 1630 Charles I had just embarked on his eleven years of government through the Privy Council, of which the watchword was to be *Thorough*. The new proclamation introduced two fresh points. In the first place it contained an additional clause about exports. No English commodities were to be shipped for exportation to the Eastland except by the Eastland company. This put a stop to export by clothiers. In the second place there was a significant change in the wording of the clause about imports.

If it is permissible to repeat what has been said before, the purpose behind the proclamation of 1622 was to stop the import of Eastland goods from any place except the Eastland, and with this object it had purported in the preamble to prohibit the import 'of any commodities traded by the Eastland merchants into this kingdom, as well by subjects as by strangers, not free of that company'. But at the same time it professed only to confirm the Eastland company's charter. The charter, however, merely prohibited Englishmen to trade in the Eastland unless they were members of the Eastland company; it did *not* prohibit them to import Eastland goods from elsewhere. And the vital words of the proclamation reflected the charter more closely than they reflected the intention for which the proclamation was granted, for they gave to the Eastland company the sole importation of Eastland commodities '*brought from*' the Eastland. The Eastland company complained almost immediately that 'there seems to be some defect in the penning...[for] some would interpret his Majesty's meaning to be, that no man shall fetch such commodities in the East country, but if he find them elsewhere he may bring them in, as if the words had reference to the places where we are privileged and not to the commodities of that country growth'. And therefore when they prosecuted interlopers the latter 'plead law for themselves'.[2] Charles I's proclamation of 1630 remedied this defect in the penning by changing 'brought from' to 'of'—it gave to the Eastland company the sole importation of commodities *of* the Eastland. It may be that the defect in the penning of the first proclamation was deliberate, since the judges had made it plain to James I that he could not make new law by proclamation;

---

[1] See interrogatories below, Appendix A6. The depositions are not printed. To each question there was at least one affirmative answer. The clothiers had exported indirectly, through Amsterdam and la Rochelle.

[2] Appendix A5.

it would then represent another Jacobean compromise, leaving final interpretation to courts of law; but there were clearly no such scruples in the proclamation of Charles I.[1]

When the Eastland company applied for this proclamation, their petition touched briefly on their troubles abroad and on 'the excessive trade of clothiers and mariners outward, and other interlopers both subjects and strangers who daily import Eastland commodities, not only through the Sound of Denmark, but from Hamburg, Amsterdam and other places'.[2] It prayed in simple terms 'for the settling and confirming of their privileges'. It was referred to a committee of the Privy Council; there was no question of referees. It was granted within a week and the proclamation is dated three weeks later. This speed is in sharp contrast to the dilatory proceedings of James I.[3]

We note also that the new proclamation was enforced more effectively than the old. In the following year the Eastland company complained again that 'divers merchants and others not free of the company' were importing Eastland commodities 'from the Sound, from Norway, Hamburg, Amsterdam and other places'. The Privy Council 'for the future more effectual preventing of such insufferable abuses' deputed one of their own messengers to attend daily at the custom house to see that the company's privileges were enforced. Twelve months later, on a similar complaint, the Council issued warrants of assistance to the company's deputies at the outports. By a practice of long standing the customs officers were supposed to pass no goods in violation of the company's privileges, but these steps were a novelty.[4]

There were the usual automatic exceptions. The merchants of Newcastle received permission to import Eastland timber in Eastland ships ('and the Board doth enjoin the said Eastland company that they be hereafter careful to have the said town of Newcastle conveniently furnished and provided with the said commodities at reasonable rates'). The Council peremptorily forbade the town to import Eastland timber in Dutch ships.[5] Merchants of the West country, as in 1623, wished to import Eastland goods in Dutch ships. (They said they had factors in Norway, of what nationality is not stated.) The Council granted some individual exemptions. The West country claimed a general freedom, quoting a precedent

---

[1] The proclamation, Appendix A4.
[2] In 1628 the company accused two Englishmen and a foreigner named Dirick Garrett of importing Prussia flax from the Netherlands under pretence that it was Holland and Muscovy flax. The Council commanded them to re-export it. PC2/38/459.
[3] For papers relating to the issue of the proclamation, see below, Appendix A7.
[4] PC2/41/272, 42/324.   [5] PC2/39/778, 40/304.

of James I. The Council confessed ignorance of their precedent but said it would search the records, and having done so declared that Plymouth was free to import masts and deals in foreign bottoms, for its own use only, the Eastland company's privileges notwithstanding.[1]

These exceptions had an interesting sequel. In 1640 we find the Eastland company apparently complaining to the Council against certain of their own members who, they said, had for many years, in defiance of the proclamation of 1630, imported timber from Norway in Danish ships. The offenders—we do not know who they were—excused themselves by producing a letter written in 1622 by the then Lord Treasurer, to permit the import of Norway timber in Danish ships notwithstanding the proclamation of that year. The Council decreed that a letter written in 1622 was no defence against a proclamation issued in 1630, and the offenders humbly promised to reform themselves.[2] As we know, English merchants had long freighted Danish or Norwegian ships from Norway with impunity. This episode seems to represent a tightening-up of the shipping policy. We have seen that English trade and shipping were exceptionally prosperous in 1640, and it must have been thought—for example, by Trinity House, which was consulted—that there were enough English ships even for the Norway trade. The government would not have compelled Norway merchants to use them unless it had been practicable; if practicable it was obviously desirable; but it would not have been possible had the proclamations of 1622 and 1630 stated specifically the exceptions that were taken for granted when they were issued. General prohibitions, preserving silence about the exceptions that were understood, permitted useful flexibility in administration. Perhaps with this sort of consideration in mind the Eastland company had asked that the proclamation of 1630 'be penned in general words'.[3]

It was soon after the proclamation of 1630 that the Eastland company moved their residence to Danzig. The proclamation was probably a help in their negotiations. Once settled there, and the Baltic war over, they embarked on a period of great prosperity. Yet their privileges at home were less secure than they perhaps hoped and expected.

In 1630, shortly after the proclamation, the flax-dressers of London and Berkshire complained to the Privy Council that their trade was much decayed for lack of flax to dress—'the Eastland merchants are the cause thereof, for that they neither bring in rough flax enough nor suffer others'. The Council temporarily threw open the import of flax, anticipating that

[1] PC2/39/779, 810; 40/29, 59.
[2] PC2/51/262, 419. SP16/448/58.
[3] Appendix A7(*b*).

the company 'will be afterwards able to bring in sufficient quantities of hemp and flax at reasonable rates'. The company had admitted a momentary inability to supply these goods, and the Council's act is not to be regarded as against their interests. Nevertheless, there was an unmistakable implication that the crown's support was not unconditional.[1]

In 1631 we find the Eastland company complaining that the city companies of London would not buy their rye, though offered at 6s. 6d. the bushel at a loss to the merchants of 1s. 6d. The harvest of 1630 had been poor and now the Eastland company had over-supplied. The Council ordered the companies to buy it. A few days later the companies reported that they had enough rye and that the price asked by the Eastland company was higher than the current market price. The Council found that this was true and their final solution was a compromise. The companies were to buy the rye, but at the market price, which was 4s. 9d. a bushel. Only afterwards did the Council give permission for the re-export of rye. It is interesting that the Eastland merchants acted here in their corporate capacity, although the import of corn was free. The Council wished not to discourage them from importing rye in future times of scarcity, but did not hesitate to force them to sell at a loss.[2]

In 1635 the company brought before the Council a test case against a member of the Merchant Adventurers who had imported five bags of Polonia wool from Hamburg. The Merchant Adventurers alleged that 'being neither heard at that time nor mentioned in the proclamation, [they] supposed themselves not restrained by it'. They said that the Eastland company's charter did not warrant the proclamation and that the Merchant Adventurers had imported up to that time Eastland goods found in their own privileges. They added that 'while the Eastland company restrained others themselves have brought in the same commodities from Holland, and sometimes in strangers' bottoms'. This (as we noted above) was true. However, after the Eastland company had replied with a description of their trade, the Council decided in their favour.[3]

After the proclamation of 1630 the Eastland company had confirmed

[1] PC2/40/222, 408–10.   [2] PC2/40/534, 41/19, 64, 87, 144.
[3] PC2/44/482. The company's description of their trade included three points: (1) that they exported dyed and dressed cloth 'and therefore hath been cherished hitherto by the state'; (2) that, since they could not import money, any diminution of their import trade would lead to a corresponding reduction of the export trade; and (3) 'that the shipping of this kingdom is exceedingly interested in the present question, if Hamburg...may be made the staple and the kingdom receive their supplies from there (though in English ships) the serviceable shipping of this kingdom will soon be worn out, barques and other small vessels, in regard of the nearness of the place, being able to do the service wherein now many great ships are employed'.

and tightened up their regulations, increasing the shipmaster's bond from £50 to £300. But evidently they could not entirely stop interloping nor even regulate their own members. Shortly after the case with the Merchant Adventurers—perhaps as a result of it—they brought before the Privy Council a disorderly brother, George Price, who had imported potash from Amsterdam in a Dutch ship 'and had in further contempt resisted and derided the messenger authorised by warrant to seize the same'. The Council ordered him to submit to the company and to re-export the potash; and others who had offended, likewise.[1] But again in 1636, at the time when the Eastland company were making their spring shipment, they complained that their privileges were daily violated 'both by strangers and by English merchants, clothiers, mariners and others not free of their company, and by disorderly brethren'. Two offenders were Humphrey Wightman and William Brunskell, who had intended to forestall the market at Danzig by shipping cloth through Hamburg. When they admitted their fault, the Council ordered them to unship their cloth and confirmed once again its directions to the customs officers not to pass goods to or from the Eastland save under the hands of an officer of the company.[2]

In 1635 the Artisan Skinners of London applied for a patent to form a joint stock for exporting the product of their industry. The Eastland company objected that for the Skinners to export skins to the Eastland would infringe their privileges. This was no more than the truth, and they obtained a stay of the patent. Still, the question was argued on other grounds than the letter of the law. The Skinners were responsible for employing the Grey Tawyers who, it was carefully said, consisted of many families. These complained that the Skinners gave them too little work. The Skinners asserted that the Eastland company took off too few tawed skins. The Eastland company said that, war having recently interrupted their trade, they would in future under peaceful conditions export a due proportion of tawed skins. The Council professed itself not entirely satisfied with the company's answer; however, after some months of spasmodic debate, 'thinking fit to afford the said Skinners and Tawyers all just relief for the support of their trades and being careful withal to uphold and preserve the rights and privileges of the said Eastland company', it commanded the two parties through their counsel to come to some

---

[1] PC2/44/519, 526. George Price's name occurs rather frequently in the Council Register, and he reappears later in this chapter. One might suppose that he had some connection at court.

[2] PC2/46/15, 17; SP16/315/89, 119. Brunskell is identifiable as probably a member of the company from 1632; see Appendix C. Later he held office. Wightman is identifiable as probably a member in 1640, see Appendix C.

arrangement for settling their differences. The question again was not of legal right but of the common good.[1]

If against the Merchant Adventurers the Eastland company had gained through the flexibility of the mercantile system, they had not gained in the case of the Skinners. Still less did they gain when they came up against the soap corporation. To encourage new methods of soap-making without potash, to reduce imports and to increase exports, was sound policy. We have described in Chapter III how James I granted privileges to new soapers under a scheme which provided for the compensation of the Eastland company for the loss of their imports of potash. The privileges were not put into effect at that time, but were revived by Charles I. Charles I's soap monopoly was perhaps the most odious of all monopolies. He allowed no compensation to the Eastland company. The Eastland company opposed it. When, after unpleasant cases in Star Chamber, the new soapers failed to produce enough soap at the price laid down in their charter, they were dissolved. The old soapers had won a victory. Not so the Eastland company. For the old soapers received in their turn a charter and became a monopoly. Potash might now be imported freely—but only for the use of the company of soapers. The Eastland company offered (in vain) against the monopoly of the soapers the classic free-trade argument which the clothiers had used against themselves, namely, that they would greatly suffer from the ability of this monopoly to fix prices in its own favour.[2]

In spite of recurrent allegations of interloping, one would have thought that the Eastland company would have been satisfied with their trade. A well-known passage of Clarendon puts the matter in another light by remarking that prosperity induced pride. It may be that the Eastland company for all their prosperity did not so much feel gratitude towards the crown for its support of them, as resentment that support was sometimes withheld. They were perhaps less conscious of the crown's support than of its control. In the naturally self-centred view of corporations and business men, it was not impossible to blame the crown for failing to support them effectively abroad and for overriding them in the soap business. The ideas of the time not only emphasized the crown's power to govern, but its duty to govern well; good government was the commonwealth's due but bad government was the crown's fault. It is generally thought that the merchant companies were among the parliament's

---

[1] PC2/45/268, 47/195; SP16/303/3, 319/30, 341/108.

[2] Above, pp. 44–5. For the Eastland company's objection to the new soapers, see Appendix A8; for their objection to the old soapers revived, see PC2/48/299, 358 and SP16/371/18.

strongest supporters against the king when the constitutional trouble came to a head. This (if true) is not easy to explain if one remembers only the great privileges they owed to him.

In 1638 a person named Henry White, who purveyed timber for building the king's houses, applied for the freedom of the Eastland company. He tendered the fine for admission and produced a letter from the king. The governor, Sir Christopher Clitherow, denied that White was eligible. (He was not a mere merchant.) White suggested that the king's favours might prove useful to the company. Clitherow used slighting words of the king's favour. White was not admitted.[1]

When the civil wars began the king used his influence with his uncle the King of Denmark to hinder the rebels' Baltic trade. He granted to individual merchants letters to authorise their passage through the Sound. One such letter was granted to George Price. The company sent representatives to Oxford to request the king to forbear. He put them in prison.[2] It was important alike for the parliament and the Eastland company to counter his negotiations with Denmark, and we recounted in the last chapter how they sent Richard Jenks of the Eastland company and Skinner of the Merchant Adventurers to conclude an Anglo-Danish treaty on their own account. Nevertheless, the Eastland company obtained from parliament, so far as can be seen, less satisfaction than they had obtained from the king. Parliament made ordinances confirming the Merchant Adventurers' and the Levant company's privileges, but none for the Eastland company. They would have valued one; petitions concerning their privileges were referred to the committee for the navy. We do not know on what grounds they were refused.[3]

In 1646 they were attacked in a pamphlet by one Mr Thomas Johnson, entitled

A plea for free-men's liberties; or the monopoly of the Eastland merchants anatomized by divers arguments (which will also serve to set forth the injustices of the Merchant Adventurers' monopoly) and proved illegal, unnatural, irrational, against the honour of the nation, tending to its ruin and vassalage, procured by evil counsellers; and lastly treasonable; with a short comment upon their oath....

Acts xxii. 27, 28. Then the chief captain came and said unto him, tell me, art thou a Roman? He said yea, and the chief captain answered, with

---

[1] This is the version given by a friend of White who accompanied him; SP 16/395/2. Perhaps he was admitted later, for at the restoration of Charles II, petitioning for re-employment, he said he 'was heretofore made an Eastland merchant by your Majesty's late royal father'; SP 29/2/152.

[2] So I interpret *Lords Journals*, v, 626, and *Commons Journals*, III, 16.

[3] *Commons Journals*, III, 38, 270, 504, 517 (1643, 1644).

a great sum of money obtained I this freedom, and Paul said, but I was born free.

2 Peter, iii. 13. Nevertheless we, according to his promise, look for new heavens, and a new earth, wherein dwelleth righteousness.

This was the voice of free trade at its most irresponsible, fortified with religion and a personal grievance. Most of the argument is a mass of unsupported assertions about natural right and liberty, but the conventional free-trade case found a place. Johnson said that the privileges of the East-land company tended to the ruin of the nation by reducing thousands of poor people to beggary; by setting low prices on cloth; by preventing the sale of five thousand cloths a year, for which buyers could be found if young men were able to roam about the Eastland instead of being tied to the staple; by causing the decay of navigation; and by reducing the import of Eastland goods, of which free traders would import greater quantities at lower prices. The author described himself as

late servant to Mr Whitlock, one of the East country monopolising merchants, which is all one in nature with the monopoly of the Merchant Adventurers...; they keep my freedom from me, for which I have so often ventured my life in the northern service these present wars [between Sweden and Denmark]...though I have served 7 years...but most inhumanly have taken from me my place of factorship in the Eastland, and all because I have rejected their diabolical oath, and this was the gallant service of Mr Burnell, governor, and his associates, the 3 October 1645....

O intolerable burden! Whither will this bottomless pit go?

Chapter VII

THE CRISIS OF 1649 AND THE NAVIGATION ACT OF 1651

The crisis in the Eastland trade

We have now completed our survey of the first half of the century and we come to the crisis of 1649. We noticed Sir Thomas Roe's gloomy prophecy of what would happen when the Thirty Years War ended. 'Our great trade depends upon the troubles of our neighbours', he had said, 'but if a peace happen betwixt France, Spain and the United Provinces, all these will now share what we possess alone.' That peace was made in 1648. We noticed that Dutch freight rates had risen during the war. They began to fall in 1646, when the Dunkirk privateers were checked by the French, and by 1648 they had fallen by about half.[1] In England at the same time a second outbreak of civil war led to the execution of the king in January 1649. Foreign princes disapproved of king-killing—not least the dead king's cousin, the King of Denmark, and son-in-law, the Stadholder of the United Provinces. The new republic was an outlaw. The royalist fleet and foreign privateers captured English merchant ships.[2] English merchants living abroad were faced with the awkward choice of identifying themselves with regicides or of being regarded as traitors to the commonwealth; they could either endanger their security in the place where they lived, or endanger it at home.

A severe commercial crisis was only to be expected. In the Eastland trade, the Sound Tables show that the number of English ships sailing from the Baltic declined rapidly: 1647, 130; 1648, 93; 1649, 64; 1650, 46; 1651, 22. The volume of cloth exports declined in the same period from 20,000 pieces to 11,000 pieces.[3] A high proportion of this cloth was ex-

[1] Schreiner, *Nederland og Norge*, 49–50; above, p. 46.

[2] In July 1649, fifteen ships laden with corn were afraid to sail from the Sound because of privateers; the Council of State feared also that the King of Denmark would detain them. *Cal.S.P.Dom. 1649–1650*, 223.

[3] Pieces of cloth exported from England to the Baltic (Sound Tables *1497–1660*, 2B, 21–23, 200);

	In English ships	In foreign ships		In English ships	In foreign ships
1621–30 (average)	31,000	400	1651	8,000	3,000
1631–40 (average)	33,000	1,000	1652	11,000	4,000
1641–46 (average)	20,000	2,000	1653	1,000	4,000
1647	17,000	3,000	1654	14,000	12,000
1648	15,000	5,000	1655	8,000	3,000
1649	7,000	8,000	1656	7,000	1,000
1650	13,000	5,000	1657	7,000	4,000

ported in foreign ships; in 1649 more than in English ships. This had never happened previously. Most of the foreign ships from England were Eastlanders, but in 1649–51 there were also a fair number of Dutch. This had not happened for twenty years. When we find Dutch ships sailing into the Baltic from England we naturally infer that they have first brought Baltic goods *to* England, either directly or (more probably) from the entrepôt at Amsterdam. The Eastland merchants said that 'the general employment of Flemish bottoms gives also a greater advantage unto the Hollander to enter upon our trade... and they keeping also at Amsterdam a magazine of Eastland goods... intercept us in the vent of our returns'.[1]

Roger Coke, who lived in the East Anglian clothing country, was much struck by the decline of the Eastland trade in these years. He tells us that English freight rates rose and that good English cloth became dearer in the Eastland than good Dutch cloth. He thinks that the Dutch learnt the art of making Suffolk cloth from emigrant weavers in Charles I's reign. As to cheap cloth he takes the view that the civil wars interrupted its export and thereby encouraged its manufacture in Poland and Silesia, but in another place, aligning himself with Sir Thomas Roe, he concedes that some setback was only to be expected: 'England of late, under King James but more especially under King Charles, did flourish by trade, and was more rich than any other kingdom in these western parts of the world: but this was by an accident of the times, not to be again hoped for.'[2]

The features of this crisis were, therefore, a decline of exports and a decline of shipping. Nothing is to be found that indicates a decline in the quantity of imports, and Thorold Rogers's wheat prices for 1647–51 are very high; but there was a reversion to the Dutch entrepôt. The crisis of 1649 looks strikingly similar to the crisis of 1620, though without the monetary disturbance. The main factor was probably freight rates. The English revolution doubtless made freight rates inordinately high, but even had they been normal they would have been higher than Dutch freight rates when the United Provinces were not at war.

The disparity in transport costs was widened further when the Dutch made an agreement with the King of Denmark to farm the Sound tolls on their own ships for a fixed annual sum. This saved money and—no less important—time. The Redemption Treaty came into force in 1650.

[1] Appendix A9. For the figures, see Appendix D. No port books survive from this period for ports that had an Eastland trade, but E190/492/11, Yarmouth 1649, shows a great increase in the number of Dutch ships.
[2] *Detection of the Court and State of England* (London, 1694), I, 420–1; *Discourse of Trade* (London, 1670), preface.

The Eastland company seeks confirmation of privileges

It cannot be said exactly when the Eastland company's privileges ceased to be enforceable, whether in 1649 or earlier. Their powers had not been taken away, they had simply lapsed for lack of will or ability on the government's part to support them.

In November 1649 the Eastland company presented to the Council of State a petition which has not survived. The Council referred the petition to one of its committees that was then considering the East India trade. This committee sat daily and became in effect a general committee for trade. In December the Council recorded that several companies, especially the East India, Levant and Eastland companies, had submitted proposals 'which carry with them some restraint to general liberty of trade', and which the Council, therefore, thought fit to refer to the parliament. What were these proposals?[1]

The Eastland company's proposal was contained in a 'representation' which is reproduced in full at Appendix A. They said that the only remedy for the decay of their trade was 'by renewing or confirming the incorporation of the traders, under such a government and such a power as they have formerly had'; that is to say, with the proclamations of 1622 and 1630.[2]

It would be tedious to recount the details of the representation, and to summarise it is not easy. They said that they used to export 14,000 broadcloths and to employ about 200 English ships, and that their cloth exports were now much diminished and the ships reduced to 'scarce twenty'. The argument was directed against interlopers and the Dutch. Interlopers debased English cloth by loose and disorderly trading; they used Flemish bottoms 'which go at half the charge of our English ships'; and the company were obliged to follow suit. The Dutch brought Eastland goods to England from Amsterdam. It is no longer said that this reduced the volume of exports, but it is said that England could not afford to see this trade in Dutch hands, because 'they may then set what prices they please upon those foreign commodities, so necessary for this land...and (which is as bad) we shall not be able then to set out a ship to sea but at their pleasure'.[3]

---

[1] *Cal.S.P.Dom. 1649–1650*, 408, 462.

[2] In the *Calendar of State Papers* it is attributed to 1659, but there is no evidence for this. Being addressed to the Council of State it does not fall in the Protectorate and must be earlier than the setting-up of a Council for Trade in August 1650. It was 'presented 10th December, to be considered 17th December'; and was in amplification of 'our late humble petition to this Great Council'. Internal evidence also puts it before the Navigation Act and the Dutch war. Its date must therefore be December 1649.

[3] It is not clear where the figure of 14,000 broadcloths came from. According to the Sound Tables (Appendix D) that figure belongs to the earliest years of the century,

The Eastland company tried to forestall two objections. First, they protested that their privileges were not a monopoly, because any man qualified for trading, at any port, could join the company upon a mean and inconsiderable fine of £20. But a government established to uphold the liberty of the subject could grant no privilege lightly; and their case about the debasement of exports was not irrefutable. Secondly, they suggested that 'if a restraint of the Hollander from this trade...may seem to reflect with inconveniency upon that state, it is answered that they have ever been (in the time of our government) wholly excluded'. This argument was sound and simple. But the greatest danger to the new republic of England lay precisely in the naval strength of the Dutch, and if there was any good will worth cultivating in 1650 it was that of the republican merchants of Holland, who alone resisted the pro-Stuart policy of the Stadholder. The Council was content to pass the requests of the merchants to the parliament. It was, however, building a great fleet of warships as fast as possible.

The representation spoke also of trouble at Danzig. This was an argument for privileges, since a united body could withstand oppression more effectively than a collection of individuals. It seems that the King of Poland was laying a tax on Englishmen's estates and was enforcing the law by which the estates of foreigners dying in Poland were confiscated to the crown. The city of Danzig began to demand a custom called *Zulag* or *Anlag*. In other words, the English were losing their special immunities. The situation became worse in 1650. In February 1651 the Council of State did what it could to help them, by sending a letter to the senate of Danzig. Their troubles were partly due to a royalist agent whom Charles II had in Poland, and there are one or two hints of a clash among themselves between royalists and republicans. Twelve of them, 'the well affected party', wrote to the Council of State in 1651. They thanked the Council for rescuing them from the oppressive tyranny of kings, confessed that some of their colleagues were royalist, and asked for an opportunity to take the engagement (that 'I will be true and faithful to the Commonwealth of England, as it is now established, without a King or House of Lords'). They also desired the Council to put a stop to interloping and to prohibit the import of Eastland goods in foreign ships. On this letter the Council commanded the company in London to send the engagement, and soon Richard Jenks was writing from Danzig that all were taking it.

unless to the single year 1633. Two hundred English ships seems an exaggeration at any time; the nearest figure is 170 in 1641; they said 'about' 200. The 'scarce twenty' ships of 1649 is also difficult; it may refer to ships freighted by the company, or to ships sailing from London. The figures may truly reflect the decline of the company's trade; they overstate the decline of the trade as a whole.

He also wrote that some were being prosecuted for refusing to pay the King of Poland's tax. If the Poles persisted in this tax, he said, the company would have no choice but to remove from Danzig for a space; he thought optimistically that this would soon bring them to reason.[1]

Meanwhile, at home, events had moved towards the Navigation Act. When the Council of State referred the merchants' proposals to the parliament, the parliament voted for setting up a Council of Trade. This was constituted in August 1650, and it took over all the papers on trade that the Council of State had accumulated. The Eastland company submitted a 'remonstrance' to the Council of Trade. They invited the outports to join in the remonstrance but they preferred to submit petitions on their own account. Evidently the outports did not stand shoulder to shoulder with London on every point. Neither the remonstrance nor the petitions survive, but the remonstrance was 'for the confirmation of our charter' and the petitions were probably for a charter somewhat modified in favour of the outports.[2]

By the beginning of 1651 the Council of State's attitude towards the Dutch had undergone a significant change. The pro-Stuart Stadholder had died. The republican merchants of Holland were in command. The Council of State were negotiating for a close alliance with them, amounting to political union. But the Dutch republicans being also merchants could not accept political union without economic union. Political union was to the advantage of England, economic union was to the advantage of the Dutch. From the English point of view the satisfactory economic relation with the Dutch was one of friendly independence: the Dutch should neither intervene in the trade which was proper to England nor strike diplomatic blows at it in commercial treaties with foreign powers. When the negotiations began to fail the English tone became threatening. It appears that the Eastland trade was one of the points where the English government was most sensitive, and the envoys were instructed to complain in strong terms about the Redemption Treaty. It is worth giving this instruction at length.

Whereas the trade of this nation through the Sound into the Baltic Sea is of very great concernment, both in respect of the usefulness of the commodities brought from thence, so necessary, among other things, for building and rigging of ships, which it is not convenient we should only receive or not, at the pleasure of other nations; but more especially in regard of the great number of ships we have employed in the transportation

---

[1] Sellers, *Acts and Ordinances*, 73, 75; SP 18/15/95, 16/36; *Cal.S.P.Dom. 1651*, 37, 287.

[2] Sellers, *Acts and Ordinances*, 73–5.

of those bulky goods, whereby mariners are bred and they and our shipping maintained; and, being also but short voyages, are often at home, to be made use of in case of any public occasions of the State requiring their service: and whereas this trade, being very much weakened otherwise, is in danger to be wholly lost by the agreement that hath lately been made between the King of Denmark and the States General of the United Provinces, wherein they have...bound up that king that he shall not grant the like to any other nation; which is directly contrary to...[the Anglo-Danish treaties of 1645 and 1646]; you are therefore to demand of the States General, and insist, that notwithstanding of the said treaty of theirs with the King of Denmark, tending so apparently to the destruction of so considerable a trade of this nation, the custom there may be left in that indifferency to this nation as they were before that treaty, that this commonwealth *be not necessitated to use other means* for the freeing of that trade from that destroying mischief which is upon it by the said treaty.[1]

Of course this demand was rejected. The envoys returned in a fury. A navigation bill was introduced into parliament and was passed after much debate in October 1651, to come into force in December.

The Navigation Act had no preamble, but its title was 'an Act for the encouragement of shipping and navigation'. Not of trade. Its provisions did encourage, and were designed to encourage, trade; but trade supported navigation. Its core was contained in two simple provisions: (i) goods were to be imported only from the place of their growth or production, and (ii) goods were to be imported only in English ships or in ships of the place where they were grown or produced. The first condition cut out the Dutch entrepôt, the second cut out Dutch ships. This was what the Eastland company wanted, but they had intended it should be done through confirmation of their charter and privileges.

The Navigation Act, The Advocate *and* Free Ports

We reprint at Appendix B a pamphlet called *The Advocate*. It contains a great deal about the Eastland trade; it shows that the problems of the Eastland trade were common to most other trades, and it throws light on the passing of the Navigation Act.

There are two editions of *The Advocate*, 1651 and 1652. In the second edition only, the preface is dated; the date is 11 February 1651/2. The editions differ only in that the second corrects printing mistakes. The printer, William Dugard, terms himself 'printer to the Council of State'; the arms of the Commonwealth are prominently displayed; every reader

[1] James Geddes, *History of the Administration of John de Witt* (London, 1879), I, 176.

must have recognised it as an official publication. The only mark of authorship is the signature of the preface—Philopatris. It was written in fact by the secretary to the Council of Trade, Benjamin Worsley. 'I was the first solicitor for the Act for the encouragement of navigation', Benjamin Worsley wrote in 1661, 'and put the first file to it, and after writ *The Advocate* in defence of it.'[1] The main part of the pamphlet is entitled *The Advocate: or, a narrative of the state and condition of things between the English and Dutch nation...as it was presented in August 1651.* Presented to whom? The bill for the Navigation Act was introduced to parliament on 5 August. *The Advocate* may therefore be, or embody, a speech or circular drawn up in the Council of Trade on behalf of the Council of State. But if so it may—it probably does—embody a report in which the Council of Trade first recommended a navigation act to the Council of State. And this would probably be the report on the Council of Trade's ninth instruction:

> They are to take into consideration whether it be necessary to give way to a more open and free trade than that of companies and societies, and in what manner it is fittest to be done; wherein, notwithstanding, they are to take care that government and order in trade may be preserved and confusion avoided.[2]

For *The Advocate* includes material which obviously came from the representations of the trading companies (though no doubt supplemented by inquiries), and those representations were for charters and privileges.

It is a complete mistake to suppose that the Navigation Act was evolved as a result of the pressure of 'interested groups', that it was the product of forces exerted on the government by pressure groups.[3] In the first place this is intrinsically unlikely. For one thing, the merchant companies relied entirely on the support of the state and were too weak to have exerted pressure in this sense, while the government in 1651 had consolidated its position and was strong enough to override them if it wished. Had the merchant companies been able to shape the policy of the government, they would have done so in 1649; and the result would not have been a navigation act. For another thing, the Navigation Act was to some extent against the interests of the companies. If what had formerly been achieved by privileges was now to be achieved by Act of Parliament, there was

---

[1] Bodleian Library, Clarendon Papers, 75/300. C. M. Andrews appears to have first noticed this claim: *The Colonial Period of American History* (New Haven, 1934–8), IV, 23, 41, 60.

[2] Instructions of councils of trade are printed by C. M. Andrews, *British...Councils of Trade and Plantations, 1622–1675* (Baltimore, 1908).

[3] This seems to be the attitude of G. N. Clark, *History*, new series, VII (1923), 282 ff., and of L. A. Harper, *The English Navigation Laws* (New York, 1939), 34–49.

clearly less reason for privileges. This was recognised by the Eastland company in 1660—'we have employed about 200 ships yearly . . . by which means this company proved a singular nursery of seamen . . . thereby performing the intent of the Navigation Act before it was in being'. And in the second place there is not a scrap of evidence that any company pressed for a navigation act. If some merchants wanted a navigation act, the companies did not represent them. Trinity House wanted a navigation act, but its interests were not those of merchants. If the companies wanted an act of parliament, it is more likely to have been an act for confirming their charters than an act which tended to destroy them.

The *Advocate* says of the Eastland trade that 'whereas we did use formerly to send thither 200 sail of shipping in a year, we now did not send 16 sail'. This is an echo of the Eastland company's representation of 1649, brought up to date. For 1651 it is, according to the Sound Tables, very near the truth, not simply for the ships of the Eastland company but for ships from England as a whole. Everyone was freighting Dutch ships, says *The Advocate*. Dutch ships were, in some commodities, 'able to go as cheap again for freight as we; in some, half as cheap; and near in all, a full third penny cheaper than we'. So not only Dutch ships had an advantage, but Dutch merchants. *The Advocate* takes for granted that when English merchants must use Dutch ships Dutch merchants tend to engross English trade. They undersold us abroad in cloth and in England in foreign goods. 'And thus they served us, as for all our Norway, Eastland and Russia commodities, so also lately in our wines, fruits, oils, currants etc. which were the commodities of Spain, Canaries and the Straits . . . concluding with themselves to weary us out at length from all trade, and to have the sole buying and selling of all commodities for us.' The Levant company had submitted complaints on these lines in December 1649 and December 1650; they desired that the government should prohibit the import of Levant goods in foreign ships and from the Netherlands, and that the customs officers should admit only the goods of members of the Levant company. This was the former state of affairs under their proclamation of 1615; they uttered no word about a navigation act. *The Advocate* says also that the Dutch had engrossed the East India trade, not so much by cheap freights as by 'practice'—'monopolising three sorts of spices almost to the whole world, as cloves, nuts, mace, and lately much cinnamon'. In December 1649 the East India company had petitioned for an Act of Parliament for confirmation of their charter, with monopoly of trade in the Indian and Pacific Oceans and the power to punish interlopers. Their later representations, if they made any, do not survive, but it is to be presumed that they reported to the Council of State what they learnt in letters from their factors at Bantam and Surat: namely, that spices are too dear because the Dutch bid high, that the Dutch engross them, that the Dutch persuade Indians to refuse to sell; and that the Dutch engross Portuguese cinnamon 'so that we shall not only at present wholly fail you therein, but even despair of supplying you hereafter'. The Eastland, Levant and East India companies are sometimes said to have exerted most pressure for the Navigation Act, and it is true that their grievances figure largely in *The Advocate*; yet their only recorded desires were for privileges.[1]

The main feature of the crisis as depicted by *The Advocate* was the fact that imports were being carried in Dutch ships and to a considerable extent handled by Dutch merchants through the Amsterdam entrepôt. Export of money and decay of the cloth industry were secondary characteristics. *The Advocate* does not speak in terms of economic theory. The crisis of 1620 had produced pamphlets on economic theory in order to explain the monetary disturbance, but in 1651 it was simply a question of freight rates, treaties and power. Some writers following W. R. Scott deny that any action was necessary, but this is hard to believe.[2] The advantages of the Dutch were firmly rooted and would increase with time, for a great merchant fleet spelt sea-power, and sea-power in turn protected and encouraged the merchant fleet. What the English lost, the Dutch gained. The consequence of loss of trade was loss of power. 'Philopatris' in *The Advocate* was not troubled about bankruptcies of merchants, he was thinking about the security of the state. He asks in his preface what the councils of God intend to bring forth for this nation, and whether he intends we shall be oppressed by other nations about us; and towards the end of *The Advocate* we learn that 'it is by trade, and the due ordering and

---

[1] Levant: SP 105/144/21–23, 55–6; SP 18/9/21. See accounts by Wood, *Levant Company*, 53–8; and especially M. P. Ashley, *Financial and Commercial Policy under the Cromwellian Protectorate* (Oxford University Press, 1934), 116–18.

East Indies: *Court Minutes of the East India Company 1644–1649*, ed. E. B. Sainsbury (Oxford, 1912), 379–80, 384–5. *The English Factories in India 1646–1650* and *The English Factories in India 1651–1654*, ed. W. Foster (Oxford, 1914–15), *passim*, refer from index under 'cloves', 'nutmegs', 'mace', 'spices', 'cinnamon'.

[2] E.g. C. M. Andrews, *Colonial Period of American History*, IV, 30ff.; England was facing 'what to many appeared to be a trade depression, of which the Dutch were thought ready to take advantage'. 'Though conditions were not as bad as these men supposed...they saw, after the fashion of merchants, only a melancholy state of affairs in the commercial world.' After much pulling of wires and matching of wits, by lobbying and pressing in parliament, they secured an Act which was not only unnecessary but injurious.

Lipson, *Economic History*, III (1943), 129–30: the Navigation Act was 'the product of a situation essentially temporary in its nature, for there is no reason to suppose that English shippers would not have regained their former share of the carrying trade, and even extended it, as the need for meeting Dutch competition stimulated the versatility and enterprise of English shipbuilders'.

governing of it, and by no other means, that wealth and shipping can either be increased, or upheld; and consequently by no other, that the power of any nation can be sustained by land, or by sea'.

We print also at Appendix B a pamphlet called *Free Ports*. It appeared in 1652 from the same printer and in the same format as *The Advocate*, with which it makes an obvious pair. (Neither pamphlet is common today, but where they survive it is not surprising to find them bound together.) The author of *Free Ports* was 'B.W.'—who other than Benjamin Worsley?—and it is possible that the text is, or embodies, a report of the Council of Trade on their fifth instruction, 'to advise how free ports for foreign commodities imported (without paying of custom, if again exported) may be appointed in several parts of this land, and in what manner the same is best to be effected'. Free ports were in the air. London wanted to be one, Trinity House recommended a number. It was an old idea. We found it in Thomas Mun, explaining the profit that would arise from an entrepôt in Baltic rye. Lewes Roberts wrote about it. The idea had been tried with success at Dover.[1]

The Navigation Act could not increase, and was not intended to increase, the volume of trade. It could rescue, and was only intended to rescue, it from the hands of the Dutch. To increase its volume was the role allotted to free ports. Free ports aimed at imitating the successful entrepôt trade of the Dutch. Eastland goods were prominent among those to be re-exported. Benjamin Worsley's pamphlet gives several reasons in favour of this scheme, but the most notable is this. There are two ways for a nation to trade: first, to trade for its own expense or consumption like country gentlemen or tradesmen, in which case it is confined to a 'stock' not exceeding its own expense or consumption, and the employment of shipping and returns of foreign goods are limited answerably; secondly, to make itself into a shop and to buy and sell for other nations, like a man that keeps a warehouse; in this case both its stock and shipping will be indefinitely or proportionately increased. This was the ambitious superstructure that was to have been fitted on to the foundation of the Navigation Act.

We do not know what the Eastland company thought about this scheme. They can hardly have opposed it. But, like the Navigation Act, it was dangerous to their existence as a company. Regulated companies were designed to trade inward and outward in the very manner castigated by Benjamin Worsley in the argument just cited, and to a government thinking along the lines of free ports their privileges must have tended to

---

[1] Ashley, *Cromwellian Protectorate*, 26–30, 150–1, describes the agitation for free ports. He takes the view that they were inconsistent with the Navigation Act.

appear not only as subordinate to the national welfare (which they had always been) but even (new and worse) as largely irrelevant to it. Their organisation did not prohibit re-export trade, but their entry fines, impositions and system of shipping were clearly capable of making it more difficult and expensive than it would otherwise be. Benjamin Worsley explained clearly why re-export must be made as cheap and easy as possible, and if, as seems likely, *Free Ports* represents the opinion of the Council of Trade, it is not difficult to understand that this idea played a part in undermining the Eastland company in subsequent years.

Chapter VIII

THE GROWTH OF THE NAVY AND THE DEMAND FOR NAVAL STORES

The decline and disappearance of the Eastland company was a corollary of the growth of the state. We are accustomed to be told that the reign of Henry VIII introduced the modern state in England, but under Elizabeth I and James I it is possible to see in some quarters a tendency that can be described as regressive. If the mark of the modern state is centralised bureaucracy, Elizabeth I and James I, when they delegated some of the functions of government to private individuals and corporations such as the Eastland company, took a step away from it. Charles I did not alter the system of delegated government that he inherited, though he controlled it more closely. But the new republican government with its Navigation Act resumed some of the delegated powers, and henceforth the process of bureaucratic centralisation was uninterrupted. At the end of the seventeenth century commerce was regulated by a permanent Board of Trade; the government imposed its will on merchants for the most part through the customs service; a statistical department under the Inspector-General of Imports and Exports furnished information; the civil service had assumed its modern shape and the day of the Eastland company was over.

If we attempt to express in simple words the several links of cause and effect by which this process came about, we must constantly recur to the idea of sea-power. Sea-power was the object of the Navigation Act. Without sea-power sufficient to win the Dutch war that followed it, the Navigation Act could hardly have become the corner-stone of a system. The republic built a large fleet which successive governments expanded further. Naval shipbuilding required Eastland naval stores and encouraged Eastland import trades which, as we have seen, the Eastland company had never strictly controlled. Further, it made the navy the Eastland merchants' greatest single customer; the necessity of a cheap and plentiful supply of naval stores tended to put the government on the side of free trade. Again, the fleet protected and promoted English trade and encouraged the building of merchant ships; this created a further demand for Eastland naval stores with the same effect. Thus in 1673 the Eastland company's privileges were curtailed by the removal of those import trades which chiefly supplied naval stores. In addition, the general development of foreign trade favoured re-export trade which also the Eastland company had never strictly controlled. At the same time sea-power gave new life to foreign policy. Even when exerted only in home waters it fortified policy in the Baltic, balancing Dutch influence and forestalling discrimination there; and in the end English warships penetrated to the Baltic itself, and the state was able to take over the functions of the Eastland company even at their foreign residence. The Eastland company was never dissolved, but at that point it disappeared.

Such is the theme of our remaining chapters. In the present chapter we shall examine the demand for naval stores.

TABLE 8.* *Naval ships built and rebuilt, 1601–88*

	Gross tonnage					
	200–400	400–600	600–800	800–1000	1000–1500	Over 1500
1601–10	1	1	4	—	1	—
1611–20	1	4	6	1	—	—
1621–30	1	—	2	4	—	—
1631–40	2	2	2	3	—	1
1641–48	5	4	—	—	1	—
1649–50	—	4	6	1	1	—
1651–60	16	3	9	14	8	1
1661–70	2	4	2	3	11	7
1671–80	5	3	1	2	22	11
1681–88	1	—	1	3	—	6

* M. Oppenheim, *History…of the Royal Navy and of Merchant Shipping…* *1509–1660* (London, 1896), 121, 202, 254–5, 330–7. Samuel Pepys's 'Register of the ships of the Royal Navy', edited by J. R. Tanner in his *Descriptive Catalogue of the Naval Manuscripts in the Pepysian Library*, 1 (Navy Records Society, 1903), 266–95.
Only those ships of which all the required particulars are given in the above sources have been included.
No account has been taken of the different methods of measuring tonnage in use over the period. Ships therefore appear after 1626 as about 5 per cent smaller and after 1650 as about 12 per cent larger than they would have appeared in the time of James I. But the figures were not in any case exact.
Pepys gives burden, not gross tonnage. His figures have therefore been corrected by the addition of one-third, since gross tonnage = tons and tonnage = burden plus one-third (Oppenheim, *op. cit.* 266–8).

Table 8 shows that warships were built in the reign of Charles I at the rate of less than one a year, and during the interregnum at the rate of more than five a year. In tonnage the rate of building increased perhaps sevenfold. It must be agreed that 1649 is an extremely important date in the history of naval shipbuilding. Cromwell's and Charles II's ships, which kept the sea for long periods and fought three naval wars against the Dutch, required more maintenance than had Charles I's ships. They were bigger and therefore required a higher proportion of imported naval stores.[1]

In 1649, in a long and carefully worded representation arguing for the restoration of their privileges, the Eastland company said that they would not fail, under a well-ordered government: 'To furnish this land with a constant supply of corn and other needful commodities of the East, at reasonable rates.' In 1656, in a similar representation, this sentence reads: 'To furnish this land with a constant supply of naval and other needful commodities of the East, at reasonable rates.'[2]

'The greatest provision of any one particular in the navy', wrote John Hollond in 1638, 'is hemp.' It was of Baltic hemp that he spoke. In or about 1659 he wrote that 'this commodity is the most absolutely necessary provision...of all other commodities in the navy both for kind and quantity', and discussed at length the best method of supplying it.[3] Riga hemp was best for quality, Muscovy hemp was cheaper but of low quality; the navy ropeyards mixed them. Pepys experimented with Milan hemp, Holland hemp, English hemp and Indian grass, but failed to find a satisfactory substitute.[4]

Riga masts likewise were the best for their size. The biggest masts were found in America, but for medium masts shipwrights preferred the slow-growing fir poles from the Baltic hinterland. Spars were found in Norway and were shipped from many harbours on the southern fjords. Norway also provided deal boards, used in the interior parts of warships. When Sir William Warren took Pepys on a tour of his timber-yard, all the deals were Norwegian,[5] and in the navy's contracts during the second Dutch war very few of any other kind were specified.[6] Most pitch and tar came from Stockholm.

Great ships required long plank. The question was whether foreign oak could replace English oak, and the answer was that it sometimes had to. Hollond wrote about 1659 that

It is a disputed case whether foreign or East country plank be fit for the State's service or not. For my part...I see no reason why it should

---

[1] The needs of naval shipbuilding are discussed in R. G. Albion, *Forests and Sea Power, 1652–1862* (Harvard University Press, 1926) and more briefly in J. Ehrman, *The Navy in the War of William III* (Cambridge, 1953). Albion's opening date is significantly chosen.   [2] Appendix A9.

[3] Hollond's two *Discourses of the Navy*, ed. J. R. Tanner (Navy Records Society, 1896), 74, 190. Hollond was successively paymaster, commissioner and surveyor of the navy.

[4] Pepys, *Diary*, ed. Wheatley (London, 1893–9), II, 293, 301, III, 58, 235, IV, 258.

[5] *Diary*, II, 265.

[6] *Cal.S.P.Dom. 1664–1665*, 131–7; *1665–1666*, 129–35. These summaries of contracts, and those for other years, show at a glance the origin of most of the navy's imports.

not, if sound wood and well cut; and this I am sure of, that when any merchants have brought the provision to the market, if not the State, yet the shipwrights of the Thames have bought it....I know the wood is poorish and 'frow' as they phrase it, and it's probable...in that regard not so lasting as our English oak, but I know withal, that they are generally gallant long plank...and that the master builders of the Thames not only know this, but also make use of it for their private profit, in building with this plank upon the sole account of its length, breadth, and growth at the top end, wherein the profit of a contractor is much concerned.[1]

In thirty new ships ordered in 1677 Pepys specified some East country plank below the water-line.[2] When the ships rotted this plank was blamed, according to Pepys unjustly. In some ships, he said, not one foot had been used, but they also had rotted. He added that at that date some of the king's ships were planked with no other; these had not rotted. The master-builders of the Thames certified in his support that they were accustomed to use a hundred loads of foreign plank to twenty of English, and that for ships over 300 tons its use was essential; the best foreign plank was from Danzig, Königsberg, Riga and Hamburg.[3]

Even for the frame of the warship, for the great timbers on which its strength depended, English oak yielded at times to Baltic oak. In the thirty new ships, according to Pepys, 'not above five hundred of five and thirty thousand loads of timber, provided for these ships, were of East country growth',[4] but he saw a note in 1692 'about the quantity and sizes of fir timber needful for supplying the want of large oak for the *Britannia*'.[5]

An easily overlooked naval store, although it is clear that warships were useless without guns, is iron. Hollond discusses the supply of iron nails and so forth, but not of guns; guns were the responsibility of the ordnance office, not of the navy. But a three-decker of this period carried about 200 tons of ordnance, the burthen of a fair-sized merchant ship.[6] Swedish iron made good guns. If English warships were equipped with guns of Swedish iron, this alone—not to mention the Cromwellian armies—must have greatly expanded the volume of Swedish imports.

There was never a time when the navy did not require Eastland naval stores. The ancient office of Queen's or King's Merchant had been established to supply them. Charles I's foreign policy in the Baltic shows,

[1] Hollond's *Discourses*, 225–6.
[2] Pepysian MSS. 2265/58, at Magdalene College, Cambridge.
[3] Pepys's *Memoires of the Royal Navy*, ed. J. R. Tanner (Oxford, 1906), 34–44.
[4] Pepys's *Memoires*, 35.
[5] Pepys's *Naval Minutes*, ed. J. R. Tanner (Navy Records Society, 1926), 218. It is necessary to distinguish carefully between timber and plank. In contemporary usage timber did not include plank.
[6] Ehrman, *Navy of William III*, 9, 65.

as we saw in Chapter V, that he was aware of its strategic importance as the source of naval stores. But the problem of supply before 1650 was never acute. Hollond was able to write in 1638 that 'of all provisions in the navy his Majesty is seldom or never necessitated of any... but masts, and those of twenty-two hands and upwards'. These great masts were not used save by the navy. Other naval stores, such as timber, plank, hemp, tar, 'although upon special occasion they may be scarce and hard to come by, yet generally are to be had for money upon demand'. But about 1659 Hollond gives another picture. 'How safe it is to hazard the service of the State to an uncertain market by neglecting pre-contracts [for hemp] is not easy to determine.'[1] He meant that it was no longer safe to rely on hemp being available for ready money upon demand; it must be imported specially for the navy. And pre-contract for deals, plank, pitch, tar and other goods was the usual procedure a few years later in the second Dutch war. A King's Merchant was appointed at the restoration of Charles II,[2] but by this time the supply was too great to be handled by one man and too important to be in the hands of a private man, and the work was really performed by the commissioners of the navy in direct contact with the trade. According to the Duke of York's instructions in 1662:

> They are, by themselves or purveyors, at the season of the year when the East country commodities come into the river, to enquire the market price of all those provisions as masts, deals, spars, hemp, tar, pitch etc. and then to buy where there is best, and best cheap, not tying themselves to any particular man....
> They are to take order, that an invoice be weekly brought them from the custom-house, of such goods as have been entered and are useful to the navy, with the names of the merchants who entered them, that so the purveyors may not delude them with the pretence of scarcity when choice may be had, or oblige them to one merchant when divers might afford more choice and easier rates.[3]...

Such was the importance and difficulty of ensuring a cheap and plentiful supply of naval stores for the navy, that during every Dutch war the Navigation Act was suspended to allow free import of naval stores.

It does not detract from the importance of the navy's demands to point out, as we must, that in terms of supply it still accounted for a rather small proportion of the Eastland trade. In Pepys's time shipwrights reckoned to use one load of square timber per ton of merchant ship, one and a half loads per ton of warship of the third rate and two loads per ton of warship

---

[1] Hollond's *Discourses*, 59, 73, 190. 'Money is the life of their trade into these parts and for that commodity', *ibid.* 192.
[2] *Cal.S.P.Dom. 1660–1661*, 212.   [3] Pepysian MSS. 2867/359.

of the second rate; and they further reckoned to use six loads of timber to one load of plank.[1] A merchant ship of 400 tons built about 1650, in which timber would probably be English, would therefore probably need sixty-six loads of foreign plank. The load was one ton of burthen.[2] The plank for this ship might therefore require between a quarter and a third of a timber ship's cargo. The pitch, tar, hemp, deals, masts and spars—if they could be put into the same ship—would perhaps not complete its lading. In warships, their increasing weight and stoutness required increasingly well-chosen materials, that is to say, more expensive materials, for as Pepys said, 'price riseth fast in the dimensions of timber and plank as in jewels and glass'.[3] But five warships of the second rate of 1000 tons would not take more than 2000 loads of plank; in the unlikely event of all the plank being imported it would require between six and ten shiploads. With 25 tons of hemp for cordage[4] and as much again allowed for ground tackle, and with masts, spars, pitch and tar, the five warships may have needed something of the order of sixteen ships, probably less. The most intense programme of navy building was that of the thirty ships planned in 1677. They cannot have consumed (with guns) more than 130 shiploads of Eastland materials. Their construction was spread over three years in which imports from the Baltic amounted to 950 shiploads. It is clear that the safe arrival of a dozen ships out of the Baltic could make the difference between losing and winning a naval battle, and that it might also make or mar a merchant's fortune; but we must not expect that the demand of the navy will radically affect our figures for the volume of imports. In fact the biggest naval shipbuilding years next to 1677–9 were during the Dutch wars, when our figures are at their lowest.

It is probable that warships were built in the interregnum at about the same rate as merchant ships in the 1630's. That had been a flourishing time for English navigation, and in 1639 Trinity House went so far as to declare that the merchant fleet had increased tenfold in thirty years. From returns of merchant ships fit for the royal service in 1629 (at least 400 over 100 tons) and of ships licensed to carry ordnance between 1625 and 1638 (some 340 English-built ships), we can, if we dare, calculate the rate of building as, very roughly, 5000 tons a year; whereas the average annual rate for warships in the interregnum was between 4000 and 5000. After 1638 there is apparently no evidence for merchant building until 1660. After 1660 the merchant fleet again increased. At first it included a great number of foreign-built ships, as it is said to have done in the 1630's; but the proportion dropped. Between 1662 and 1668 nearly half the

[1] Pepysian MSS. 2870/456, 466.   [2] Albion, *Forests and Sea Power*, 149.
[3] Pepysian MSS. 2870/456.   [4] Pepysian MSS. 977/66.

accessions were foreign-built, but from 1684 to 1688 nine-tenths were English-built.[1]

Taking merchant ships and warships together, then, it is possible that the demand for Eastland naval stores was little or no greater under Cromwell than under Charles I, and that it rose more or less steeply perhaps about 1670. But naval stores differed little from house-building materials. The Restoration by all accounts was a period of great house-building. Especially the rebuilding of London after the Great Fire created a heavy demand for Norwegian goods.

These suggestions about the demand for Eastland goods tally fairly well with what we know about their supply. This will be discussed in the next chapter.

[1] Harper, *English Navigation Laws*, ch. 22. See for the early Stuart returns of shipping, Oppenheim, *The Royal Navy*, 269–71.

Chapter IX

THE TRADE IN THE SECOND HALF OF
THE CENTURY

From the Navigation Act to the third Dutch war: 1651–74

The state of English commerce in the interregnum is obscure, but in the Eastland trade there are signs that it was bad. During the first Dutch war (1652–4) the King of Denmark closed the Sound to English ships. This war was hardly ended when Cromwell declared war on Spain, and Dunkirk privateers rode off the mouth of the Humber. In 1656 there was war in the Baltic and the English merchants were expelled from Danzig.[1] Accordingly we are not surprised to discover from the Sound Tables both that English cloth exports to the Baltic were low and that they were shipped to a considerable extent in Eastland ships.[2] The number of English ships in Baltic trade was low, and a high proportion of imports both in English and Eastland ships was handled by foreign merchants. Table 9 shows that of ninety-five identified shiploads of imports in 1655, only forty-three belonged, at the Sound, to Englishmen. As to the volume of imports, the figures in Table 9 possibly understate it. Baltic ships sailing to England are identifiable only when they returned to the Baltic *from* England. Nevertheless, there is no reason to suppose it was high. We have suggested that the demand for naval stores was not greater than hitherto, domestic corn prices were low, and conditions did not favour re-export. It is true that one must not take too literally, in wartime,

TABLE 9*

	1625	1635	1646	1655
English ships westwardbound, laden	80	114	85	50
English ships with cargoes not English-owned	2	4	1	10
Other ships westwardbound, laden	11	25	27	45
Other ships with cargoes not English-owned	2	1	5	42

* The sources are as for Tables 4 and 5 in Chapter III above.

[1] Chapter x, below. Dunkirkers, e.g. *Cal.S.P.Dom. 1655–1656*, 200.
[2] Above, p. 84 n.

indications about the nationality of ships or the ownership of cargoes. We shall notice in Chapter xi below a practice which the Eastland company called 'collusion', whereby English merchants and native merchants of the Eastland entered into an arrangement or partnership which enabled goods to be English at one place and foreign at another. It was therefore not impossible for the English merchant to continue to trade. But he could not hope for prosperity. From the point of view of the commonwealth the low cloth exports and the lack of employment for English ships were traditional signs of crisis. A long lament by the Eastland company in 1656 appears to be justified.[1]

There are no Sound Tables for 1658–60. Dunkirk was captured and at some point the English returned to Danzig. It is reasonable to suppose that the trade improved. An isolated record of trade at Stockholm shows an improvement in Anglo-Swedish trade in 1659. No less than thirty-four English ships arrived at Stockholm in that year, of which twenty-one had sailed from England, four from Portugal and the rest from Norwegian, German and other Baltic ports. This shows that English ships had become safe carriers. Cloth and salt predominated in their cargoes. All the English ships returned to England. Their cargoes homeward were chiefly iron. There was only one Swedish ship from England and there were only three to England.[2] In the Sound Tables up to 1657 never more than ten English ships passed through the Sound from Sweden in a year. Evidently the Anglo-Swedish trade had shifted suddenly from Swedish ships to English. The war between Sweden and Denmark in 1658–60, which caused the cessation of the Sound Tables, was no time for Swedish ships to sail with safety. This bears out what the English ambassador to Sweden, John Robinson, wrote in his *Account of Sweden*: that Swedish trade was 'transported by both or either party according to the various junctures of affairs. When Sweden has been engaged in a war, the English ships have had the whole employ; but in times of peace...English bottoms cannot be used in that trade.'[3]

In 1660 with peace in the Baltic the trade returned to normality. There were four years of peaceful trading before the total stoppage of the second Dutch war, and four years of peaceful trading before the less complete stoppage of the third Dutch war. Examination of the trade in these years permits some comparison with the analysis of 1625–46 in Chapter iii.

In the first place, the decline of cloth exports had continued. This is plain

[1] Appendix A9, an appeal for restoration of privilege.
[2] *Svensk Handelsstatistik, 1637–1737*, ed. B. Boethius and E. Heckscher (Stockholm, 1938), 666ff.
[3] John Robinson, *An Account of Sweden* (London, 1694), 145. Robinson speaks as if the ships were really different, not simply the same ships under different flags.

in the figure at Appendix D below. In 1662 English wheat prices reached, according to Thorold Rogers, the highest point in the seventeenth century; Baltic rye prices in Polish price histories reached the highest level of the century between 1657 and 1663; more favourable conditions for the sale of English cloth cannot be imagined. Yet exports were low. Complaints of local competition seem justified.

It is not for want of merchants to transport cloth into foreign parts, that our trade decayeth [said the Eastland Company in 1661] for that all places are sufficiently supplied with English cloth, most of which cannot be sold to profit, by reason of the great quantities both of broadcloth and kerseys which are made beyond seas, not only...in Holland, but also in Germany, the marks of Brandenburg and Silesia, and divers places in Poland, and also in Prussia, and the cloth can be afforded cheaper than any such like that can be carried out of England, though in the wearing it prove not so good.[1]

In the second place, however, the development of colonial re-exports can be observed. Occasional consignments of pepper, sugar and tobacco had been shipped to the Baltic in the 1630's. After 1660 the re-export especially of tobacco considerably increased. The following are annual averages of colonial re-exports from England to the Baltic:

1621–30	8,000 lb.
1631–40	34,000 lb.
1641–50	63,000 lb.
1651–60	73,000 lb.
1661–70	172,000 lb.

After 1670 the large number of Swedish ships, which were toll-free at the Sound and whose cargoes were not registered, makes exact calculation impossible; but in four years when there were no Swedish ships the annual average was: 1676–79   1,132,000 lb.[2]

[1] *Reasons offered by the Merchants Adventurers of England and Eastland Merchants residing at Hull for the preservation of their societies*, 1661. Note also in Appendix A9 below, representations of 1649 and 1656: 'Great hath been of late the industry of strangers in Poland and Prussia to advance their manufacture of cloth.'
Add. MS. 36785 in the British Museum gives exports from London to Poland, Sweden and Denmark. It is unsuitable for comparison because it omits Ipswich exports. It indicates that Poland was still the best market for quality: a short cloth to Poland was valued at £8, to Denmark and Sweden at £7; a Spanish cloth to Poland was valued at £14, to Denmark and Sweden at £12. Sweden and Denmark took few of these dear cloths.
[2] *Sound Tables, 1497–1660,* 2B, *Sound Tables, 1661–1783,* 2 (i). The Sound Tables, *1661–1783,* ed. N. E. Bang and K. Korst (3 vols., Copenhagen, 1930–45) differ in several particulars from the earlier series. There are no values and certain details are omitted. The goods in this table correspond to the 'spices' in Table 2 in Chapter III above, and they include Mediterranean fruits, East and West Indian spices, drugs and dyestuffs, but it is safe to assert that the chief English colonial re-export after 1660 was tobacco.

In the third place, as to imports, whereas the volume (so far as we can measure it) shows little or no change, a significant change had taken place in the relative proportion of commodities. We now have, as before, about one hundred English ships bringing Baltic goods to England. The number of Baltic ships did not exceed fifty before the second Dutch war; afterwards it reached one hundred, reflecting in all probability the demand for house-building materials after the great fire, but even so the figures were well below the corresponding figures in the import boom of 1641, and the value was probably of the same order. The list given in Table 10 of commodities imported at London in 1663 and 1669 is to be compared with the list of imports in table 6 in Chapter III above. If we ignore wood as an

TABLE 10.* *Imports from the Eastland to London only, at selling prices*

	1663 (£)	1669 (£)
Wood	55,000	135,000
Iron	41,000	42,000
Flax	41,000	17,000
Hemp	26,000	27,000
Pitch and tar	19,000	22,000
Potashes	13,000	29,000
Linen and canvas	4,000	8,000
Total imports including some not given above	220,000	302,000

* B.M. Add. MS. 36785. For a close examination of this document see Ralph Davis, 'English foreign trade, 1660–1700', *Ec.H.R.* 2nd series, VII (1954), 150ff. It gives exports separately to Denmark, Sweden and Poland but lumps together imports under 'Eastland'. If the values are halved to give first cost, multiplied by four to convert approximately to rixdollars, and doubled or trebled to give the total import of all England, a highly inexact but not altogether meaningless comparison is possible with values in Table 6 (above, p. 39) and with estimates of value in the year of high imports, 1641 (above, p. 48 n.).

import chiefly from Norway, the remaining commodities give a fair picture of Baltic trade to London. There is no corn. There had been corn imports every year in 1625, 1635 and 1646, even though the price of English wheat had been lower than in 1663. Iron is the most valuable commodity. Its importance in 1625 and 1635 had been slight, though in 1646 somewhat greater. It is reasonable to estimate that the value of iron imported at London alone in 1663 and 1669 was at least double the total import in 1646.

We have seen that Swedish trade normally preferred Swedish to English ships. We shall see that English merchants frequently complained of obstructions to their trade in Sweden. Nevertheless, it was a profitable and expanding trade in which English merchants played an indispensable part. John Robinson writes of it in these words:

> The management of the trade of Sweden has always in the main been in the hands of strangers, most of the natives wanting either capacity or application, and all of them stocks to drive it; for without credit from abroad, they are not able to keep their iron-works going: and therefore at the beginning of winter they usually make contracts with the English and other foreigners, who then advance considerable sums, and receive iron in summer.[1]

Lastly, from 1669 it is possible to observe the development of Swedish and other branches of Baltic trade in terms of shiploads. In 1669 the Sound toll registers began to record ships' destinations. Hence all ships bound for England are known, with their ports of departure. There were eighty-nine from Sweden, sixteen from Riga, six from Narva, and only sixty-three from Danzig, Elbing and Königsberg. In other words, the number of ships from Prussia was appreciably less than in 1625, 1635 and 1646, and from other places far more.[2] The trade from Prussia accounted for only about one-third of England's imports. Table 11 shows the future development of the above-named four trades. The most striking feature is the continued growth of the Riga and Narva trades.

It is important to recognise that the history of the Eastland trade up to the third Dutch war is one of dispersion rather than of growth. The successful trading of Charles I's reign culminating in the import boom of 1641 was not paralleled under the 'normal' trading conditions after the English Restoration. It is true that signs of an apparently natural growth of commerce can be seen in the Swedish iron trade and the tobacco re-export trade, but they were offset by the decline of corn imports and cloth exports. It would be natural for English public opinion at this juncture to regard the Eastland trade as decayed.

We come now to the great expansion which gave it the shape and size well known from the ledgers of the Inspector-General of Imports and Exports at the end of the century. This expansion coincided significantly with a decline of Dutch Baltic trade. The middle of the seventeenth century was characterised in England by an almost hysterical hatred of the Dutch, combined with a desire to emulate them. The Anglo-Dutch wars struck hard blows at Dutch commerce from which their Baltic trade never wholly recovered. The English thought that their commerce could not advance save at the expense of the Dutch. Table 12 shows that this belief

---

[1] *Account of Sweden*, 148–9.
[2] Table 7, p. 41 above, gives the ports of departure of English ships in 1625, 1635 and 1646.

TABLE 11.* *Ships bound for England*

Year	From the Baltic	From Prussia	From Riga	From Narva	From Sweden
1669	172	63	16	6	89
1670	204	79	32	6	72
1671	166	52	22	10	64
1672	99	20	13	2	54
1673	148	34	48	6	49
1674	226	84	32	9	52
1675	356	134	60	25	97
1676	363	95	69	26	137
1677	337	133	69	25	99
1678	294	84	43	21	127
1679	244	89	28	21	87
1680	219	56	30	22	97
1681	302	116	33	32	87
1682	331	86	72	46	99
1683	360	76	91	49	122
1684	264	79	49	29	94
1685	321	93	70	35	101
1686	339	93	77	47	111
1687	358	92	73	51	128
1688	324	69	90	45	108
1689	201	32	70	25	63
1690	205	37	51	23	82
1691	253	43	61	40	101
1692	224	50	65	44	58
1693	226	53	60	37	69
1694	210	40	50	34	78
1695	188	27	52	33	71
1696	229	44	73	34	68
1697	126	24	41	17	41
1698	271	70	49	33	107
1699	331	78	89	48	101
1700	294	101	3	71	106

* Sound Tables, *1661–1783*, 2 (i). Includes ships in ballast, but there were very few. There were generally a few ships from ports in Pomerania, Kurland, Finland, Denmark and so on, so that the first column in the table is not simply the sum of the remaining columns.

TABLE 12.* *English and Dutch ships passing through the Sound, westward bound; annual averages by decades*

	Dutch	English		Dutch	English
1591–1600	1609	91	1651–60	879	34
1601–10	1350	94	1661–70	672	67
1611–20	1699	95	1671–80	581	220
1621–30	1076	76	1681–90	946	245
1631–40	1017	127	1691–1700	571	133
1641–50	1178	88			

* From the figures in Appendix D.

was plausible. English ships generally numbered less than one-tenth of Dutch ships in the first half of the century, but in the second half they came to number generally about a quarter. The Dutch decline dates from the 1650's, the English expansion from the 1670's. In fact the English expansion began in 1675.

From 1675 to the end of the century

In the Eastland trade 1675 was *annus mirabilis*. The westward traffic out of the Baltic roughly doubled. English ships passed the Sound destined for Dutch and French ports.[1] There were large and altogether exceptional imports of Baltic corn, evidently for re-export.[2] English ships entered the Baltic from the Netherlands, France and Portugal, laden with wine and salt; and as these far outnumbered those that sailed *to* these places, we deduce a triangular trade with one leg from the Baltic to England, another from England to France or Portugal, and the third from France or Portugal back to the Baltic.[3] All this trade the English literally seized from the Dutch.

The merchants ought to have thanked Charles II for their prosperity, unless they were blinded to material benefit by thoughts of morality or constitutionalism. Charles had learnt from experience. The first Dutch war was fought by Cromwell without allies, under the disadvantage of having the Sound closed to him. For the second (1665–7), Charles II tried to get Denmark on his side as well as Sweden, and he had hopes of France also; but his optimistic diplomacy came to nothing, and both France and Denmark aligned themselves with the Dutch. In the third war he achieved two notable successes. First, he made sure of the alliance of France by means of the Treaty of Dover. Secondly, he deserted her at the crucial moment, in 1674. In 1675 England was not only at peace, but neutral among nations still at war. A great part of Dutch trade—especially the trade with France—was free for the taking. In 1671, the last year of general peace, the Sound Tables have, from France, 144 Dutch ships and fifteen English. In 1673, when both nations were at war, they have no Dutch ships and no English. In 1675, when England was neutral, they have one Dutch ship and 121 English.[4]

The fruits of neutrality were also found in Swedish trade. In 1675 (not unconnected with the war in the west) war broke out between Denmark and Sweden, and Swedish ships became unsafe. Accordingly, the English trade from Sweden and the Swedish dominions fell entirely to English ships. In 1674 the Sound Tables have seven English and forty-seven foreign

---

[1] Appendix D.   [2] Sound Tables, *1661–1783*, 2 (i).
[3] The ships possibly touched at English ports without unloading. The goods would not appear in English customs records.   [4] Sound Tables, *1661–1783*, 1.

ships bound for England from Sweden, in 1675 they have ninety-five English and two foreign.[1]

This made for a shipping boom even more pronounced than the trading boom. In 1671, 104 English ships sailed out of the Baltic; in 1676, 403.[2] The extraordinary rapidity of these alterations in shipping figures opens many questions, but we need not enter into them here. Whatever made the English flag safe and prosperous at sea made the English merchants' trade prosperous and great.

When the war in which Charles II had so cleverly made himself neutral ended in 1678, English ships lost the trade of Baltic goods to the Netherlands and France. English ships entering the Baltic from France dropped from 119 in 1677 to thirty-eight in 1678, while Dutch ships rose from none in 1677 to 144 in 1679. Likewise when Denmark and Sweden made peace in 1679, Swedish ships came back into the trade from Sweden. But the relapse was not complete. The Baltic trade continued after 1678, through ten years of general peace, at a higher level than it had reached before 1675, did not drop excessively in the war of 1689–97, and at the close of the century was rising.

The chief explanation of the new prosperity is not to be found in the third-party trade with France and elsewhere. The triangular trade which took English ships back to the Baltic from France and Portugal did not, indeed, die away completely, but it was not very large by the new standards. Nor are significant signs of re-export of corn to be found in the years after the peace. The important thing in the long run was probably the import of Eastland goods for home consumption.[3]

[1] Sound Tables, *1661–1783*, 2 (i).
[2] The Sound Tables actually record passages of ship *masters*. Every tenth year they say how many passages were made by each master. English masters generally made two passages, sometimes four, i.e. one or two trips. But 1675–8 may be exceptional.
[3] The following are laden English ships entering the Sound from (A) the Netherlands, (B) France, (C) Portugal, (D) Spain (Sound Tables, *1661–1783*, 2 (i)). From the three last-named hardly any sailed unladen:

	A	B	C	D		A	B	C	D		A	B	C	D
1661	2	4	1	0	1675	36	121	31	1	1688	4	12	4	1
1662	0	2	3	0	1676	48	121	39	4	1689	2	0	2	1
1663	0	0	1	0	1677	7	119	25	1	1690	7	0	1	0
1664	0	1	2	2	1678	16	38	9	1	1691	1	0	0	0
1665	0	0	0	0	1679	2	67	10	0	1692	1	0	2	0
1666	0	0	0	0	1680	0	24	19	1	1693	1	0	0	0
1667	0	0	0	0	1681	3	10	20	2	1694	2	0	1	0
1668	0	2	1	1	1682	5	23	9	1	1695	3	0	0	0
1669	0	3	1	1	1683	7	14	18	0	1696	2	0	1	0
1670	0	3	1	0	1684	1	25	9	0	1697	1	0	0	0
1671	2	15	2	0	1685	3	7	6	0	1698	2	2	2	1
1672	0	0	0	0	1686	0	11	4	1	1699	2	2	5	2
1673	0	0	0	0	1687	2	13	6	1	1700	3	1	11	0
1674	2	11	3	0										

The boom in the Eastland trade was part of an expansion in English foreign trade as a whole. Ralph Davis, in a comparison between Add. MS. 36785 and the figures in the Inspector-General's ledgers of imports and exports beginning in 1696, finds that exports expanded by about 50 per cent and imports by about 25 per cent. Most of the increase in imports is accounted for by an increase in the import of colonial goods, and a big part of the increased exports were colonial re-exports. The re-export of tobacco trebled. This change, says Davis, was accomplished by 1688; it began for 'English shipping and distant trades' in 1674 and for 'England's most important markets' in 1678. These few years, from the end of the third Dutch war in 1674 to the beginning of the French wars in 1689, saw what may well be called the commercial revolution of the seventeenth century—a change from the straightforward scheme of import-export in which almost all exports were native woollen textiles to a scheme with wider horizons in which England served as an entrepôt as well as a producer and consumer.[1]

This expansion required an expansion of the merchant marine and called for a greater import of naval stores. No great or permanent expansion of English trade was possible without a large native-owned, home-built, economical merchant fleet: native-owned, because it was necessary for merchants and owners to be in close touch; economical, because freight charges were very important; and home-built, not because native builders were better than others, but because the use of foreign-built ships would necessarily imply that foreign merchants—to whom those ships were native-built—had an inherent advantage over their English rivals. England gained this merchant fleet in the period we are considering. We have seen that in the 1660's nearly half the new ships were foreign-built, but by the 1680's less than a tenth were foreign-built. There was at the same time (remember the thirty new ships in 1677–9) a continuing increase in naval building. There was intense pressure on shipyards, in spite of the growth of some of them. All this activity called for bigger imports from the Eastland, while the demand for iron was subsequently swollen by the needs of William III's land forces.[2]

Simultaneously the price of Eastland naval stores fell. The price of hemp, pitch and tar paid by the navy in England had risen steeply in 1652, the beginning of the first Dutch war; thereafter the price of pitch and tar had fallen but that of hemp went higher and higher until it dropped to the

[1] R. Davis, 'English foreign trade, 1660–1700', *Ec.H.R.* 2nd series, VII (1954), 150ff.
[2] On shipbuilding see D. C. Coleman, 'Naval dockyards under the later Stuarts', *Ec.H.R.* 2nd series, VI (1953), 134ff.

pre-1652 level, almost as suddenly as it had risen, at the close of the second Dutch war; it rose again during the third Dutch war but immediately afterwards fell away to a very low level in the 1680's, and this last downward movement in the late seventies and eighties is also visible in pitch and tar. The same upward and downward tendency can be seen in Polish price histories: after about 1646 some very high prices are observed and the five-year periods 1646–50 and 1651–5 have the highest averages of the century; the five-year period 1656–60 has a lower average, but rye reached the highest price of the century in the years 1657–63. After that there is a general cheapness. Rye was exceptionally cheap in 1668 and again in 1680. If these figures are a guide to naval stores they indicate that prices in England reflected prices in the Baltic both in the initial rise and in the subsequent fall. Who can calculate the demands of builders of merchant ships when they saw the price of some of their commodities nearly halved?[1]

By this reasoning we may conclude that the expansion of the Eastland trade was a sign of increased activity in other trades, which in turn was facilitated by an improvement of conditions in the Eastland trade. The process was circular. Cheapness of naval stores promoted trade in general, the expanding trade increased the demand for naval stores. The bigger the demand, the greater reason for more frequent and therefore more economical voyages. Eastland merchants put capital into colonial trade, and this provided them with goods to sell profitably in the Eastland. Cheaper ships in the colonial trade made for better profit on colonial goods when re-exported, and better profits on exports enabled imports to be sold cheaper. A wider range of exports meant a greater return to the shipowner for freight on the outward voyage, and this correspondingly reduced the burden of freight charges on imports.[2]

This sort of consideration was sufficiently well understood for an apt policy on the part of the government to have produced a foreseeable result. It was not only a case of clever foreign policy giving four years of happy neutrality. In 1669 the government had taken steps to introduce sixty cheap, economical, foreign-built ships into the Eastland trade, and in 1673, actually during the third Dutch war, it—or some of its members—had engineered the partial overthrow of the Eastland company. Denmark, Norway and Sweden, where the trades were import trades, were removed from their jurisdiction, and the company was thrown open to anyone

[1] The hemp, pitch and tar prices are Beveridge's (above, p. 42 n.) and the Polish prices are those of Pelc and others (above, p. 15).

[2] On investment see K. G. Davies, 'Joint-stock investment in the later seventeenth century', *Ec.H.R.* 2nd series, IV (1952), 299. Baltic merchants invested in the African company founded in 1671. Swedish iron was re-exported to Africa.

who wished to trade, at a nominal fine for entry. Most Englishmen would probably have assented to Sir Dudley North's *laissez-faire* dictum that 'no people ever yet grew rich by policies; it is peace, industry and freedom that brings trade and wealth and nothing else'. But what are we to say when peace and freedom are themselves a policy?[1]

The ledgers of the Inspector-General of Imports and Exports, 1697–9

We come to the end of the century and to the comprehensive figures of English trade compiled by the Inspector-General of Imports and Exports. His ledgers begin at Michaelmas 1696. We use three twelve-month periods ending Michaelmas 1697, Michaelmas 1698 and Christmas 1699. The ledgers give particulars of individual trades. The Eastland trade comprised the trades of Denmark and Norway, Sweden and the East country. The East country may be taken to cover all the southern and eastern shore of the Baltic.[2]

The year 1697 was a bad one, 1698 was better, 1699 was good. The figures are given in Table 13. Average total imports and exports were £477,000 and £249,000 respectively. Compared with 1625, 1635 and 1646, exports were a little higher and imports had about doubled. We estimated English trade out of the Baltic in 1625, 1635 and 1646 at an

TABLE 13.* *English imports and exports: current prices, first cost (without freight, etc.)*

		Denmark and Norway (£)	Sweden (£)	East country (£)	Totals (£)
1697	Imports	64,000	150,000	152,000	366,000
	Exports	80,000	41,000	126,000	247,000
1698	Imports	91,000	219,000	197,000	508,000
	Exports	37,000	52,000	150,000	240,000
1699	Imports	87,000	246,000	225,000	557,000
	Exports	38,000	58,000	166,000	261,000

* The Inspector-General's prices are probably reliable. Exports to Denmark and Norway in 1697 look too high; this may arise from shipmasters giving their destination as 'the Sound'. The total figure for the whole Eastland is likely to be more correct than the figures for individual areas.

[1] North is quoted by K. G. Davies in the article just cited. The sixty ships and the reduction of the Eastland company's privileges will be discussed in Chapter XI.

[2] For an account of the Inspector-General and his work see G. N. Clark, *Guide to English Commercial Statistics, 1696–1782* (Royal Historical Society, 1938). Davis prints figures from the ledgers in *Ec.H.R.* (1954); he uses 1699, 1700 and 1701. My sources are the fair copies in the Public Record Office, Cust. 2/1–4, 6 (5 is Michaelmas 1698 to Christmas 1698).

average of 114 shiploads, and the corresponding figure for 1697–9 is 242 shiploads.[1]

Imports are given in Table 14. The seven specified commodities account for nine-tenths of the total. Iron easily comes first, making a third of the total. Hemp, second, makes one-fifth. There is no corn worth mentioning. In the corresponding table for 1625, 1635 and 1646 hemp and flax came first with corn a close second; iron was very low.[2]

TABLE 14. *Imports from the Eastland at first cost*

	1697 (£)	1698 (£)	1699 (£)
Iron	124,000	147,000	166,000
Hemp	62,000	98,000	117,000
Wood	62,000	106,000	83,000
Linen and canvas	30,000	46,000	39,000
Pitch and tar	27,000	42,000	31,000
Potashes	22,000	25,000	14,000
Flax	14,000	13,000	44,000
All imports including some not specified above	366,000	508,000	557,000

It is chiefly to be noticed about the commodities which increased most, that they drew the trade away from Prussia—away from the Eastland company's market at Danzig, Elbing and Königsberg. Iron came from Stockholm, and pitch and tar were also peculiarly Swedish products. In 1697–9 one-third of the ships in Anglo-Baltic trade were from Sweden. We have seen that Riga masts and Riga hemp were highly favoured in England; in 1697–9 about a quarter of the ships were from Riga. The Riga trade was generally greater than the trade from Prussia. In 1697–9 there was also a considerable Narva trade; the commodities normally included hemp, and in 1700, on the interruption of the Riga trade, Riga goods were brought from Narva.[3]

The bulk of these imports were for home consumption. The Inspector-General's ledgers show that not more than 10 per cent was re-exported in 1697–9. The main re-exports were iron, hemp and cordage.

In 1697–9 the Sound Tables show virtually no English ships bound out of the Baltic for non-English ports.[4] It is possible that some of the English

[1] For 1625, 1635 and 1646 see pp. 36, 38, 41 above, and allow say £20,000 and £60,000 for Norway exports and imports.

[2] Above, p. 39. That table omitted Norway, but this only invalidates comparison as to wood.

[3] For shipping figures, see above, p. 107. Sound Tables *1661–1783*, 2 (i), gives glimpses of their cargoes, obscured to some extent by toll-free Swedish ships.

[4] Appendix D.

ships bound for England, having merely touched here, went off for France and other places without unloading, and in this case the Inspector-General's figures would be an understatement of the complete Englishmen's trade from the Baltic. But there is no evidence for this practice.

Exports, we saw, had increased a little in value over 1625, 1635 and 1646, but the most conspicuous change was an increase in their variety. In the Inspector-General's ledgers, cloth accounts for only 61 per cent, as against 90 per cent in 1625, 1635 and 1646. And whereas the greater part of cloth exports used to consist of short Suffolks and kerseys, at the end of the century short cloths, long cloths and Spanish cloths together make about 40 per cent, kerseys, dozens and perpetuanas make 30 per cent and a mass of bays, says, stuffs, cottons and other types make the remainder. This perhaps explains the decline of Ipswich; the problems of the Essex and Suffolk clothiers have found no solution, and even in this northern trade we see a victory of the new drapery over the old.

In the Inspector-General's ledgers other goods of English origin account for 21 per cent of exports. These were lead, tin, pewter, malt, coal, salt, skins (chiefly rabbit), leather, silk, haberdashery, glass, grindstones, alum, corn-flour, corrupt bark, butter, hops. In this class the products of the industrial north-east are prominent, but there is no sign of an industrial revolution.

The remaining 18 per cent were re-exports. Some typical European goods, wine, salt and fruit, are found, but most were colonial. Tobacco was the biggest single item, making three-quarters of all re-exports, or 12 per cent of the total export. The re-export trade was mainly handled from London.

Over and above this, the Sound Tables show a regular but not great trade in English ships from France, Portugal and Spain: nine ships in 1699, twelve in 1700. The connection with Portugal was the mainstay of this trade, at the end of the century still a new thing. No doubt this trade was handled by English merchants.

The Sound Tables and the Inspector-General are in close agreement as to the destination of the export trade; far and away the biggest part went to the East country. The Inspector-General puts 59 per cent to the East country, only 20 per cent to Sweden, 21 per cent to Denmark and Norway; and the last figure may be too high. The export trade had not followed the import trade. While imports came from all over the East-land, exports predominantly went to Prussia as in the past.

The Inspector-General's ledgers had space for the export of bullion and foreign coin (which was legal since 1660), but little or no silver was entered for the Eastland. From this the Inspector-General himself concluded that merchants were meeting the adverse balances with those countries by secretly exporting *English* coin, but there is no need to suppose that he knew more about trade than how to record it, and the question was not so simple as he appears to have thought.[1] In the Norway trade, indeed, there is repeated evidence for export of silver. This was one of the three trades which were held in 1660 to be unmanageable without it.[2] But the same was not necessarily true of the rest of the Eastland trade. The Inspector-General's ledgers show an export surplus in the whole trade of England by about £6 million to £5 million, and it was therefore possible for English debts to the Eastland to have been settled in France or Amsterdam. The trade of Sweden proper (omitting the possessions across the Baltic) was commonly supposed to balance; the Swedes had an export surplus in their English trade and an import surplus in their French and Portuguese trade. England's trade with Sweden probably did not entail export of silver either from England or from any other place.[3] In our

---

[1] 'Upon the several trades of Sweden, Denmark and Norway, East country and Russia, the excess is very much on the importation side (which is a demonstration these trades are less profitable to us) and the same may reasonably be supposed to arise from their clandestinely carrying away of our milled money instead of our manufactures.' *House of Lords MSS.*, new series, IV, 430–6; a report on the years 1697–9. Evidence for the export of silver and the use of bills of exchange was discussed by C. H. Wilson and the late Professor Eli Heckscher in *Ec.H.R.*, 2nd series, vols. II, III, IV. See above, pp. 48–9.

[2] The others were the East India and Turkey trades. 'For the Norway trade which gives a very large employment to a great number of shipping and furnisheth us with a very necessary supply of timber and tar, it cannot be carried on without the liberty of exporting money and bullion, because that Kingdom of Norway gives no vent to any of our native commodities in proportion to the value of what we fetch thence, and therefore money and bullion must pay for it, and should the ships first go to Holland or Hamburg to fetch the dollars, the very time expended in deviating from their designed ports of lading would make the price of timber twice as much as now it is, the freight of it being at least two thirds of the value of it when it is imported.' Report of Council of Trade, B.M. Add. MS. 25115, 42ff. I have seen entries of silver exported to Norway in London port books of 1670 and 1671, E190/52/9, 10; there are also entries of silver to India, France, the Mediterranean, with two or three to Sweden and none otherwise to the Eastland. *Reasons offered against the Navigation Act* (1668: B.M., 816. m. 11 (108)) says that before the Navigation Act the Norway trade was driven 'in barter of our growths and manufactures', but that it is now driven 'in dollars and the treasure of the nation'. In 1677, in *England's Great Happiness*, Complaint asked Content 'What think you of the Norway trade that takes away so many of our crown pieces?'

[3] Swedish trade figures for 1685 show a small favourable balance equal to one-ninth the value of imports: Heckscher, *Svensk handelsstatistik*, liii, 139–40. John Robinson writes in the *Account of Sweden* (1694), pp. 146–7, that 'the chief commodities Sweden vends are…[worth] £700,000 a year, in return of which they receive from abroad…goods which are supposed commonly to balance their exportations, and sometimes exceed them'. 'Their trade to Portugal', he says, 'for salt is accounted most necessary, as without great quantities of which they cannot subsist. That with England is more beneficial, because it takes off almost half their own commodities and brings in near two thirds of money for one of goods. The worst is their French trade.'

trade with the East country, which balanced most nearly, £50,000 a year would have covered the deficit in the Inspector-General's ledgers, and some of this was doubtless accounted for by the direct trade from France and Portugal. John Holland had said that money was the life of the hemp trade,[1] and it may be that Riga and Narva took silver while Prussia did not; but, again, it does not necessarily follow that the silver was directly exported from England. It is possible that the Baltic trade involved an immediate indebtedness to France, and that this helps to explain the suspicion with which French trade was regarded in the second half of the seventeenth century. It is also possible that silver was more urgently needed for freight than in payment for goods.[2] But the whole question of the financing of foreign trade seems really to require some merchants' letters and account books.

The merchants

According to English port books, the Eastland trade was as predominantly handled by English merchants in the second half of the century as in the first. It was said that the Norwegians warmed their hands at the Fire of London, but by far the greater quantities of Norwegian goods in London port books in 1669 were entered for Sir William Warren, Edmund Lee, John Sharp, and Charles and John Shorter. At all times, and particularly at the outports, we find Norwegian shipmasters importing in their own name, but more often foreign ships' cargoes were entered for Englishmen. In Swedish trade an occasional cargo is entered for the shipmaster, but usually the trade from Sweden was entered for Englishmen even when the ship was Swedish. Foreigners' entries from the East country are extremely rare. Exports to all parts of the Eastland were habitually entered for Englishmen. It is a merchants' trade; English shipmasters play a small part.[3]

The English merchants did not conduct their trade in the second half of the century exactly as they had conducted it in the first half. There were changes that had an important effect on their attitude towards the Eastland company and the state.

In the first half of the century their trade was inwards and outwards, to and fro, in barter of commodities and silver, and they specialised in an

---

[1] Above, p. 99 n.

[2] Danzig shipmasters insisted on silver: see below, p. 161 n.

[3] London: 1664 (searcher, outward, E 190/50/1), 1669 (inward, merchant strangers, 52/4); 1670 and 1671 (outward, merchant strangers, 52/9, 10). Ipswich: 1666 and 1670 (607/2, 13). Hull: 1666, 1670, 1672, 1699 (320/6, 10; 321/4; 334/21). Newcastle: 1661, 1670 (193/1; 194/7).

area of trade rather than in any particular commodity. A few years after the Restoration this was said to be still the case by Josiah Child. He deplored it:

The Eastland, beside our native commodities, spend great quantities of Italian, Spanish, Portugal, and French commodities; viz. oil, wine, fruit, sugar, succades, sumach etc. Now in regard our East country merchants of England are few, compared with the Dutch, and intend principally that one trade out and home, and consequently are not so conversant in the aforesaid commodities, nor forward to adventure upon them, and seeing that by the company's charter our Italian, Spanish, Portugal and French merchants, who understand those commodities perfectly well, are excluded those trades, or at least, if the company will give them leave to send out those goods, are not permitted to bring in the returns; it follows, that the Dutch must supply Denmark, Sweden, and all parts of the Baltic, with most of those commodities, and so it is in fact.[1]

This was an important opinion, because Child was an important man. The new trades were sapping the foundations of the Eastland company.

The Eastland company's rule was never intended to embrace the trade instanced by Child. The general object, as expressed in the charter, was the 'service of us and our land in venting our commodities...and serving our land and country with the most necessary commodities' of the Eastland.[2] James I's proclamation concerned imports; Charles I's concerned exports, but only exports of English commodities. Thus the merchant who wished to re-export to the Eastland the goods of southern Europe, or of the colonies, and likewise the merchant who wished to trade direct from those parts to the Eastland, found himself under the company's jurisdiction almost by accident. The company did not prevent those trades, but it imposed certain handicaps; unfree impositions were higher than those paid by members, while Child tells us that the company withheld permission to bring in returns. If the merchant was prepared to pay £20 (no great sum for a man of any standing) he became a member and could trade more freely, but he could hardly expect to gain an effective voice and there was no certainty that his interests would be properly regarded.

The man who felt this most strongly would be the colonial re-exporter. Child's merchant wanted to bring in returns, and was therefore interested in Eastland commodities. The tobacco merchant, on the other hand, was not interested in Eastland commodities; he traded to many places but he traded only in tobacco. A Hull port book enables us to see how the tobacco trade was conducted in 1670. In the *Relief* for Danzig Thomas

[1] Sir Josiah Child, *New Discourse of Trade* (1694, but written before 1669), 104-5.
[2] Sellers, *Acts and Ordinances*, 143 (the charter).

Berket exports Virginia tobacco which 'paid custom by himself' in the *Supply* (meaning that he himself imported it from America in the *Supply*) ten months previously. In the same ship Thomas Nisbet exports tobacco which paid custom by himself in the *Adeline*. These men also export tobacco to the Netherlands. In the *Hope* of Stralsund for Stockholm and in the *Seaflower* of Bridlington for Norway William Idle exports tobacco which paid custom by himself in the *Supply*. In the *Release* of Hull for Danzig, Gawen Hodgson exports tobacco which paid custom by George Bottomly and company in the *Nightingale*, John Berket exports tobacco which paid custom in the *Nightingale* and *Supply* by Edward Nightingale and company, and John Bottomly exports tobacco which paid custom by himself in the *Nightingale*. Gawen Hodgson also trades outwards to Virginia. William Idle is master in the *Supply* of Hull outward-bound for Dort. In the *Love's Increase* of Hull for Danzig, Thomas Carter exports tobacco which had paid custom by himself. The impression is of a small group of merchants and shipowners who specialised in tobacco. Their appropriate association, if they needed one, was an association of tobacco merchants. The interests of the Eastland company were largely irrelevant to them.

An increasing class of exporters who may be called industrialists felt, in all likelihood, a similar disinterest. Newcastle was the home of this class, and at the Restoration the Newcastle residence of the Eastland company had a big membership, but they were miners or manufacturers first, merchants second. They exported wherever they found markets, and the Eastland was only one market. In the Eastland, according to the Inspector-General's ledgers in 1697–9, the 'East country' claimed a low proportion of their goods and the best market was Denmark, Norway and Sweden. This outport probably, therefore, put its weight against the Eastland company in 1673, or at least was lukewarm in support.[1]

Lastly we have the specialist importer. Sir William Warren imported a great deal of Eastland timber but he cannot be called an Eastland merchant —he was a timber merchant. He cannot be seen to have taken part in the Eastland company's affairs, and it is possible that he was not a member. Another big importer was Sir William Ryder, who handled many shiploads of hemp, pitch and tar for the navy in the second Dutch war. He was associated with William Cutler and, less closely, with George Cock. Cock we know as a member of the Eastland company and Cutler may

---

[1] Miss Sellers, in her introduction to *Acts and Ordinances*, points out that Newcastle led the northern outports against London until about 1670. Thereafter she considers that York led them. The improvement in relations between Newcastle and London may be attributed to the curtailment of privileges in 1673.

have been a member, but Ryder's name does not occur in their available records. Among fourteen prominent naval suppliers in the war of 1689–97, seven are known as members; but the greatest (Sir Peter Rich) was not a member, while only three of those who were members were prominent in the company's administration and the most senior of them was about the smallest supplier. Men of big calibre in the import trades were perhaps embarrassed rather than assisted by membership of an association in which the export of cloth to Danzig was the primary interest. It is a sign of constitutional weakness in associations when they include great men who do not bother to take the lead.[1]

It must not be thought that the Eastland company could do nothing useful for these men. Although the company remained most interested in exports, as in the first half of the century, and although most of their internal rules concerned exports, they took trouble to oppose a projected additional customs duty on imported iron in 1664, and the import of canvas, hemp and linen attracted their attention until the end of the century.[2] But of course powerful importers, who were in close touch with the government by virtue of supplying the navy, were capable of speaking for themselves. The company's chief defect, however, was lack of power abroad.

The Eastland powers enjoyed the advantage in their relations with England of having a monopoly of supply in goods that England could not dispense with, while England had no such monopoly. With the growth of the English import trades, and assisted by the Navigation Acts, the Kings of Denmark and Sweden were able to indulge in protective practices in favour of their own ships, merchants and manufacturers. We shall notice

---

[1] The treasurer's account book of the company at London, beginning in 1660, survives. It belongs to the Russia Company with whose permission I have used it. It gives among other things the names of treasurers, governors and the annual auditors. It does not give assistants, but I suppose that everyone of note in the company's administration took his turn at auditing, and that people whose names do not occur did not reach the company's higher ranks.

The book also gives the names of persons admitted to the company after 1660, of whom a list will be found below, at Appendix C4. Appendix C1–3 gives certain names for the period before 1660, but is incomplete, especially as regards Norway merchants and men who were only importers. For this reason it is not possible to say whether Sir William Warren and Sir William Ryder were members. (The company settled a debt to Warren in 1671 but this is inconclusive.) The surname Cutler occurs among cloth exporters from Ipswich in 1624 and 1625, but William Cutler does not occur. George Cock was a member in 1656 (Appendix C). These men's trade in the second Dutch war is touched on in Chapter XII. The names of the navy suppliers in 1689–97 (not including iron importers) are taken from J. Ehrman, *The Navy of William III*, 58–62.

[2] These items are mentioned in their records in Sellers's *Acts and Ordinances* and in the treasurer's book.

several complaints against the King of Denmark. The King of Sweden's policy began to create grievances during the interregnum and at the end of the century it gave rise to the following.

Several grievances of the English merchants in their trade into the dominions of the King of Sweden, whereby it doth appear how dangerous it may be for the English nation to depend (as now they do) on Sweden only, for the supply of the naval stores; where they are subjected to so many and great grievances...

The English merchants are denied liberty to stay in the King of Sweden's dominions, above four months in the year.

The English merchants have not liberty to demand their debts of their debtors at country fairs in Sweden, on pain of forfeiting those debts.

The English merchants are not suffered to keep houses of their own, but are forced to lodge in burghers' houses.

The English merchants have not liberty to lay up salt, and other bulky goods; but are forced to sell them on the ship's keel. And although they are permitted to land and house some other goods; yet they are forced to put them into a warehouse under the city lock, where the owners can't come at them, but at certain days, when the city gives them leave.

The English merchants are forced to pay custom on goods, when they are brought into Swedish ports, though they are neither landed nor sold; and are not permitted to draw back any part of the customs so paid, though they would carry them away to another port.

In the dominions of Sweden, where English merchants die, they demand one third of their estates.

The English factors in Reval cannot receive any goods from an English merchant. But the burghers there must receive them, and have the benefit of the commission for them.

The English merchants are not suffered in Sweden to buy of, or sell to, any person but those who are burghers there.

At Riga, the English merchants are forced to sell salt within twenty days after its arrival, on a penalty.

The English merchants are not suffered in Sweden, to go up into the country, to buy or sell.

The English merchants are not suffered to have the rates of the Swedes' town-duties, (which ought to be made public) by which means they frequently alter the customs and town-duties on a sudden, upon the arrival of ships, as they think fit.

The English woollen manufactures, imported into Sweden, are rated in their customs one third more than the woollen goods of other nations, (pari gradu); and the duty on our northern manufactures, is so great, that that trade in a manner is totally lost.

At Stockholm when the King of England has no resident there, the English are denied the exercise of their religion, and the liberty of a minister of the Church of England.

The English merchants are forced to pay 34 per cent for the tobacco they import into Russia by way of Narva, whereas other nations pay but 2 per cent for the commodities by them so imported.[1]

For the redress of these supposed wrongs the English merchant did not turn to the Eastland company, but to the crown. He wanted ambassadors and treaties of commerce, retaliation against Swedish merchants in England, embargoes—actions far beyond the scope of a private corporation. In the first half of the century the English merchant often required and obtained the help of the crown, but less immediately, less bluntly— the king would support the company's commissioners, or would lend them an ambassador (so to say) with whom they established direct liaison on the spot. But in the second half of the century things became more formal and were conducted at a higher level. There was a more continuous diplomacy; there were resident embassies; there were councils of trade. The Eastland company, in the middle of the century, boasted of being able to make or divert trade, to oblige cities, to procure immunities;[2] but this power did not extend to the places where the import trades had developed, nor even, it seems, after 1660, to Danzig. After 1660 they stopped boasting of it. In the next two chapters we shall see how the conduct of mercantile affairs was progressively taken over by the central organs of government at Whitehall—or rather how it was resumed by Whitehall, for the crown had always been responsible for it even when it exercised its responsibility by delegation. And we shall see in the end that the death of the Eastland company followed closely the first royal treaty with Danzig.

We need not look among the merchants for strong outright hostility to the Eastland company, but we may expect perhaps a growing intangible indifference on the part alike of old members, new members and non-members. This perhaps is how institutions commonly decay, and is at the bottom of the late seventeenth-century movement towards free trade.

[1] B.M., 816. m. 11 (121).
[2] Appendix A 9, 10. The immunities were some of those that were said to be lacking in Sweden.

Chapter X

GOVERNMENT POLICY DURING
THE INTERREGNUM

The Dutch war

We discussed the passing of the Navigation Act in Chapter VII. A few months later came the first Anglo-Dutch war. Had the government not been ready for a war, this act would perhaps not have been passed. Had the war ended in defeat, it would probably have lapsed. The war and the Navigation Act bring the history of the Eastland trade to a new phase. They mark a new effectiveness in the action of the state in matters of trade. Henceforth the policy of the government is far more important than the policy of the Eastland company.

The Eastland policy of the government of the interregnum did not differ from the policy of Charles I. It was, first, to keep the trade open, and, secondly, to secure all possible advantages in it. The government of the interregnum had no more strength in the Eastland than Charles I. It was able to be more effective because it was stronger in the North Sea and the Channel.

The first Dutch war was won by fleets operating in home waters. The Council of State refused to make war on Denmark in spite of provocation. The redemption treaty had given great offence, and soon after the outbreak of war the Council of State learnt that Dutch men-of-war had captured English merchant ships off Elsinore. When they sent a squadron to the Sound, the King of Denmark declared that his sovereignty had been infringed; he arrested all English merchant ships he could lay his hands on, and closed the Sound to them. At the end of the war he held twenty-two English merchant ships. The English seized Danish merchant ships in English ports but continued to regard Denmark officially as neutral. This policy was correct. The Danish ships were useful. English merchants were permitted to charter them for trade with Norway, and they were allowed to sail freely so long as they sailed to England.[1]

The obvious counter-move against Denmark was an alliance with Sweden. But the ambassador to Sweden, Bulstrode Whitelocke, did not

---

[1] *The King of Denmark his Declaration concerning the English merchants ships lying in Copenhagen* (London, 1953). *Cal.S.P.Dom. 1651–1652*, 421, 423, 428, 448; *1652–1653*, 131; *1653–1654*, 163, 293.

sail until November 1653. This inaction was also correct. Sweden was more useful as a neutral than as an ally.[1]

The closing of the Sound to English ships was Dutch policy in all three Anglo-Dutch wars. It was embarrassing but could not be fatal. In all three wars, the Dutch Baltic trade was interrupted as absolutely as was the English. Not the Sound but the North Sea was the decisive area. Neither side carried the vital naval stores in its own ships. Both sides relied on neutrals. It was in the interest of the Scandinavian and Baltic countries to supply these goods. Some naval stores were bought for England at Hamburg, some were shipped over from Dunkirk. The fleet intercepted neutral ships and forced them into English ports. On one occasion seven or eight large Swedish ships, said to be bound for Portugal, were diverted into the Downs in this way. The shortage of naval stores can be exaggerated. Since the navy's demand was unlimited, supply was bound to be short of requirements. In fact supply was adequate, though no doubt expensive.[2]

These expedients were fatal to the Navigation Act so far as it applied to naval stores. English merchants told the Council of State that they would cancel contracts for Riga hemp if they could not import it in ships of Danzig, and in response to many similar requests the policy emerged of permitting the import of Eastland naval stores in any ship and from any place. The toleration was not supposed to extend to goods other than naval stores. It was an exception with defined limits for a definite time.[3]

At the end of the war there was no treaty with Denmark, save in so far as Denmark was included in the Anglo-Dutch treaty. This provided for the English merchants' claim for damages, on account of the ships arrested at the Sound, to be paid, after arbitration, by the Dutch. The King of Denmark cancelled the redemption treaty and bound himself not to discriminate in future against English trade through the Sound.[4]

When it was clear that England had won the war, Bulstrode Whitelocke concluded a treaty with Sweden which contained, with expressions of mutual amity, some innocuous provisions for free commercial intercourse according to the laws of the two nations.[5]

---

[1] Whitelocke's *Journal of the Swedish Ambassy* was first published (London) in 1772. He was a member of the Council of State and had introduced the navigation bill in parliament in 1651. Men of the same name were members of the Eastland company, but no relationship has been established.
[2] Albion, *Forests and Sea Power*, ch. 5.
[3] *Cal.S.P.Dom. 1651–1652*, 305, 438, 443, 447, 448; *1652–1653*, 20, 50, 344, 372, 442.
[4] The merchants claimed £157,000, about half and half for goods and freight; B.M. Add. M.S. 22546/164, SP 18/42/150.
[5] The treaty of Uppsala; G. Chalmers, *A Collection of Treaties* (London, 1790), I, 20ff.

Cromwell boasted of this outcome in the following words:

> You have now...peace with Sweden; an honourable peace.... You have a peace with the Dane.... Satisfaction for your merchants' ships; not only to their content, but to their rejoicing.... You have the Sound open; which was obstructed. That which was and is the strength of this nation, the shipping, will now be supplied thence. And, whereas you were glad to have everything of that kind at the second hand, you have now all manner of commerce, and at as much freedom as the Dutch themselves there, who used to be the carriers and vendors of it to us, and at the same rates and toll;—and I think I may say, by that peace, the said rates now fixed upon cannot be raised to you in future.[1]

But this was not really the end of the Anglo-Dutch war, if we may believe the Secretary of State, John Thurloe. In 1655 Cromwell made war on Spain, and this was partly, says Thurloe, with the idea of subduing the Dutch still further. One of the aims of the Spanish war was to capture Dunkirk. 'The safety of our own trade was also considered', says Thurloe, 'that it was in all times greatly disturbed and prejudiced by the Dunkirk and Ostenders.' Furthermore 'there were no greater considerations in England in reference to foreign interests than how to obviate the growing greatness of the Dutch'; Dunkirk in English hands would set

a bridle upon the Dutch, who not being able to sail through the Channel ...without passing by the English harbours on the one side or the other, where ships of war have their stations, would be necessitated to manage their trade under the favour and goodwill of the English, the benefit whereof England could not but find in all their negotiations and interests relating to that state either in time of war or peace.[2]

For Oliver Cromwell religion and policy went hand in hand. Convinced that England was the main bulwark against the Counter-Reformation, he knew that England could only be strong through foreign trade. He sent to the Mediterranean a fleet which helped the Levant merchants, and which for the first time made English sea-power effective in that sea. He gave the Eastland merchants a standing convoy.[3] He would in all probability have given the Eastland company a charter, had not unfavourable circumstances intervened.

[1] Carlyle's *Letters and Speeches of Oliver Cromwell* (ed. Lomas, London, 1904), II, 355–6.

[2] See Thurloe's memoranda on foreign policy for Charles II, in S. von Bischoffshausen, *Die Politik des Protectors Oliver Cromwell* (Innsbruck, 1899), 207, 221.

[3] *Cal.S.P.Dom. 1655–1656*, 304; *1657–1658*, 53, 67.

1655 and 1656: the question of the company's charter

The Eastland company was in abeyance. As a corporate person it lived, but as a regulated trading company it was dead. To remove its power no deliberate act of state had been necessary, it sufficed that the state had ceased to give it support. Already in 1649 the members said that their government had 'desisted'.[1] They continued to hold courts but lacked the power to levy money and had contracted debts which they could not pay. At a court at York in 1655 a member refused to conform to the company's rules, saying 'there was no company but when there was one he would take the oath and not till then'.[2] The surviving treasurer's book of the company at London opens in 1661 with debts outstanding from 1651, 1652 and 1653; in 1651, at the outports, expenses had exceeded income.

In January 1656 the company addressed to the Protector a petition for privileges and a long representation setting forth their case in detail. The petition was as follows:

Your petitioners want means to express their due acknowledgements of so eminent and noble a favour as they have lately enjoyed, by the unparalleled action of your Highness, in reference to 22 full laden ships detained in Denmark, and by your sole means (under God) recovered; to the ample satisfaction of all persons concerned; many of whom had been, with their whole families, ruined by that sad accident, who do now rejoice and will leave the memory thereof unto their posterity, to bless God for the interposition of so great wisdom.... The sense of which great blessing already obtained by your Highness' means animates your petitioners to a most humble address for the further improvement of this so necessary trade into the Baltic Seas; which in all former times hath been regarded by the state with an extraordinary eye of favour, and hath of late suffered in nothing more, than in the want of good regulation.... [For] to their grief they find, that the irregularity or obstinacy of any one of the traders (which they have not a power to remedy) renders the exactest course they can take, ineffectual. By which means a most licentious and confused kind of commerce is now exercised, as the humour or private interest of every person prompts him; without the least respect had unto the public....[3]

The petition and representation were passed to the Council of State's committee of trade with a note that the Protector conceived it 'a business very fit and worthy of their consideration'. Five months later, in June 1656, the committee recommended a new charter.

---

[1] Appendix A9.   [2] Sellers, *Acts and Ordinances*, 76–7.
[3] SP 18/123/16.

The proposed charter differed in two principal respects from that granted by Elizabeth. First, it extended the membership. The fine for admission was reduced from £20 to £10, and all merchants *and other persons* were made eligible, except clothiers, and except retailers, artificers and handicraftsmen within ten miles of London. Secondly, the proposed new charter made the company more democratic. Whereas law-making and election to offices were by the old charter in the hands of the court of twenty-four assistants, these functions were now vested in the general court of all members meeting twice a year, and there were only twelve assistants. Further, an upper limit of 5 per cent was placed on penalties exacted by the company, and their impositions were not to exceed a shilling a cloth. Otherwise the new charter followed the old, even to the extent of repeating the clause in which the purpose of the charter was explained in terms far removed from the language of free trade:

And for that divers persons being not brought up in merchandise or use of traffic, but altogether ignorant and unexpert as well in the orders and rules of merchandise as in the laws of the said realms of the East parts aforesaid, and in the customs, usages, tolls and values of money, weights and measures, and in other things belonging to merchants very necessary, through their ignorance and lack of knowledge commit many inconveniences...we willing to assist, and prevent such inconveniences, and intending to further and help the expert and exercised merchants in their lawful and honest trade, will and command, and also forbid and prohibit...that no person [1579, subject]...which is not...made free of the said company shall...intermeddle in the trade of merchandise...in the said parts of Eastland.[1]

But the charter was not granted. We hear no more of it. It is improbable that the Eastland company refused it. The reason is probably to be found in the Baltic.

The timing of the petition makes it appear that the company intended to link their fortune with the new King of Sweden, who came to the throne in 1655 and whose warlike adventures dominated the Baltic until 1660. This is not the place to discuss whether Charles X really hoped to turn the Baltic into a Swedish lake; however, he behaved as if he did. His first

---

[1] SP 18/128/7. In the committee's report there was also a postscript about Narva, formerly reserved to the Russia Company, but where the Eastland company had traded 'by connivance for divers years'. The Eastland company were to be free to continue to trade there, because it was now not Russian but Swedish, and the Russia Company traded wholly to Archangel; but only with the consent of the Russia Company ('whose charter is by Act of Parliament') and for so long as Narva remained Swedish. 'It is very necessary that the said trade should be kept on foot for the supplying of this Commonwealth with hemp and other Eastland commodities.'

action was to attack Poland. He had held on his accession a council to decide the question, 'Wer von der benachbarten Potenten, weil Krieg zu führen nötig erachtet worden, zu attaquieren sei?' It was understood that the most valuable prize was to be gained by attacking Denmark, but it was borne in mind that an attack on Denmark would involve war with Denmark's traditional allies, the Dutch. England was a natural counterpoise to the Dutch, but English assistance could not be expected in this case since England had the same interest as the Dutch in seeing that no Baltic state completely dominated the Baltic. The council therefore concluded that it would be better to proceed by stages, and that the first stage should be an attack on Poland. They foresaw that this would antagonise the Dutch, but believed that the friendship of England would sufficiently offset it. Poland having been defeated, and control having been won over the places where both Dutch and English principally traded, the attack could be turned against Denmark with better chance of success. Their trade held as a hostage, the reaction of England and the United Provinces might be moderated. This appreciation was astute.[1]

At Danzig the position of the Eastland merchants had been unsatisfactory for some time. We saw that in 1649 they were being taxed, losing, as they said, privileges 'not easily to be recovered, if once lost'.[2] Now in 1656 one of the objects for which they desired a charter was 'to recover and preserve... foreign privileges, now lost'. The representation of 1656 was word for word a copy, with some changes, of the representation of 1649. The most significant change was the omission of three paragraphs about the Dutch. The Dutch were now not a danger to their trade, from which they were excluded by the Navigation Act. The argument for privilege in 1656 rested mainly, therefore, on the need for unity and discipline in order to secure favourable treatment abroad.[3]

In 1655 Charles X moved against Poland. By the end of the year he occupied Elbing and blockaded Danzig. He either possessed or commanded all the Baltic ports where the Eastland company traded. Up to this point his progress imitated that of Gustavus Adolphus. But he intended to go further. He intended to make Polish Prussia a Swedish province. This, at least, was the assumption of the Eastland company. They submitted to Cromwell 'articles of trade desired to be settled in the Baltic seas'. The document is undated but must have been submitted at about the same time as the petition for a charter, and is a list of privileges,

---

[1] Guernsey Jones, *The Diplomatic Relations between Cromwell and Charles X Gustavus of Sweden* (Lincoln, Nebraska, 1897), 20.

[2] Above, p. 87.

[3] The representation of 1656 is compared with that of 1649 at Appendix A9.

including privileges at Danzig, which were to be obtained by treaty with the King of Sweden. Some of the articles were as follows:

1. That the goods and estates of Englishmen dying, may be reserved without diminution for the use of the true proprietors.

2. That if any Englishmen's son, servant or factor lie under delinquency for any fact personal or criminal, his principal's goods remaining in his hands and custody may not be subjected to arrests....

[3–5. Free exercise of religion, house for meetings and for residence of officers, power to decide 'causes mercatorial' arising among themselves.]

6. That the customs in all the ports of Prussia be moderately set, according to the ancient constitution of the land of Prussia, and by no means enhanced above customary or ordinary rates formerly paid. And that the customs in all ports of Sweden be abated, and the English eased of the excessive rates now paid by them on goods both inwards and outwards....

7. That customs and Toolag may be paid in such coins and species as are current in the place, without any enhancement or upgelt of ducats and dollars....

8. That the English merchants having paid their sea customs...shall not be liable to...other municipal duties (vulgarly called Zulag or Anlag) since the same ought properly to be paid by the citizens, and not by strangers.

9. That they may be free to choose such place or places of residence as may be most fit and convenient....

10. That all ports and havens may be alike open unto them, to buy and export their commodities called returns....

[11–16]. Search of ships, wreck, piracy, retaliation, right to hold assemblies.]

17. That it shall be free for the English merchants to buy their returns in the inland 'emporean' towns and cities of his Majesty's dominions... without any inland, bridge or river tax or custom.

18. That whereas in anno 1650 by instigation of one Crofts, an Englishman, a constitution of parliament was procured at Warsaw for all English and Scots inhabiting within the Polish jurisdiction to pay...the tenth part of all their personal and real estates; who in pursuance thereof obtained from the King of Poland in 1651 an edict of execution; which to this day remain, the one unrepealed, and the other uncancelled; whereby those of both nations (still residing in those parts) which have not conformed, lie under imminent danger of life and goods; the said unjust constitution and edict may be annulled, which mainly strike at the root of all national intercourse of trade.

19. That it be free for the English to carry and transport their moneys by water or land in such coins and species as are most portable and useful for them, without stop or tax laid upon them.

20. That if any difference or misunderstanding arise in future concerning these articles...the same shall be decided and removed by commissioners on both parts deputed, according to the equity and rule of the civil law and custom of merchants.[1]

Some of these desires found their way into an Anglo-Swedish treaty which was concluded a month after the committee of trade had recommended the Eastland company's charter:

VIII. The subjects of the said most Serene Lord Protector...shall also hereafter enjoy all the prerogatives, in the several branches of trade which they used to carry on in Prussia and Poland, or elsewhere in the dominions of the said most Serene King of Sweden, which they enjoyed heretofore in preference to other nations; and if at any time they desire further privileges, their desires shall be gratified by all the means possible. And if the said most Serene King of Sweden shall grant greater and more ample privileges than the abovementioned, in Poland and Prussia, to any nation besides, or people not subject to him, or shall suffer any nation or people to enjoy such larger privileges there, then the people and citizens of this republic shall enjoy the same privileges in all respects, after they have desired it of his most Serene Royal Majesty. And moreover, if any edicts that have been published since 1650 happen to be burdensome to the English and Scots dwelling or trading in Poland and Prussia, the same shall after this time be of no force, as far as it can be rendered so, in the dominions of the most Serene King of Sweden; but the subjects of the said Lord Protector shall hereafter be entirely free from those burdens.[2]

In thus tying themselves to the King of Sweden the Eastland merchants either thought that there was no doubt of his success, or were taking a calculated risk. Their growing trading interests in Sweden itself and at Riga and Narva impelled them, in either case, towards the Swedish side. Cromwell's attitude to Charles X was favourable: he welcomed a Protestant anti-Hapsburg ally while he himself was attacking Spain; so that the interests of the merchants either coincided with or could easily be accommodated to the interests of the state. Charles X had only to occupy Danzig and to force a peace treaty on the King of Poland, and the Eastland company with privileges at home and abroad might look forward to trading under more favourable conditions than they had ever enjoyed.

It happened otherwise. Charles X failed to take Danzig and began to suffer reverses in the interior of Poland. He is often blamed for having

---

[1] Bodleian Library, Rawlinson MS. A 30, 129 ff., with a copy of the representation and a summary of the petition, representation and articles. The last is entitled 'The sum of three papers humbly tendered to his Highness by the Eastland merchants'. All are in the same hand.

[2] Chalmers, *Collection of Treaties*, I, 29 ff.

undertaken a campaign far inland, but it was perhaps necessary unless he were to leave behind him, when he moved against Denmark, a kingdom not only still at war but still capable of fighting. Meanwhile, at Danzig, at the time when the committee of trade's draft charter for the Eastland company reached the Council of State, and when the Anglo-Swedish treaty was nearly completed, the Eastland company were on the point of expulsion.

The news from Danzig reached England in a series of letters from the body of merchants and from an anonymous intelligencer who was one of them. Letters written in January 1656 tell us that when the city was blockaded the city government required foreign merchants to take an oath, to pay a tax, and to bear arms; and that the English refused:

[They] required the English merchants to bear arms and take an oath of fidelity to the city, which they have generally refused, alleging the Swedes would then seize their estates in Elbing and other parts; but they fear they shall be constrained to do it, or be put out of the city, if they receive not countenance from his Highness....It seems their ancient privileges with that city are now but little regarded.[1]

Cromwell accordingly provided the merchants with a letter. But in June the merchants wrote that the city government paid no attention to it:

Of late some of us in the name of the rest have been sent for to appear before the president of this city.... We (according to his Highness' letter) desired, in case we could not be suffered to remain here free (as formerly) from those taxes, or [from] being engaged in the present war against those with whom we have daily commerce; we say, that in such case we might (together with what goods belong to our principals in England and selves) freely leave the city, and have some convenient time allowed (which we entreated might be six months) to fit us for such a departure; to which the president replied not six weeks; and that withal if we would be gone, we must leave the tenth part of our estates here.... Yesterday their officer coming to levy their hundredth penny from one of our nation, by way of distress did (finding nothing else) seize upon his wearing clothes....[2]

---

[1] *The State Papers of John Thurloe*, ed. Birch (London, 1742), IV, 441–2. This series contains a letter with remarks about the cloth trade, dated October 1655; see IV, 85–6. It refers to a toll exacted by Charles X at the entrance to Danzig: 'There are yearly in the upper parts of Poland towards the border of Silesia...220,000 cloths made... besides the cloth as is made in these parts; and at this town 15,000 pieces of rash... which manufactures will increase, and ours be totally overthrown, if the Swede be permitted to burthen our commodities.... The Duke of Brandenburg hath bespoke a livery for his soldiers, 100,000 ells of all of Silesia cloth, and not one ell of English, which used to be altogether in request.'

[2] *Thurloe Papers*, v, 88.

This story excites little sympathy for the disingenuous if not hypocritical Englishmen. A few days later the intelligencer added:

And now our cause with this town, which we have defended so long, is come to a conclusion, that we must either swear, pay taxes, and serve in persons, as the Hollanders do (who do so much for them, whereas his Highness contra assists the Swede with men, as they say) or else we must depart this place by the 15th instant [i.e. in ten days], which is very short warning to dispose of our affairs, break up housekeeping, and depart; but I hope we shall be introduced again, the troubles being over, in better conditions than now we are upon.[1]

We at another place have nothing to do [said a third letter] for indeed this place is best for sales etc., with returns sooner and later, and lying so near to the sea for dispatching of ships hence to all other ports of those Baltic seas. Sir, we that are here are the representatives of the nation in this place, and what is done to us concerns the whole.[2]

The intelligencer went to live a mile outside the city gates. We do not know if others did likewise or returned to England, or if, on the other hand, some acceded to the city's demands and stayed. In 1657 Richard Jenks wrote from Danzig that the outbreak of war between Sweden and Denmark 'conjecturally will prove a further obstruction of the small residue of trade in the Baltic Sea'.[3] In 1658 a Danzig agent came to England and received a gold chain.[4] In 1660 we shall find the merchants back at Danzig and still complaining of unjust taxes. Of what happened to them in the meantime we know nothing.

1657 to 1660: Baltici dominium maris

Attention now turned from the inner Baltic to the Sound, the entrance and key to power within it. When it was seen that Charles X was in difficulty in Poland, those who feared his success gathered together to bring about his downfall. The King of Denmark with Dutch encouragement declared war on him. Charles X replied to this by leaving Poland, marching through Germany, invading Denmark and occupying Jutland. Three years of war and diplomacy followed, in which England and the Netherlands were as interested as Denmark and Sweden.

At the end of 1657 Charles X occupied the Danish mainland but, without sea-power, could not reach the heart of Denmark in the islands. A coalition of enemies supported by the Hapsburg emperor gathered in

[1] *Ibid.* 158.   [2] *Ibid.* 176.
[3] *Ibid.* VI, 315.
[4] *Ibid.* VII, 130, 407; *Cal.S.P.Dom. 1658–1659*, 287.

his rear. His position seemed weak. Cromwell tried to persuade the parliament that Charles X's danger was their own. The root of danger, he said, was the Pope and Emperor, 'armed and prepared to make themselves able to destroy the whole Protestant interest':

> Who is there that holdeth up his head to oppose this great design? A poor prince...a man that hath adventured his all against the Popish interest in Poland....He is now reduced into a corner: and...men [even] of our religion...seek his ruin. I beseech you consider how things do co-operate. Consider if this may seem but to be a design against your well-being? It is a design against your very being....If they can shut us out of the Baltic Sea, and make themselves masters of that, where is your trade? Where are your materials to preserve your shipping? Or where will you be able to challenge any right by sea, or justify yourselves against a foreign invasion in your own soil? Think upon it; this is in design.[1]

Cromwell therefore dispatched, like Charles I in similar circumstances, a mediator. This was Sir Philip Meadowe. Meadowe's instructions were to persuade the King of Denmark to peace by representing, first, that the war was harmful to the Protestant cause in view of the growing power of the Roman Catholics, and, secondly, that it damaged the trade and navigation of England—'it being well known what need we have of the commodities of those parts in reference to our shipping'.[2]

But Meadowe had not been long in Copenhagen when the situation was radically altered. Charles X crossed the ice, reached the island of Zealand, and advanced on Copenhagen. It was now the King of Denmark who was in danger.

The Protector, though he wished in general the prosperity of the Swede his ally, hoping that at last his arms might be directed the right way, yet did not like that the Swede should conquer the Dane and possess all those countries and, being thereby become powerful, engross the whole trade of the Baltic Sea, wherein England is so much concerned.[3]

Meadowe therefore shifted his effort to Charles X. Charles demanded as the price of peace, says Meadowe, all the kingdom of Norway. Meadowe says that this would have given him 'the sole and entire possession of the chief materials...for the apparel and equipage of our ships, too great a treasure to be entrusted in one hand'; and that he therefore suggested that Sweden should take instead the Danish provinces across the Sound: 'thus

---

[1] Carlyle's *Letters and Speeches*, III, 165, 168–9.
[2] SP 75/16/241.
[3] Thurloe's memorandum, in von Bischoffshausen, *Die Politik des Protectors Oliver Cromwell*, 215.

the power over that narrow entry into the Baltic being balanced betwixt two emulous crowns, will be an effectual preventive of any new exactions or usurpations in the Sound'.[1]

On this basis was concluded the peace of Roskilde. The division of the Sound between Denmark and Sweden suited the Dutch as much as it suited the English. However, the peace did not last. Charles X required a general pacification in the inner Baltic. If he withdrew from his commanding position outside Copenhagen he would be too weak to secure a general pacification on acceptable terms. He did not withdraw in the time laid down in the treaty of Roskilde. Meanwhile Dutch troops were put into Copenhagen and the city was made defensible. Charles X attacked the city, failed to carry it by assault, and settled down to besiege it. But he himself was virtually beseiged on the Danish islands. His enemies now occupied the Danish mainland. With the Dutch in Copenhagen and the imperialists behind him it looked as if he faced total disaster:

> The Protector very much apprehended the issue of this conjunction. He thought it equally dangerous for England, that the Swede should be ruined and the Dane preserved by such saviours who, after they had broken the King of Sweden, would also make a prey of the Dane himself. The Emperor in his assistance he gave against the Swede, revived the old design of the Austrian eagle, stretching her wings towards the eastern sea and planting herself upon the Baltic. The Dutch aimed at the command of the Sound and, under pretence that the Dane was too weak to keep it against his neighbours, would have kept it for him.[2]

This appreciation seems to be typically ambiguous. It is hard to imagine real danger from the Baltic design of the Hapsburgs, if the Dutch were as powerful and ambitious as Cromwell represented them. It did not, however, affect his policy. Meadowe (retrospectively) defined English policy at this juncture as if it were concerned only with the Dutch:

> England though sorry for this second rupture with Denmark, thought it not their interest to see Sweden overset and sinking under the mighty weight of so powerful a confederacy, but to buoy it up out of those quicksands it was fallen into.... Without which counterpoise England in every war with Holland (her emulous and rival state, and that which

---

[1] Sir Philip Meadowe, *A Narrative of the Principal Actions occurring in the Wars betwixt Sweden and Denmark* (London, 1677), 58 ff. Meadowe does not hesitate to praise himself in this retrospective account, but his delineation of national interest and policy is both vigorous and accurate.

[2] Thurloe's memorandum, von Bischoffshausen, *op. cit.* 216.

stands in the eye and aim of all her greatness and glory in point of trade and sea-dominion) would run a great risk of being excluded from the Baltic, and by that means shut out from the market of all her naval stores.[1]

It was decided to send a fleet to the Sound. Thurloe broached the subject in parliament on behalf of Richard Cromwell, Oliver being dead. He began by speaking of the Baltic design.

His Highness considered that the Emperor was likely to arrive at the design of the House of Austria, to command the Baltic and the eastern seas....I think the King of Denmark is in more danger from those that are allied with him, than from his open enemies....He considered that when the Emperor had done his business there, he and his confederates would next pour themselves into Flanders, and from thence hither into this Commonwealth, where they intend to bring in another government, when they are ready for it. Such counsels, we know, are on foot, *de facto*, already.

Thurloe then said that the Protector was fitting out a fleet 'to interpose upon the account of amity'. 'Unless he hath considerable fleets, as well as the Dutch, his bare interposition as to peace will signify nothing.' It is fairly clear, in spite of the long preamble about the Hapsburgs, that Thurloe thought the most immediate danger arose from the Dutch. In the debate most speakers ignored or discounted the Hapsburgs. They discussed whether it were more dangerous for the Sound to be controlled by Denmark or by Sweden. One said that it should be left to Denmark: 'The King of Denmark hath but the door into the Sound. But what if we should help to put it into the hands of Sweden, that hath [would have] both the door and house too?' Against this it was said that the King of Denmark was a vassal of the Dutch, whereas Sweden would be unable to hold the Sound without our help. A third 'would no sooner trust Sweden than the Dane'. But, indeed, nobody trusted anyone; it was a question of interest. True interest was easily discerned. All agreed that 'he that is master of the Sound is master of all the trade of Europe', and the tenor of the debate was summed up by one who said that 'some think it most dangerous to fall into the Dutch hands, others to the Emperor's, others to

[1] *Narrative*, 114–15. It would be natural for Meadowe to have forgotten about the Baltic design when his book was published in 1677, but even so his sole preoccupation with the Dutch is very striking. He thought the Dutch were entirely masters in Copenhagen. 'The old King of Denmark, Christian the fourth, was too stomachful to truckle under the Dutch lee....But in the reign of his son and successor, the now Frederick the third, the Dane...twisted his interest, too weak of itself to hold against the Swede, with that of Holland....And from that time forward the Danish court, which in the old king's time was used to lofty Danish, spoke nothing now but low Dutch' (*ibid.* 115–17).

the Swede's: and indeed, for my part, I am of opinion it is best in his hands that, it seems, is least able to keep it'.[1]

The English policy was simple: to divide the Sound between Denmark and Sweden according to the treaty of Roskilde, while obtaining from Sweden, in return for support, certain concessions about trade. These concessions were perhaps never distinctly formulated. Meadowe says: 'The Swede was to give real gages and pledges.... [The English mediator] proceeded so far as to nominate Stade upon the Elbe and Landskrona upon the Sound... which taking vent afterwards, gave occasion to that frivolous report how that England and Sweden had agreed together to share Denmark between them.' Thurloe says: 'A sum of money was to be paid to England and freedom given to the English for ever from paying any toll for the passage to and from the Baltic Sea.' To this time perhaps belongs a proposal for the management of the whole export trade of Sweden by an English joint-stock company; all Swedish exports would have been brought to England and re-exported. At the least, it could be hoped to obtain the removal of some of the restraints on English trade in Sweden.[2]

[1] *Diary of Thomas Burton, Esquire*, ed. J. T. Rutt (London, 1828), III, 376–403. One is inclined to suspect that Thurloe introduced the Baltic design in order to give the debate a higher tone than it deserved. He perhaps hoped thereby to avoid the constitutional wrangle that in fact developed.

The Baltic design was useful in diplomacy in a similar way. George Downing, the envoy to the United Provinces, reported a conversation with the envoys of Brandenburg in which the latter pointed out that if the King of Sweden made himself master of the Sound 'he will neglect England; yea, he will then become formidable to it, as having the sole disposition of the Baltic Sea, and consequently of all materials for building shipping, and of those magazines of corn'. 'I told them', Downing said, 'that I perceived they were much afraid of the growing greatness of the Swede, but very little sensible of the growth of the House of Austria; and that I thought they had sought a very ill remedy, for fear of the Swede, to throw themselves into the hands of the Emperor to the making him master of all at last.' *Thurloe Papers*, VII, 533.

[2] New envoys with fresh instructions accompanied the fleet to the Sound. Their instructions are SP 75/16/262. In case the King of Sweden refused to make peace, they were to transfer their support to the King of Denmark in return for trading concessions. See Meadowe's statements, *Narrative*, 119–20; Thurloe's statement, in von Bischoffshausen, *op. cit.* 219.

The joint-stock scheme is in an undated paper called 'Considerations and propositions to be represented to his Highness the Lord Protector for the managing the trade of Sweden and the King of Denmark'; SP 95/5 B/154. The scheme does not mention Denmark or Norway. The company was to be established at Stockholm. The Protector was to join the company as an assurance of the state's support against expected reprisals by the Dutch.

'Propositions in order to a treaty with Sweden', SP 95/5 B/152, undated, in the same hand, is a list of grievances in trade with Sweden, with appropriate remedies to be embodied in a treaty. It is practically identical with the Swedish part of a representation by the Eastland company to Charles II, which is printed at Appendix

This optimisim was short-lived. If at the beginning of 1659 it seemed that something might still be gained from the long association with Charles X, a few months later it looked as if all was lost. Richard Cromwell abdicated and the English government tottered. The fleet returned from the Sound, leaving the Dutch absolute masters of the situation. The Swedes were defeated in a battle on one of the Danish islands. Charles X died and was succeeded by a regency anxious to make peace. Meadowe says of the politicians at home—a little unfairly, since they had no choice—that 'they made no great scruple, at least for that one time, to come under the stern of their neighbouring commonwealth, thereby to have better leisure to recollect and refit the scattered planks and pieces of their own broken republic'.[1]

Yet the settlement that was made by the treaties of Oliva and Copenhagen (May 1660) was not so bad as the English might have expected. We never see more clearly than in this settlement the interaction of two balances of power. While England and the Netherlands played off Sweden against Denmark, Sweden and Denmark played off England against the Netherlands. Sweden was a far stronger power than Denmark, but Denmark's unique topography rendered an aggressor by land weakest when at the furthest point of his attack and most vulnerable when nearest to success. Denmark survived all the Swedish attacks because the centre of her power was in the islands. This circumstance both created a state of natural stalemate between the two Baltic kingdoms, and permitted the western sea-powers to intervene. As between England and the Netherlands, the Dutch were stronger by far at the Sound, but the balance was in England's favour in the Channel, especially after the capture of Dunkirk. It followed that the politics of all four states were restricted by the interests of the others. Thus, although Sweden in a military sense was thoroughly defeated, Denmark was not permitted to recover the provinces across the Sound:

The Dane expected no less [says Meadowe] than to be reinvested in all those dominions and possessions which the former war had wrested from him. . . . But unhappy that prince who wages a war against a stronger than himself, not by his own strength, but by that of his confederates. . . . The alliances of states are conveniences not friendship, interest not affection,

---

A 11 below. We know that the English were in a favourable position in Anglo-Swedish trade in 1659 (above, p. 103). These proposals should perhaps be associated with a representation by some Eastland merchants in January 1658 (*Cal. S.P. Dom. 1657–1658*, 268), or with petitions by the Eastland company in May 1658 and June 1659 (*Cal.S.P.Dom. 1658–1659*, 23, 373). A petition made in March 1658 concerned re-export of hemp (*Cal.S.P.Dom. 1657–1658*, 316, 320, 322).

[1] *Narrative*, 122–3.

a reason of the head not a passion of the heart.... The dividing of the banks of the Sound betwixt the two crowns accommodated Holland as well as England. That necessity which first cast the Dane upon the Dutch alliance, if removed, might make him recoil from it; to keep him poor was to keep him humble and so dependent.[1]

Likewise, although the Dutch had all power at the Sound, their gains were surprisingly modest. The English had credited them with pretensions to territory at the Sound, but they only secured a favourable commercial treaty with Sweden. In 1656 they had negotiated a treaty with Charles X at Elbing, but as Charles was then very strong the terms were not wholly favourable to them; in 1660 they obtained 'elucidations' which conceded a low customs tariff in Swedish ports. The abrogation of this treaty became one of the objects of English policy after the Restoration.[2]

[1] *Narrative*, 141–5. Denmark recovered, however, the Norwegian province of Trondhjem and the island of Bornholm, which Sweden had taken at Roskilde.

[2] J. Dumont, *Corps universal diplomatique du droit des gens* (Amsterdam, 1726–31), vi (ii), 293. C. E. Hill, *Danish Sound Dues and the Command of the Baltic* (Durham, North Carolina, 1926), ch. 6, describes the diplomacy of 1658–60.

Chapter XI

THE DEVELOPMENT OF STATE CONTROL
AFTER 1660

The restoration of the Eastland company

The restoration of the Eastland company followed by nine months the restoration of the king. But it was incomplete. The company asked for a renewal of the proclamation of Charles I, but they received only a confirmation of their charter. We learn, in a letter written some ten years later by the governor of the company to the Secretary of State, that a second application for the proclamation was on the point of being successful when it was obstructed by the Earl of Clarendon. This is his account of what happened:

His Majesty directs a second and his own especial warrant to his Attorney General...forthwith to prepare a bill for his royal signature, suitable to the proclamation desired by the company. In conformity whereto the draft of a proclamation was prepared by Mr Attorney General, and by Mr Secretary Morice presented to the Council: where the same was at the point of being passed, when the late Lord Chancellor appeared at that instant, and obstructed it: but for what reasons the Eastland company never understood.

We can probably understand the Lord Chancellor's reasons better than the governor professed to do.[1]

Without a proclamation the company had no power over foreigners. It was originally granted as a weapon against the Dutch, but, since one of the first acts of Charles II's first parliament was a Navigation Act similar to that of 1651, a proclamation against the Dutch would have served no purpose. The company wanted it as a weapon against Eastlanders. They either believed or disingenuously pretended that the charter and proclamation formed a single body of privilege which was necessary in its entirety

---

[1] The company's application for restoration of privileges, Appendix A 10, is an undated copy. It is attributable to October 1660 on the strength of the governor's letter, SP 29/289/124, 1671. This is an account of their applications for privilege to that date, enclosing copies of documents. One enclosure is a copy of the warrant for a proclamation, just referred to, said to be dated August 1661. The governor said that a confirmation of the charter 'with some enlargements' passed under the Great Seal in February 1661. Elsewhere (PC 2/55/155-6, March 1661) the company said that the patent was 'ready to be engrossed for the Great Seal but...retarded by the many public business intervening'. In May 1662 'the copy of the charter renewed by his Majesty was now wholly read over', Sellers, *Acts and Ordinances*, xlviii n.

for good trading. The sole question, they said, was 'whether the carrying on of the trade...should be in the hands of his Majesty's subjects, or of strangers'. But the logic of their case on this occasion was far less convincing than it used to be. 'Our native commodities', they said, 'are incredibly debased in the foreign places of our trade; which hath happened by the confused and uncontrolled trading of interlopers and unskilful persons of late years, and the continued trading of foreigners now.' This is the argument that we discussed in Chapter IV, namely, that inexpert traders of small means 'carry over what their stock and credit will amount unto' and, for the sake of quick returns, 'being there necessitated to take the present market, though to loss, do in a manner give away our native commodities';[1] by which, in the end, exports were reduced. It was a coherent argument, though never entirely compelling: but it was hardly applicable to trading by native merchants of Danzig. On firmer ground the company declared that free trading encouraged the use of foreign ships. The Navigation Act, having prohibited Dutch ships, did encourage Eastland ships. It encouraged also the native Eastland merchant. The company had some justification for wishing to protect both English ships and merchants against the Eastlander. But the government had already protected them by other means. The government raised the aliens' custom on exports so that aliens' goods now paid as much again as Englishmen's goods, and for imports it defined as aliens' goods all goods imported in foreign ships.

We do not know exactly how the Eastland company would have used a proclamation had it been granted, but we can see that a prohibition of foreigners in general words would have been of service in the recovery of their lost privileges at Danzig. On the other hand, it would have interfered with the administration of the Navigation Act. Charles II was negotiating at that very moment a series of treaties of amity and commerce, and these treaties were based on the Navigation Act. Charles II was going to maintain permanent diplomacy with Sweden and Denmark. Too great powers for the Eastland company would have limited his freedom of negotiation.

He set up a Council of Trade. This body, rather than the trading companies, was now responsible for trading interests. It was the first of a series which periodically lapsed and were reconstituted. It interposed between the Eastland company and the crown.

The council received merchants' suggestions for the treaties then under negotiation, and passed them to the Privy Council with suitable supporting arguments. The Eastland company submitted grievances

[1] This phrase is taken from Appendix A9.

concerning their trade in Sweden, Denmark and Danzig, all of which the council accepted.[1] In the Danish treaty (which revived Cromwell's treaty of 1654) the Eastland company's aims were realised by a provision that in each country the merchants of the other were to be charged no higher duties than Dutch or other merchants. (There was also, as in 1654, a provision to protect the English timber trade in Norway; this, however,— rather strangely—the Eastland company had not asked for.)[2] The Swedish treaty was less satisfactory. Sweden wished to be guaranteed in her gains at Oliva, but England could not agree to this. It would have thrown the Danes into the arms of the Dutch. Accordingly Sweden refused commercial concessions. The Eastland company had complained of exorbitant customs duties, of their arbitrary alteration; of the restriction of English goods to packhouses appointed by the Swedes; of the prohibition against re-export; of the fixing of salt prices; and of the monopoly of pitch and tar. By the treaty, each nation accorded to the merchants of the other 'such full and ample privileges, and as many exemptions, liberties and immunities, as any foreigner whatsoever'; 'saving nevertheless those treaties heretofore entered into by both nations with other kingdoms republics and states, which shall subsist in full force'. Thus the elucidations of Elbing continued to give the Dutch an advantage.[3]

A treaty with Brandenburg protected the Königsberg trade (English merchants to pay no higher duties and to enjoy no less privileges than the Dutch or other foreign nations) and made provision for transferring the English staple there in the event of the abrogation of the Danzig seal, which the Elector promised to try to secure; an illusory prospect.[4]

At Danzig the Eastland company had objected to the seal and to the tax of *Zulag* or *Anlag*; but in each case to no avail. To representatives of the Hanseatic towns Charles II granted free trade under the Navigation Act. Danzig might import in its own ships goods which were the product of Poland or normally shipped from Danzig. Lübeck might import in its own ships, as from a normal entrepôt town, goods of Germany, Norway, Sweden and the rest of the Baltic Sea.[5]

There was no precedent for treaty-making on such a scale. The interests of the merchants were by no means ignored, but one may say that the interests of the state transcended them. There was no treaty with Poland. Of all the Eastland countries, from 1660, only Poland remained outside the sphere of regular English diplomacy.

Under these treaties, without a proclamation, the Eastland company attempted once more to regulate the Eastland trade. They admitted their

---

[1] Appendix A 11.   [2] Dumont, *Corps diplomatique*, vi (ii), 346.
[3] *Ibid.* 384.   [4] *Ibid.* 364.   [5] *Ibid.* 378–9.

first members in January 1661. In two years they admitted about forty persons by name, as well as batches of twenty-eight from York, eighteen from Hull and sixty from Newcastle.[1] On complaint to the Privy Council that 'divers unfree and irregular persons contrary to his Majesty's intention...daily ship cloth and other goods for the East parts', they received warrants to empower their searchers to seize such goods.[2] In a case in the Privy Council against a Merchant Adventurer who, they said, had imported goods from their privileges, the Council adopted the familiar device of ordering an amicable settlement.[3]

Some cases against foreigners, in which their searcher had seized goods imported, show how the company's rights in this respect were interpreted according to the Navigation Act and treaties. The Council register is reticent in these entries. We do not know exactly what the company demanded, nor if they were demanding the same in every case. John Vanderhoven, a Fleming resident in London, who had imported iron and potashes from the Baltic, was required to submit to the company and pay a fine to them.[4] He was unprotected by Navigation Act or treaty. But Jacob Jacobson, the aldermaster of the Hanseatic Stillyard, who had imported Swedish iron, was not required to submit.[5] His brother Theodore Jacobson, who had imported deal boards, was not required to submit.[6] In a case brought by the Swedish resident, the company having seized pitch and tar imported in Swedish ships, the Council commanded the company

not to give any hindrance or molestation unto any Swedish-built ships, navigated or manned with the subjects of the King of Sweden, and laden with goods of the natural growth and product of that kingdom, trading into any ports of his Majesty's dominions, according to the late Act of Navigation...it being his Majesty's will and pleasure that the subjects of the King of Sweden, paying the ordinary customs due unto his Majesty, may in all full measure enjoy the freedom and liberty of trade and commerce, which the said treaty between the two crowns, the said late Act of Navigation, and the usual custom and practice with all other neighbouring kingdoms and states do allow.

The company restored the pitch and tar but retained 'what hath been paid down in ready money'.[7]

---

[1] Appendix C. [2] PC2/55/155–156.
[3] PC2/55/471, 480. [4] PC2/56/164, 172. Appendix A 12.
[5] PC2/56/275, 279; SP29/67/152. The company referred to a late judgement of the Council concerning Danes importing their own goods, that 'they ought not to import the same without the company's duties'.
[6] PC2/58/253. [7] PC2/56/398, 401, 409.

The company had one rate of imposition for freemen, another for unfreemen. The unfree imposition was probably normally double. It is likely that in these cases the crown upheld the principle that unfree impositions were to be levied only on foreigners who were not native Eastlanders importing their own goods in their own ships; unless it upheld the principle that nothing *above* unfree impositions should be levied on Eastlanders importing their own goods in their own ships. Whatever the principle, the yardstick with which it was applied was the Navigation Act.

The company's chief difficulty was to obtain a 'settlement' at Danzig. Without a settlement beyond the seas—in their own words—'better no company'.[1] Their status at Danzig is unclear. Complaints of taxes do not recur. They resented, however, the law that compelled them to buy and sell only with burghers.[2] The Dutch in the Eastland became burghers wherever they traded. But the Eastland company wished to remain foreigners with liberties and immunities. This was hardly possible. Burghers had advantages over them at Danzig, just as they had advantages in England. Doubtless for this reason, we find from 1660 repeated complaints by the Eastland company about 'combination' or 'collusion' with burghers. The procedure with exports was described in 1685 as follows:

There are some of our company (who we could name) who patronise such foreigners' goods and so defraud the company of those impositions due for strangers' goods. And lest they should be discovered at home they do consign the goods specified in their bills of loading to themselves or their order, and afterwards endorse one of the bills unknown to the masters of ships, to whom till the foreigners here produce the endorsed bill of loading.[3]

By collusion they evaded aliens' custom in England (which on a short cloth was 7s. 10d. against 3s. 4d. paid by an Englishman) and various expenses and difficulties at Danzig. The Eastland company set their face against collusion. Naturally they encountered opposition from their own members. It is doubtful if they ever succeeded in quelling it, and their attempts were probably not in the best interests of the cloth trade. There was also collusion in the Swedish trade, but of this the Eastland company did not complain.[4] They were preoccupied with the situation at Danzig.

---

[1] Sellers, *Acts and Ordinances*, 84.
[2] Appendix A 12.
[3] Sellers, *Acts and Ordinances*, 118.
[4] Instructions for a consul at Elsinore about 1671: 'Prevent collusion betwixt English and Swedish merchants, who pass all out of England as English goods, and when they come by the Sound and Stockholm they have dockets to show them all Swedish; so likewise from Stockholm they are Swedish and when they passed the Sound they are good English, whereby the three crowns are defrauded.' SP 75/17/501.

It was partly with an eye to stopping collusion that they decided to send a deputy to Danzig in 1662. At Danzig were Englishmen who had never been admitted to the Eastland company and who would not come to England to be admitted. The company at London wrote to the company at York that 'by the increase of interlopers, and by means of false brethren, and combination with the burghers at Danzig, much cloth and other goods are carried into our privileges, which they are the worse able to prevent, in regard of the want of an orderly government there'.

They therefore have found it necessary (sooner indeed than they supposed at the general meeting would have been needful) to send over a person to remain for this ensuing year at Danzig, in the quality of a deputy, to endeavour what redress may be had to these evils; by administering an oath of admission to the factors (for which they must otherwise come to England) and reducing them to a regulation, and giving advice of concernments there; and as he may see occasion, privately to understand how the magistrates of that city stand disposed to treat for a more complete settlement.[1]

But William Barker, George Cock and other members alleged before the Privy Council, with truth, that the appointment of the deputy had not been made at a general court; and they added that he was a republican. He was John Collins. They said that he was

formerly notorious for the observation of a triumphant anniversary in Danzig for the murther of his late Majesty, and by his influence corrupting the most part of the English factory there, where himself and his adherents became so obnoxious to the King of Poland that they were proscribed his kingdom, and that the said factory and assistants have displaced others of his Majesty's best affected subjects for celebrating at Danzig the day of his Majesty's happy restoration.

The Eastland company craved pardon. Ordered by the king in Council, John Collins not to go.[2]

The tendency of William Barker's and George Cock's action was to undermine the existence of the company of which they were members. If this was not their intention, it is clear that they felt no compulsive obligation to support the company. Nor did the company find a deputy who would be more acceptable. Instead they appointed in 1664 a committee at Danzig, from which, they said subsequently, they received 'but small benefit'.[3]

---

[1] Sellers, *Acts and Ordinances*, 80–1.
[2] PC2/55/635, and the last page of that volume where the entry is perhaps incomplete. [3] Sellers, *Acts and Ordinances*, 83, 87, 93.

Nevertheless, we may say that at home the company prospered. The treasurer's book which survives from 1660 gives an insight into their affairs which is lacking earlier. The first annual feast was defrayed by subscription, but later feasts were charged on their funds. Impositions were now collected in England, both inward and outward. Impositions and entry fines gradually paid off the debts with which they began: arrears of salary, liabilities to the outports, and borrowings from the difficult times at the beginning of the interregnum. (One of the creditors was George Cock.) In spite of considerable outgoings the balance in the treasurer's hands at the audit of 1663 was nearly £300, and at the audit of 1664 over £400. York then thought that the debts were paid off, but in fact the company still owed £1590.[1] In 1667 it looks as if they were clear.

If it is permissible to speculate about the attitude of George Cock, we may suggest that, while he was unwilling to promote the establishment of orderly government at Danzig, he would welcome it, as a creditor, at home. The company's indebtedness was an inducement to continue the company. If in hard times trading companies fell into debt, the demands of creditors necessitated their re-establishment when the hard times were over. This fact helps to explain their vitality.

The treasurer's book allows us to see on what items the company spent their income. 'July 1664, to money paid for 100 pieces of gold presented the Lord Chancellor, £107 10s.' 'November 1644, to money paid for 50 pieces of gold presented the Lord Ashley, £53 6s. 8d.' These entries are exceptional, but presents of thirty pieces to Mr Secretary Morice recur. Presents to Danish customs officers at the Sound recur: for example 'paid Zephaniah Parker [a shipmaster] for eight hogsheads of beer and cask being the company's present to the customers at the Sound, £11 2s. 6d.' Regular small presents were made to secretaries, clerks and doorkeepers in the Privy Council office and the Secretary of State's office, and to English customs officers, especially the searchers. The recipients, from the Earl of Clarendon to the lowest doorkeeper, were those with whom the company had official business. Only Clarendon's single £100 looks faintly like bribery, and that was given too late to be of much use.

The company paid for copies of entries in the king's customs books. They paid fees to lawyers. They settled the expenses of their searcher, Mr Chaplin.[2] Chaplin's expenses echo the Privy Council cases mentioned above and show, incidentally, that they were the complete list of such cases. Thus in 1662, 'to paid Mr John Chaplin in going to Gravesend, £2',

---

[1] The statement given to York tallies with the treasurer's book (Sellers *op. cit.* 84).
[2] Chaplin also acted as searcher to the Canary company (*Cal.S.P.Dom. 1665–1666*, 31).

'to paid upon account of Vanderhoven's arresting Chaplin, £1', 'to paid John Chaplin upon account of the lawsuit with John Vanderhoven, £1 11s. 2½d.'

When the expenses of courts of assistants were recorded separately, it emerges that there were twelve or more a year. Assistants received £1 a meeting. The expenses run continuously through the year and give an impression of uninterrupted activity.

Their payments at home far exceeded payments abroad. It is probable that they maintained a 'correspondent' at the Sound who received possibly £20 a year. But they made no presents in Sweden or at Danzig, nor to English or foreign ambassadors. They were not required to bear any of the costs of diplomacy. A person of free-trade sympathies, examining their accounts, might well come to the conclusion that their impositions were bringing in more than they could usefully spend on the welfare of the trade as a whole.

Four years of peaceful trading followed the Restoration. Exports remained very low. Imports were lower than in the good period under Charles I, and showed but slight tendency to rise. In 1665 the trade was completely interrupted by the second Dutch war.

The second Dutch war

Cromwell's Dutch war was a war of preservation. Charles II's was a war of aggression. Cromwell wished to defend himself against the Dutch, Charles II wished to make himself their master.

He prepared the way in the Baltic by an alliance with Sweden. He guaranteed the Swedish gains at Oliva, and the Swedes bound themselves to annul the elucidations of Elbing. Now the English could trade in Sweden no less favourably than the Dutch. Provision was further made for some sort of pre-emption by English merchants of Swedish goods, and there was a mutual arrangement for free ports at Gothenburg and Plymouth. The English received permission to establish residences at Stade, Landscrona and Narva. The treaty was calculated to give England the greatest possible share in Sweden's expanding foreign trade.[1]

At the same time Charles II tried to keep his friendship with Denmark. His ambassadors worked hard to prevent Denmark falling into line with the Dutch. He tried to embroil Denmark against the Dutch through a combined attack on Dutch ships sheltering at Bergen. All failed. The Danes were stiffened in their resistance by the King of France. When the

---

[1] A transcript of the treaty is in the Public Record Office, PRO 31/17/32.

war broke out, France and Denmark took the side of the Dutch. The Sound was closed to English ships.[1]

In all this planning it is not recorded that the Eastland company took any part.

The needs of the navy were met by shifts and turns. There was great reliance on supplies from Germany and Hamburg. The Navigation Act was suspended for goods of the Eastland. For Norwegian goods, licences were granted to permit their import in Danish ships. Edmund Lee was the first mover for this; there is no evidence that the Eastland company were involved.[2]

Two important men in the supply of naval stores were Sir William Ryder and William Cutler. At the outset of the war, press warrants were issued for five of their ships destined for the Sound. Later they applied for convoy for seven hemp ships from Riga and six ships with pitch and tar from Stockholm, and they had two or more ships detained at Pillau by the Elector of Brandenburg.[3] One might expect these influential men to have been leading personalities in the Eastland company, but they were not; we do not even know that they were members.

The war was lost. Peace came in 1667. The Eastland company in the Great Fire had been burnt out of their usual meeting-place, Founderers' Hall. Their records had been damaged and dispersed.[4] The fire enlarged the Norway trade, but the war had ended the favourable Danish treaty of 1661 and the King of Denmark imposed restrictions. The next year saw a thorough review of the conditions of the Eastland trade.

The encouragement of the Eastland trade

The immediate problem in 1668 was to ensure an adequate supply of cheap imports from Norway and the Baltic for the rebuilding of London. The same materials were also required cheaply and plentifully for shipbuilding. The Privy Council had set on foot an inquiry into the cause of the high freights of English ships, and half the battle was to build them of cheap materials.[5] The course immediately adopted was to suspend the Navigation

---

[1] H. L. Schoolcraft, 'England and Denmark, 1660–1667', *E.H.R.* xxv (1910), 457 ff.

[2] PC 2/58/363.

[3] *Cal.S.P.Dom. 1664–1665*, 345, *1665–1666*, 26, 31, 67.

[4] The Treasurer's book has the following items in 1670: to the secretary for 'charges of removing things at fire, £5', 'allowed him for transcribing books burnt, £5', 'paid Alderman Asty [treasurer] his charges of removing the company's books and cash at fire, £5'. Sellers, *Acts and Ordinances*, 89, refers to the confusion into which they fell through the dispersal of their records.

[5] E.g. PC 2/60/143–4.

Act for those goods, not only from Norway but from the Baltic.[1] As a long-term solution this was unsatisfactory. Its effect was to encourage foreign shipping at the expense of English; and the more so, as the King of Denmark had begun to discriminate against English traders. The Council of Trade examined the question. They took note that the King of Denmark had raised the Sound tolls, that he was exacting in Norway 'greater tolls and impositions of the English than of the Dutch and French, about one third more than was paid since the treaty of 1660', and that he was persecuting the English traders in Norway in other ways.[2]

One opinion saw no harm, under these circumstances, in using Dutch ships, and therefore believed that the suspension of the Navigation Act ought to be continued. This was Roger Coke's advice, and he implies that some Norway merchants agreed. Roger Coke's remarks are often quoted as a valid criticism of the Navigation Act, but they completely ignore its original intention.[3]

Another suggestion was to enforce the Navigation Act and to place a sixfold imposition on goods imported in Norwegian ships. Otherwise 'so many Hollands ships and mariners will be made free in the several parts in these seas, that few English ships will be freighted'. This, however, would have made imports too dear.[4]

The solution preferred by the Council of Trade was to naturalise foreign ships taken prize during the war and sixty newly purchased. They estimated that of £200,000 of wood imported annually, £100,000 went to the carrier for freight. Sixty ships would cost £60,000. Therefore one year's trading would cover their cost. They were to be employed 'in the

---

[1] Granted on application of 'East country and Norway merchants'; PC 2/59/221.
[2] Some of the Council of Trade's papers concerning the Norway trade, including their report, are printed by A. F. W. Papillon, *Memoirs of Thomas Papillon* (Reading, 1887), 64 ff. Thomas Papillon was a member of the Council of Trade.
[3] *Detection of the Court and State of England* (London, 1694), II, 476–7:
Before the Act of Navigation the English traded to Norway in Dutch vessels... and then imported masts, raff, pitch...so cheap, that the Norwegians could build but six small vessels to trade into England; but after the Act of Navigation, when the Norway trade was restrained to the Norwegians, and [to] English in their inconvenient dear-built ships, the Norwegians increased their ships from six to above sixty, and those of double dimensions than the former were; but after Oliver dispensed with the Act of Navigation, the English Norway merchants imported goods so cheap, that the Norwegians were forced to sell their vessels for want of employment: this Mr Lee and Mr Smith, Norway merchants, were ready to have testified before a committee of the Commons, when endeavours were used in 1667 for the free importation of timber, board and raff, after the burning of the City of London; these be dead, yet I am assured Sir William Warren and Mr John Hammond, Norway merchants, know this to be true.
[4] SP 88/11/105; a letter from a merchant at Danzig, Francis Sanderson, of whom we shall hear more.

Norway trade, or the Baltic Seas, or for salt from any place'. 'His Majesty having spent two several days in hearing divers members of the said Council of Trade thereupon', it was ordered that sixty ships be naturalised. The suspension of the Navigation Act was not continued.[1]

In a new treaty with the King of Denmark, England undertook to defend Denmark against aggressors. In return the commercial discrimination was removed. It was agreed, especially, that the English should pay no higher duties and enjoy no less privileges than the Dutch.[2]

There is no evidence that the Eastland company as such took part in these affairs. Their contribution to the Council of Trade's business was an application for a proclamation. Their representation on this subject concerned only the trade with Danzig. The burghers of Danzig, said the company, were fitting out ships of their own and had formed a company to manage trade with England. They had great advantages at Danzig 'where we never enjoyed any privileges at all', and their ships sailed more cheaply. This 'invites the English to manage their trade in strangers' names, and to use strangers' vessels.... And of what consequence this may prove, by the destruction of English shipping and trade...the petitioners humbly refer to your royal wisdom'.[3]

We are fortunate in possessing the Council of Trade's report on this application and the Eastland company's comments on the report. The council were in favour of a proclamation, but with limitations that the Eastland company found not entirely acceptable.[4]

The report begins by rehearsing the council's terms of reference. It explains that the proclamation was chiefly recommended in order to make the company 'more esteemed and considerable in foreign parts':

May it please your Majesty.

In obedience to your Majesty's order made in Council the 16th of November last [1668], your Majesty's Council of Trade did humbly offer

---

[1] One of those who presented the Council of Trade's report in the Privy Council was John Shorter, a Norway merchant. Another was Josiah Child. His opinion, written at this time, was as follows (*New Discourse of Trade*, 1694, ch. 9): 'The trade of Denmark and Norway is advantageous to the kingdom, not only because it gives or would give employment to two hundred or three hundred sail of English shipping (if we did a little mend our Act of Navigation) but principally because the commodities imported from thence...are of such necessary use, in order to the building and supplying our shipping, that without them other trades could not be carried on.'
[2] Dumont, *Corps diplomatique*, VII (i), 126, 132.   [3] Appendix A 12.
[4] The petition of the Eastland company for a proclamation was read in Privy Council on 18 September 1668. On 6 November this was referred to the Council of Trade, and the question whether a proclamation would be consistent with the Swedish and other treaties was referred to a committee; PC 2/61/16–17, 92. This is described accurately in the governor's letter to the secretary of state (1671), with which copies of the Council's report and the company's comments were enclosed; SP 29/289/124.

their opinion and advice to your Majesty concerning the Norway trade; and now in further conformity to your Majesty's said order, requiring them to report unto your Majesty their opinion and advice touching a proclamation desired by the Eastland company, how far the restraints and prohibitions desired by the said company might be advantageous or disadvantageous to the trade of this your Majesty's kingdom, they do in all humility, after serious debate and consideration of the matter, being of very great moment and general concernment to trade, tender unto your Majesty their humble opinion and advice thereupon, as followeth.

That the corporation of Eastland merchants, by your Majesty's royal charter in a way of association and regulation, may be convenient and advantageous to the trade of your Majesty's kingdom, as well for the obtaining and upholding the privileges, trade and honour of the English abroad, as for other reasons.

That in consequence such a proclamation as is desired (if limited as is hereafter expressed) may be useful to render the company (by your Majesty's owning of them) more esteemed and considerable in foreign parts, and will not be prejudicial to your Majesty or your subjects.

It looks from this as if the proclamation was to be a key to unlock the door of privileges at Danzig. It was not to interfere with the pattern of trade prescribed by the Navigation Act and the Danish and Swedish treaties:

As to foreigners and how far they should be permitted and allowed, your Majesty's Council of Trade do not offer any limitation to be inserted in the proclamation in reference thereunto; apprehending the general terms for their exclusion (as is desired) to be more effectual for the advantage of English trade, and cannot (as they humbly conceive) be made use of by the said company, to debar or hinder the subjects of such princes with whom your Majesty is in treaty of alliance, from enjoying the privileges of those treaties, in regard the charters of the said company (on which the proclamation is desired to be grounded) do limit that the rules, orders etc. of the said company shall not be contrary to any treaty, league or covenant made or to be made by your Majesty or your successors with any other prince or potentate.

This was a straightforward assertion of the absoluteness of the state. The absoluteness was not new. It had been asserted in the charter. But, so far as we know, before the Restoration it had not been enforced in practice.[1]

'The limitations to be inserted in the proclamation' were four. The first

---

[1] The charter gave the company power to make laws for their good government 'so as the said laws...be not repugnant or derogatory to the laws and statutes of this realm of England or contrary to any treaty, league or covenant between us, our heirs and successors and any other prince or potentate made or to be made'. Sellers, *Acts and Ordinances*, 145.

was most important to the constitution of the Eastland company. It shows that the Council of Trade had adopted the opinion that the Eastland company was too exclusive. They were probably thinking along free-trade lines that the cloth export trade could not be in too many hands.[1] We remember also that Josiah Child believed that the Eastland company hindered re-export trade to the Baltic.[2] Benjamin Worsley, an exponent of free ports, was on this council.

1. That to the intent none of your Majesty's subjects who are willing to conform to good order may be excluded, and thereby the trade restrained; it may be provided, that any English merchant (requiring the same) may be admitted to the said company; and that the fine to the company for such admission do not exceed five pounds.

This reminds us of the recommendation concerning a new charter by the Council of Trade of the interregnum. The Eastland company objected that £5 was too little. It would destroy apprenticeship. 'The whole body of traders will consist of unskilful members, to the ruin of the whole.' They asked if the Council of Trade meant by 'merchant', mere merchant; for mere merchants could not possibly hold trade with shopkeepers, 'but must lie still whilst the others are furnishing their shops'. This admission was damaging, especially at a time when cheap imports were a prime consideration. The objection to the low entrance fine was in effect merely a flat contradiction of the point of view of the Council of Trade.

The second limitation showed the council's concern for cheap and plentiful building materials for the rebuilding of London:

2. ... That for the space of two years next ensuing, all Englishmen whatsoever may be free to import timber and deals in ships sailed with English master and mariners; paying only to the said company the same impositions that have been paid for one year last past. ...

To this the company raised no objection.

The third limitation showed the council's concern about the cloth trade.

3. That in regard the enlarging and increase of the trade of our native manufactures is much the interest of your Majesty and your kingdoms; it may be provided, that the said company do not, nor shall for the future, levy or take any imposition whatsoever upon the exportation of any English manufactures.

The company did not object to this. They pointed out that their imposition on a short cloth was only 6*d*. They said that they would have to increase their impositions on imports.

---

[1] Above, p. 56.   [2] Above, p. 117.

The fourth limitation showed the council's determination to admit no exceptions to the Navigation Act.

4. And for an additional encouragement to English shipping and for the increase of English mariners, that it be provided that the said company be obliged to take care that the Acts of Trade and Navigation be duly observed.

On this the company only asked that they might continue to use Eastland ships when English ships were not available. 'Otherwise the English may often stand still, while strangers enjoy the trade, and goods bought and lying ready in the East and in Norway may be in England by a foreign ship before any English ship can arrive there.' This was not strictly an objection and did not run counter to the Navigation Act.

The Council of Trade's report was read in the Privy Council on 29 October 1669. It was ordered that some of the Council and some of the Eastland company attend on 3 November. On 3 November the same were ordered to attend on 10 November. There is no subsequent entry. The Eastland company had failed to obtain a proclamation but they had successfully avoided the limitations.[1]

The next two years were the Eastland company's swansong. They obtained warrants of assistance for searchers at London and the outports.[2] They brought before the Council one William Strangh, who had forcibly rescued a parcel of copper seized by their searcher; and who submitted and took his freedom.[3] They raised the duty on unfreemen and appointed a deputy at Danzig:

And because we cannot expect they [interlopers] should be totally excluded the trade on a sudden, and know they have not been very sensible of the easy fine paid by them the last year, we have ordered that any unfree men trading shall pay a fine to the value of treble what they have paid the last year, namely six times the imposition ourselves pay. And to the end they may be also the easier met with abroad, we have instead of a committee from whom we received but small benefit, appointed Mr Francis Sanderson to be our deputy at Danzig, who may be our constant correspondent, and answer all our occasions.[4]

Sanderson was at Danzig in 1651 and 1656 and was a member of the committee in 1664 and 1669.[5] Since 1655, if not earlier, he had maintained an almost weekly correspondence with Joseph Williamson in the office of

[1] PC2/62/29, 35. The governor says that the Council of Trade reported to the Privy Council in May 1669; SP29/289/124.
[2] *Cal.SP.Dom.* *1670*, 427; *1671*, 124, 180.
[3] PC2/62/323, 325. For his admission see Appendix C.
[4] Sellers, *Acts and Ordinances*, 92–3.   [5] Appendix C.

the Secretary of State, Lord Arlington. The letters, which are not unlike the letters of intelligence to Thurloe during the interregnum, consist of short notes about Polish affairs with occasional digressions into personal and commercial business. They were frankly intended to win Williamson's patronage. Even after Sanderson's appointment as deputy they have the form of private letters, but even before his appointment he performed semi-public functions which Williamson must have found useful. He published at Danzig the English gazettes and other propaganda sent him by Williamson, and forwarded them to Riga on the way to Moscow. Sometimes dispatches from the envoy at Constantinople passed through his hands. He sent Williamson from time to time a present of sturgeon (the Eastland company at home also gave presents of sturgeon) and once put him in the way of making £100 for freeing a Danzig ship seized in England. Both before and after his appointment as deputy he asked Williamson for information on the state of war and peace, on the prospects of trade with France and Spain, on the best course for ships leaving the Sound to avoid Dutch men-of-war and Ostend privateers. We have noticed his suggestion for a heavy imposition on timber imported in foreign ships. He explained to Williamson how Dutchmen made themselves burghers at Danzig and sold English cloth on the same terms as natives, having brought it from England as freely as Englishmen (he ignored the double duties paid by aliens).[1] Occasionally he warned Williamson that it was unwise to treat Danzig ships harshly, in case they retaliated against English merchants at Danzig. He never directly expressed the Eastland company's case for a proclamation, but he supported it indirectly. 'You may please to take notice', he wrote in 1672, 'that about three years ago, when very few ships were belonging to this place, a party of able burghers laid together a joint stock for the building of ships, to whom many more are since come in, so that they have already built seven large ones, and made preparation for more.'[2] The correspondence was likely to be of value to Sanderson and Williamson personally, and also to the Eastland company and to the state.

In 1671 the governor, Richard Chiverton, wrote to Lord Arlington to reopen the question of the proclamation. Nothing was done.[3]

Late in 1671 the Privy Council supported the company in a case which must have had considerable importance. Alderman Richard How, Captain John Clark and others, not members of the Eastland company, had imported from the company's privileges some goods (deals are

---

[1] SP 88/11/110. Sanderson's letters run through several volumes of State Papers from SP 88/11.   [2] SP 88/13, 24 September 1672.
[3] This is the letter with enclosures, to which we have often referred; SP 29/289/124.

mentioned) which the company's searcher had seized; they 'arrested the officers who detained the said goods and do prosecute actions against them'. The company prayed that the actions be stopped. The Council summoned How, Clark and sixteen others. Ten days later How, Clark and some of the company presented a 'composure and settlement' with which the King 'was pleased to declare himself well satisfied', and it was copied into the Council register. It was in fact an Act of the Eastland company, and as it is all we know to exist of the Eastland company's post-Restoration court book we give it in full.

At a court of Assistants of the Eastland Company 13th November 1671

Major Richard How and Captain John Clark appearing in behalf of themselves and the rest concerned in the company's complaint now depending before his Majesty and Council, desired that an amicable composure might be made thereof, by way of reference, without troubling that honourable Board; and named two persons for their arbitrators, praying the company to do the like. But the court not inclining to any motion tending to a reference of his Majesty's letters patent (without his Majesty's consent) proposed to them, either to submit to the judgment of this court, or else to stand to that of his Majesty and Council, where the matter was now lodged. And both of them at last, leaving themselves to the judgment of the court, and Major How promising in behalf of all the rest concerned therein that they should do the like, and withdraw their actions at law, and both of them likewise desiring their admission into the freedom, the court took the business into debate; and being willing upon their submission to deal kindly with them, resolved upon a moderate sum to be paid for their broke; and that their goods in custody be released; also that the said Major How and Captain Clark, being represented as persons capable, be admitted into the freedom of this company, on the fine of £20 apiece, with all which they being acquainted did kindly accept thereof; and were admitted and took the oath. Which being thus composed it was thought fit that some on each side attend the Council Board on Wednesday, to give an account thereof.[1]

The members of the Council of Trade must have watched this case with disquiet.

In 1672 began the third Dutch war. We have seen the astonishing increase in trade that resulted from Charles II's policy in this war. The

---

[1] PC2/63/86, 100, 107. How and Clark were admitted; Appendix C. The treasurer's book notes the following expenses: 'to paid for order of Council to summon Alderman How, Captain Clark etc., £3 2s. 6d.', 'to paid Mr Deputy to give Mr Attorney and Solicitor General their fees to attend at Council about Alderman How etc., £15 17s. 6d.', 'to paid Mr Henry Travis attorney, who managed the company's suit against Alderman How and Captain Clark, £5'.

secret of success, which he cannot fail to have learnt from the second Dutch war, was the alliance with France. The master-stroke was to make a separate peace after two years. If Charles planned this outcome from the beginning, he could not have planned more astutely.[1]

It is therefore interesting to notice that also in 1672 a new Council of Trade and Plantations was set up. This body united functions previously exercised by two councils. It was a small body, smaller than the 1688 Council of Trade. Its members were statesmen rather than merchants. It looks more like a department of state and less like a body of advisers than does any previous council. It was instructed to consider

how our native commodities and manufactures may be vented in greater quantities...about the building of...great ships for the more convenient carriage of masts, timber and other bulky commodities...how free ports may conveniently be opened about our coasts....And of the several advantages that may accrue unto these our kingdoms by giving way (according to the example of other nations) to a more open and free trade than that of companies and corporations.[2]

The secretary of the Council of Trade and Plantations was Benjamin Worsley. He had been a member of the Council of Trade in 1668. Another member was Sir George Downing. He also had been a member of the Council of Trade in 1668. Pepys tells us of Downing's energy. He had the reputation of a ruthless man of affairs to whom tradition was not sacred. He was secretary of the Treasury. To ensure the best use of the Treasury's money he was added to the Navy Board. No stranger to the affairs of the Eastland company, he was now to supervise the buying of Eastland commodities. He was also a member of parliament. He both hated the Dutch and admired their methods.

An Act was passed in the parliament then sitting to remove the extra duty paid by aliens on all English commodities exported. This looks like an answer to one of the instructions of the Council of Trade and Plantations. They had decided that it was more important to encourage the cloth trade than to keep it in the hands of Englishmen.

On 13 February 1673 the House of Commons appointed a committee 'to enquire into reasons of the decay of the Muscovy, Eastland and Greenland trade; and by what means these trades may be advanced and improved'. Sir George Downing headed the committee; all merchants and all members of the Council of Trade and Plantations were invited to

---

[1] Above, pp. 108 ff.

[2] Andrews, *British...Councils of Trade and Plantations*, appendix III; for its composition, see 106–7.

attend. A bill about the Greenland trade was introduced and had its second reading on 22 March, when 'a clause tendered, and twice read, concerning the Eastland trade'. The whole bill had its third reading on 27 March, and it had its first reading in the Lords on the same day. The Eastland company appealed against it on 28 March but it received the royal assent on 29 March. The sections concerning the Eastland trade were as follows:

viii. For encouragement of the Eastland trade be it enacted...that it shall and may be lawful to and for every person and persons native or foreigner...to have free liberty to trade into and from Sweden, Denmark and Norway; anything in the charter of the Governor, Assistants and Fellowship of Merchants of Eastland...notwithstanding.
ix. And it is hereby further enacted...that whatsoever person or persons subjects of this realm shall desire to be admitted into the said Fellowship of Merchants of Eastland, that every such person shall be admitted...paying for his admission the sum of forty shillings and no more.[1]

The journal of the House of Commons does not say who introduced the clause about the Eastland trade, but the Eastland company said that it was upon the motion of Sir George Downing. They also said, probably truly, that it was done 'without any complaint that we know of from abroad', that is to say from outside the House. Miss Sellers calls Downing 'a statesman whose chequered career had developed his natural talent for crooked ways', and indeed there is something unnaturally swift about a bill introduced on 22 March and made law on 29 March. But it is probable that the Council of Trade and Plantations was behind him. The clause throwing open trade with Sweden, Denmark and Norway seems to reflect the needs of the navy and the instructions of the Council of Trade and Plantations about free ports and the carriage of timber. The clause making all subjects eligible and reducing the entrance fine to 40s. seems to reflect the instructions about free ports and the cloth trade, and was in line with the act that removed aliens' custom. After the stalemate between the company and the last Council of Trade in 1669 over the proclamation and the limitations, some such blow as Downing dealt them was only to be expected.[2] The Act was called 'an Act for the encouragement of the Eastland trade'.

[1] 25 Car. II, cap. 7. *Commons Journals*, IX, 252, 273, 275, 279, 281. The appeal was against clause viii only; H.M.C., *Ninth Report*, II, 31–2. The company said that the Swedish trade was successful and prosperous under their government and that Swedish goods were not cheaper at Amsterdam, even though Dutch ships sailed cheaper.
[2] Sellers, *Acts and Ordinances*, xlix, 93.

The end of the Eastland company

The Eastland company thus truncated had a quarter-century of active life before them, but a few pages will suffice to describe it.

'Although the condition of our company in some respects seem to remain not so prosperous as we could wish', they wrote from London to York in 1674, 'yet we would willingly maintain and uphold such privileges and authorities as we have left us, which we do apprehend may be to the future advantage and benefit of a regulated Eastland trade, conceiving ourselves to be much strengthened by the late Act of Parliament.'[1]

After 1675 many persons took their freedom every year and there was a high number of admissions by redemption at 40s. These people were probably not interested in the cloth trade. The Act of 1673 had no visible effect on cloth exports.

Francis Sanderson in 1674 gave Williamson an account of the Eastland company's trade in which he attached no importance to exports other than cloth and dealt cursorily with imports. He said that Danzig served Poland, Königsberg, Lithuania. At Danzig the burghers had every advantage: 'if they had money to manage it, no strangers could trade in those parts'. All trade in Poland depended on the price of corn: 'When it's sold at a low rate, all other commodities do generally find but bad markets.' Reasons for the decay of the cloth trade were, first, that the consumption had fallen, owing partly to repeated devastations of Poland since 1646 and partly to the fact that 'since 1663 to this year (exclusive) their corn...hath been sold at very low rates'. Secondly, the market was supplied from other sources. For fine cloth,

the Hollanders do in spinning, dressing, dyeing and pressing, so far exceed ours (especially in outward appearance, which pleaseth the Poles best) that I dare well say: for one fine English cloth, twenty Hollands are sold here.

For ordinary cloth,

the clothiers of Silesia...can and do much undersell us: they having wool and workmanship cheaper than we in England; besides their customs and charges are incomparable less than ours....We pay here at its landing about 4s. 3d. sterling for each ordinary cloth, and when it passeth out of Prussia ...into Poland each half-cloth is rated at 100 gilders Polish or £7½ sterling (though the most sent thither are worth little more than half of that price) and the customs thereof come to nine gilders, which is above 12 per cent....

As for stuffs called perpetuanas and says, whereas we sold here formerly 8 to 10,000 pieces yearly, we can now scarce vend one tenth thereof, that

[1] *Ibid.* 95.

manufacture, especially for ordinary sorts, being wholly supplied by says or rashes made here at Danzig.

'Thus', says Sanderson, 'have I given your Honour the reasons of the decay of our trade in those parts, which by some (who perchance are disaffected to all government) hath been, through ignorance or envy, imputed to the Eastland company.'[1]

When this sort of explanation of the decay of the cloth trade was given in the past, it strengthened the opinion that the trade should be made more free. After 1673, when the trade did not improve with freedom, it justified the Eastland company.

In 1689 a bill was introduced in parliament to throw open completely all export trade in cloth. The governor of the Eastland company, Nathaniel Tenche, produced *Reasons* against it. He was able to admit frankly the decay of the cloth trade and to argue convincingly that it would not be helped by the overthrow of the Eastland company. Of all the Eastland company's statements in the seventeenth century this seems to be the most honest, sensible and forceful, for after conventional arguments against unregulated trade he was able to add:

And if it be now objected to us, that after all our endeavours to prove that a general permission will not increase the vent of our manufactures, we have in the meantime nowhere affirmed what will; we must declare, that at present we know but one of these two means: either to put a stop to its making in other parts; or to make it so cheap here, that we may be able to undersell our neighbours. The first of which we know to be impossible; the latter, we have reason to believe, might give offence to the sellers of its materials; though it is sufficiently evident to any common understanding, that the cheapness of the materials is the most proper means of increasing the vent of the manufacture.[2]

The Act when passed made an exception in favour of the Eastland company (also of the Russia and Levant companies).

Tenche's *Reasons* contained one false statement. He said that the Eastland company deserved to be supported on account of their import of naval stores, for which reason it had been established by Queen Elizabeth and favoured by successive governments. This was anachronistic. But in the second half of the seventeenth century, and especially after the expansion of the import trade in 1675, it was natural.

---

[1] SP 88/13, 15 December 1674.
[2] *Reasons humbly offered by the Governor, Assistants and Fellowship of Eastland Merchants against the giving of a general liberty to all persons whatsoever to export the English woollen manufacture whither they please* (London, 1689).

Sanderson's letter to Williamson, just quoted, had noticed the exact beginning of this expansion. After shortly describing the commodities available at Danzig, Königsberg and Riga, he added that the Dutch trade in these goods far exceeded the English, 'their cheap freights in such bulky commodities giving them an advantage before all others. But now', he added, 'their war with France doth much obstruct that trade.'[1]

Other letters convey the advantages of neutrality. Sanderson in 1673 was building a ship of about 350 tons at Danzig for the carriage of plank and masts to London. 'I most humbly beseech your Honour to... acquaint me what probability you have of peace, the knowledge whereof may highly concern me as a merchant.' Sanderson's problem was whether to give the ship Swedish, Danish or Danzig nationality. Swedish or Danish nationality would afford more safety against Dutch and Ostenders so long as Sweden and Denmark remained neutral, but 'if they should side either with us or our adversaries at sea then the danger would be greater than if the ship were a Danziger'. She was nearly ready, but Williamson kept silent. Sanderson grew more and more worried. At last he received news of the English peace. (Williamson did not tell him in advance.) Immediately he asked Williamson's favour to procure English nationality for her. Her name should be the *Concord* of London.[2]

The company prospered. In 1680 they were carrying forward a balance little short of £2000, with all debts paid. In 1684 they invested £500 in the Mercers' Company at 5 per cent. In 1697 they held an Exchequer tally for the same amount, and the cash in hand exceeded £1000. They refunded impositions on goods subsequently re-exported. When the goods are specified we get a glimpse of an entrepôt in Baltic goods. It is especially noticeable about 1678.

They took a high line with the outports. Miss Sellers prints a splendid letter to York in 1677, in which they acknowledged one 'full of discontent and controversy'. They wished that, if York intended to break away, they would say so plainly, not 'hint it darkly in a smothering manner by the signs of your murmur and discontent'.

As for our part it is plainly and openly our resolution to preserve the company and its government, notwithstanding the averseness of some

[1] 'The vent of our English manufactures is more at Danzig than all other port towns in the Baltic seas; our returns from thence are small, excepting potash, linen and canvas, with some wax and wood [and corn on occasion]....We are furnished with the best hemp from Riga and Königsberg and it's hard to say from which place the most is exported; we have also our flax from thence, but most from the latter place; likewise some potashes; but they are not ordinarily so good as those from hence [Danzig], which in times of peace come most out of Wallachia.'

[2] SP 88/13, 13 May 1673 to 7 April 1674.

members, who it may be would (if they could) bend the whole frame of our government to their private humour, which we will prevent if possible; for we will always persuade ourselves, that by the tenor of our charter, the acts and orders we make are not required of necessity to be acceptable and grateful to every restless and unquiet member, but such as we judge fit and wholesome for the commonweal of the whole fellowship, and not accommodated to the temper of every ungoverned man.[1]

The outports did not break away. They desired more independence, but they did not desire that the company should cease to exist.

Complaints of interloping and collusion continue. In 1686 the name of John Vanderhoven recurs. The company's searcher seized some goods imported by him, for aliens' account, for non-payment of the unfree imposition. He, acting on behalf of subjects of the kings of Sweden and Poland, the Duke of Brandenburg and others, alleged that the unfree impositions were unlawful. He retained the attorney-general as his counsel, who pointed out before the Privy Council that the company's charter gave no jurisdiction over foreigners. But the Council decided in the company's favour, on the ground that unfree impositions were paid by natural subjects if they traded in the company's privileges without their freedom.[2]

The Eastland company were not overthrown by opposition from outsiders. Their passing was not a case of entrenched privilege being carried by assault. It was a result of the extension of the activity of the state.

In the third Dutch war the company was much concerned with the arrangement of convoys. These entries in the treasurer's book speak for themselves:

To given...for procuring an express to be sent to Captain Guy with the order from the Duke of York about convoy, 4 guineas, £4 6s.

To given his Royal Highness' secretary...about the convoy, 10 guineas, £10 15s.

To given Captain Guy, commander of the Portland frigate, for convoying our ships from the Sound, as a gratuity per order of court, £40.

To paid Captain Wetwyn, commander of the convoy to the Sound, for his care in bringing home our ships from thence, the company's gratuity, £60.

In the war of 1689–97 the treasurer's book is again full of entries relating to convoy. But they are different: 'to be spent at the Bell about a convoy', 'to going to the Admiralty to request further convoy'. 'Coach-hire to

---

[1] Sellers, *Acts and Ordinances*, 99.
[2] Sellers, *Acts and Ordinances*, 122–3. Note also an entry in the treasurer's book, 1681: 'charges of a lawsuit with Mr Jacobson, £11'.

the Admiralty' recurs constantly. The expenses were petty. Convoy was being provided as a normal naval service. We may say that the navy in this respect had come of age.

Up to 1673, for several years running, the Eastland company gave gratuities of £100, £40 and £80 to John Paul at Elsinore. He was or became the king's consul there. In 1680, on his removal, the company disclaimed any interest in the appointment of a successor. They took for granted the performance of his useful duties in regard to shipping, and said that the appointment was useless to them as a company. Had there been no consul at the Sound, they would have been obliged to supply some of his functions on their own account.[1]

In 1696 the Board of Trade was established to look after foreign trade. An Inspector-General of Imports and Exports was appointed to supply the Board with vital information. Commercial intelligence was forthcoming from embassies in foreign countries. At Stockholm was John Robinson, who began in 1678 as secretary and chaplain and rose to be the ambassador. This embassy bombarded the government with detailed reports on the trade of Sweden and the Swedish dominions across the Baltic. Diplomatic connections with Sweden and Denmark had been continuous since 1660, but there had been no permanent connection with Russia or Poland. A permanent embassy in Russia was started in 1699. We may perhaps count one in Poland from 1700, where the English representative had credentials to the city of Danzig as well as to the king.[2]

Simultaneously with these innovations English warships appeared in the Baltic Sea, although not till 1715 did a squadron go every year. The war against Louis XIV not only made the state anxious about its naval stores, they drew even the most distant countries into the orbit of active diplomacy; and this diplomacy was now supported by warships. We may say that the flag had caught up with the merchants.[3]

In 1703 John Robinson came from Stockholm on a four-year visit to Poland. He passed the time chiefly at Danzig. In 1706 he negotiated the first English commercial treaty with Danzig. This was the Eastland company's fatal blow. But the text of the treaty says that it was initiated at the request of the English merchants at Danzig. The treaty did not recognise the existence of the Eastland company, but it provided a number

---

[1] Sellers, *Acts and Ordinances*, 112.

[2] Reports from Stockholm are printed in G. N. Clark, *The Dutch Alliance and the War against French Trade 1688–1697* (Manchester, 1923). On diplomatic representation see *British Diplomatic Representatives 1689–1789*, ed. D. B. Horn (Royal Historical Society, 1932).

[3] Sir Herbert Richmond discusses convoys and naval operations in the Baltic in *The Navy as an Instrument of Policy, 1558–1727* (Cambridge, 1953).

of privileges that the company had been seeking since the middle of the century.

The treaty limited Englishmen to trade only with burghers, but otherwise left them free to store and dispose of their goods as they pleased. It exempted them from taxation unless they maintained a house and family. It protected them in the law courts and gave certain facilities at the customs. It guaranteed the security of their estates on death and provided for the free transfer of them to England. And if any greater privileges should ever be granted to any other nation 'the British subjects shall in like manner fully enjoy the same for themselves, their ships and commerce'.[1]

The Eastland company were sufficiently alive in 1698 to attack the Russia Company in parliament. From 1700, although the treasurer's book has fewer entries, they continued to visit the Admiralty and to receive impositions. The last sign of an outport is the settlement of a debt to Hull in 1708. They admitted a member in 1713. From 1715 the only income was dividends. One page of the treasurer's book covers entries from 1717 to 1728, by which time the only expenditure was on dinners.

[1] Chalmers, *Collection of Treaties*, I, 100ff. There were also provisions to safeguard the trade and shipping of Danzigers in England. Danzig shipmasters were protected in several particulars against English hirers, and it was specified that they should be paid in ready money, not bills.

CONCLUSION

In the sixteenth century English merchants began once more to trade in Norway and the Baltic. They expanded their trade under favourable conditions. In dyed and dressed cloth they had a relatively cheap export commodity which they sold in the Baltic Sea to people who were being enriched by the export of Polish grain to western Europe. Accordingly, when harvests were bad in western Europe English cloth exports were high. If the harvest in England was bad, they had a profitable import trade of grain. If the harvest in England was good, they probably were able to import silver. The trade was subject to sharp fluctuations but increased fairly steadily up to 1597, when several very bad harvests running, in England as well as in other parts of western Europe, brought exports and imports to a peak. After this the situation changed. First, competition arose in the export trade through Dutch cloth exports and through the development of local industry; English cloth, the price of which continued to rise, became too expensive, and the quantity exported began to fall. In addition, the Dutch began to offer to England, from the Netherlands, Baltic goods which competed with those imported direct from the Baltic by English merchants. The Baltic trade in this period was by all accounts bilateral. Imports were therefore desired in order to keep up the level of exports. This Dutch intervention was therefore dangerous. For most of the seventeenth century we are dealing with a trade in decline, at best static, capable of acute depressions and with little resilience.

There was a continuous urge to make cloth exports as cheap as possible. The Eastland trade (since 1579) being in the hands of the Eastland company, this inevitably raised the question of free trade. But the more acute problem concerned imports. Two serious crises showed that imports needed protection. In 1620 and again in 1649 the Dutch broke into the import trade with disastrous results, taking advantage in 1620 of monetary disturbances in eastern Europe, and in 1649 of the English political crisis that made English ships unsafe. At all times, other things being equal, their cheap freights gave an advantage. Their Eastland trade was far and away greater than the English Eastland trade, and they were potentially able to take over the English market and put English ships and merchants out of business. When for a short period about 1640 the English Eastland merchants enjoyed considerable prosperity, this was because England was neutral while the Dutch were involved in the Thirty Years War; war meant high freight rates, neutrality brought great trade. But merchants could not rely on accidents such as this. An active policy of protection was thought necessary. This policy took the form in 1622 of a proclamation to prohibit the import of Eastland goods from the Netherlands, and in 1651 of a Navigation Act to prohibit the import of all goods save from the place of their origin. And this, we may say, was the standard defensive economic policy of the seventeenth century.

It was not sufficient to make trade *great*. They wished in the seventeenth century not merely to protect themselves against the Dutch, but to emulate the Dutch. As an island nation the necessity to be strong at sea was ever in front of their eyes. Strength at sea was impossible without a flourishing mercantile marine. But, in turn, the merchant navy could not flourish without sea-power. From this vicious circle it was hard to escape. It led the early Stuarts to some rather shifty diplomacy and eventually to ship money. The circle was broken in the interregnum under pressure of necessity, through the creation of a large professional navy and the winning of a naval war against the Dutch. Charles II continued the policy of the interregnum and after three Dutch wars England emerged as the dominant sea-power with the safest merchant fleet. Further, by a notable stroke either of luck or policy, she emerged, in 1674, as a neutral sea-power, while the Dutch were still involved in war with France. The result is seen in the history of the Eastland trade, in the sudden and great expansion of the import trade in 1675. The English Eastland merchants had never encountered such favourable conditions for import trade and, at the same time, the expansion of English foreign trade as a whole enhanced the demand for Eastland shipbuilding materials. This expansion was maintained by and large for the rest of the seventeenth century and into the eighteenth. There was a place in it for re-export trade on the model of the Dutch, and in the Eastland trade, though we know little about the re-export of Eastland goods, we know that there was considerable re-export of colonial and other goods to the Eastland. This expansion well deserves the name of commercial revolution which is sometimes bestowed on it.

It did not come about by accident. It was not the effect of beneficent economic competition. It was the result of deliberate policy consciously pursued by successive governments, and at last pursued successfully. The decisive turn of events can be identified in 1649: the weakness of the state made strength essential, the revolution gave money to build a navy, and the energy of the revolutionaries carried them to success.

In general, it appears that the most potent item of economic policy was war.

The subject of this book has been the formulation of policy, its execution and results, in regard to the Eastland trade, but one hopes that it has thrown some shafts of light on seventeenth-century mercantile policy as a whole. The influence of the Eastland company on the formulation of policy appears to have been small. The Eastland company never looks like a 'pressure group', still less an effective one. Indeed, the concept of pressure groups cannot usefully be applied in seventeenth-century history. Groups indeed there were, and the Eastland company was one of them, which did not hesitate to put their particular interests before the government. But the government had a will of its own and was not ruled by them. The government listened with sympathy, but there is never the least hint that it was not the master. The government's decisions were based on ancient and conventional ideas about the common weal, which the subjects abundantly shared and which easily transcended the interests of particular groups.

The Eastland company accepted the mastery of the state because they drew from it their life as a company and considerably relied on it for their prosperity as individuals. When the state turned its back the company died. There is no history of the Eastland company without a history of the state. Even under James I, when devolution of government was carried to extremes, the company knew that they enjoyed their measure of power not by virtue of their own wealth and cohesion but because they were in some sense servants of the crown, promoting the common good as the crown saw it. They were not outside government, they were part of it. In the first half of the seventeenth century they may be thought of almost as a government department, only one degree less 'official' than, for example, the commissioners of the navy. They were on a par with those necessary organs of government, Trinity House, the City of London, and the farmers of the customs. The fact that all these were self-interested groups with private rights must not blind us to the fact that they were departments of state at the same time. Pressure groups, on the other hand, stand outside government. Groups which are an integral part of the machinery of government do not 'press', they make representations and produce reports like ministries of today. Pressure groups are an eighteenth-century phenomenon on the whole; their existence denotes that the strictly official machinery of government has developed sufficiently to take over most of the work of government, leaving them to advance their private interests with some degree of irresponsibility. In the seventeenth century the Eastland company were never able to base suggestions for policy on their own profit. They were made to follow the national interest at every step. They had the same freedom, perhaps, as an English university has today.

When the state grew the Eastland company withered away. By the end of the seventeenth century the state had established over the Eastland merchants what is from one point of view an umbrella of protection and from another point of view a machinery of control. In the growth of direct state control a notable landmark is the Navigation Act of 1651. The Navigation Act is a corollary of the creation of the republic's new navy; it asserted the power of the state at home as the navy asserted it abroad. It took an old policy and freshly articulated it on a truly national basis. Formerly the Eastland company and other companies had executed that policy, now it was to be executed by the customs officers. What had formerly been done by privileges conferred by letters patent was now to be done by a statute. The Navigation Act therefore made a great part of the Eastland company's privileges redundant. Henceforth their exercise of those privileges was curtailed lest they should interfere with the Navigation Act, or with the treaties that were based on the Navigation Act. In addition, the perennial argument for making the cloth trade as free as possible received new strength. When the Eastland company's privileges were the only defence for the import trade, it was difficult to set them aside for the export trade. When the Navigation Act defended the import trade, the free-trade case had full rein. The free-trade case played its part in the death of the Eastland company.

It is commonly said that the Eastland company desired the Navigation Act. They are said to have used their influence to obtain it. This is the event where they are often said to have behaved as a pressure group. *A priori* it is unlikely, and our examination of some of the scanty evidence has shown that what the Eastland and some other companies were seeking was not a Navigation Act, but privileges that they had recently lost. It was the government that decided on an Act. The Council of Trade and the Council of State emerge as stronger bodies than is generally implied. This seems to be a point of general importance, and two pamphlets which seem to disclose the mind of the government, *The Advocate* and *Free Ports*, are reprinted in our appendices.

But it must be admitted that we know very little about the Eastland company, for all that we speak about it so freely. Institutions range between two extremes. At one extreme stand those whose *raison d'être* the members never question, whose existence the members struggle unthinkingly to preserve; such may be a college, a church, the state. At the other extreme stand institutions of which their members take a more detached view, regarding them merely as associations for individual convenience, as devices for securing personal aims; these evoke little loyalty and easily collapse when they fail to serve their purpose or when an alternative device will serve it more effectively; such may be a tennis club or a company for regulating trade. The Eastland company had a charter, courts, records, officers, funds, dinners; but it had not its own hall, the members had other and perhaps conflicting loyalties to cities and other companies to which they might happen to belong, and although the chief officers were evidently in constant communication the whole body met but once a year. We must not, therefore, take for granted that the voice of the Eastland company demanding privileges was the true voice of all the members. It may be that individual members simply demanded protection and were indifferent what form it took. Perhaps they did not mind if the company withered away. It is possible that they actually disliked being regulated by the company and looked for greater freedom under the aegis of the state, in which case the Navigation Act would have delighted them and they may be thought to have actually welcomed the death of the company in later years. We know nothing of this. The internal politics of the Eastland company remain hidden, except as to relations between London and the outports. Probably, had there existed internal differences such as split the Virginia company in the reign of James I, they would have left some sign. We notice only some trace of dissidence in the matter of the appointment of a deputy at Danzig in the reign of Charles II; we do not know what, if anything, this incident conceals. Even without internal quarrels, institutions may decay through indifference. This cannot be measured. It has been possible only to suggest in the foregoing pages that grounds for indifference increased as the century moved to its close.

Appendix A

DOCUMENTS CONCERNING THE EASTLAND COMPANY[1]

1. (a) Petition of the Eastland merchants, 1620
   (b) Report of the referees, 1620.

2. Two papers concerning the Eastland trade from the parliament of 1621.

3. An Act of the Privy Council, 17 May 1622; in favour of clothiers of Suffolk and Essex.

4. Text of the Levant company's proclamation of 1615, compared with the Eastland company's proclamations of 1622 and 1630.

5. A petition by the Eastland company about the soap business, 30 January 1624.

6. Interrogatories administered to witnesses in the case between the Governor, Assistants and Society of Eastland Merchants complainants and Mr George Acton, Thomas Hales and John Goodwyn defendants, in the Court of Exchequer, 1629.

7. Papers relating to the Eastland company's proclamation of 1630.

8. An undated copy of a petition by the Eastland company about soap (? 1632).

9. Two representations by the Eastland company desiring restoration of privilege (? 1649 and 1656).

10. A paper submitted by the Eastland company to a Council of Trade (? 1660). On privilege at home.

11. A representation by the Eastland company to the Council of Trade, 1660. On troubles abroad.

12. A copy of a petition by the Eastland company, read in Privy Council on 18 September 1668.

---

[1] Printed in modern orthography.

I

(*a*) *Petition of the Eastland merchants 1620*[1]

To the King's most Excellent Majesty.

The humble petition of your faithful subjects the merchants trading to the eastern parts.

Humbly show unto your Majesty that whereas in time past the English merchants have had an ample trade into those parts whereby they sold great numbers of dyed and dressed cloths and other English commodities in those countries, and have in return thereof laden great numbers of English shipping to the increase of the navigation of this kingdom and vent of their commodities, but now of late years the Netherlanders by reason of their great shipping and cheap freight have much decayed the navigation of this land and in short time if some good course be not taken by your Majesty they are like to carry the whole trade and in their own shipping, to the damage and undoing of your Majesty's loving subjects and the great increase of the strangers' wealth and strength in navigation.

In tender consideration whereof they humbly beseech your Majesty by your royal proclamation to forbid both English and others not to bring into this land any pitch, tar, hemp, flax, ashes, deal boards, spars, masts, or any other eastern goods except the native commodities of their own several countries but in English ships. And they shall according to their bounden duties daily pray to God for the long and prosperous reign of your Highness over us.

Reasons to induce the granting of the said petition.

Inprimis the Netherlanders have eaten out the shipping belonging to the eastern cities, who have left the trade wholly to the Hollanders for transportation of their native commodities into other countries, so that now themselves have only small barques who trade within their lands from port to port.

The Netherlanders by their practice, as in the aforesaid petition, have much decayed the trade and shipping of this land and will also in time bring our shipping into utter decay.

There is employed in that trade about 200 sails of ships yearly in bringing into this land hemp, flax, cordage, pitch, tar, corn, ashes, copper, wax, Polish wool, yarn, poldavis, coarse linen, masts, deals, spars, wood of divers sorts and divers other commodities.

The Netherlanders return little or no commodities for the goods they bring in, other than coin, gold or silver, as well for their freight as the proceed of their goods, which may by circumstance be proved for that they return their ships empty without employment of their money in any commodities, and heretofore they have for their goods and freight made

---

[1] SP 14/115/109. See above, p. 13.

their bargain to receive groats, pieces of ninepence and such other coins as have best fitted their profit.

The Netherlanders buy the aforesaid goods at the same market the English buy, and with their ready money they carry they buy 30 in the hundred better cheap than the English, because the English carry cloths and other native commodities which they have heretofore given in barter for the eastern commodities, whereby they overthrow the English merchants and shipping, and besides they have a great advantage in the cheapness of their freight.

Heretofore the English merchants have vented in the eastern parts yearly 25,000 cloths worth £250,000, whereby [whereas] now they vent not above 7,000 or 8,000 cloths which are sent from London, Ipswich, Newcastle, York, Hull and the western ports.

More the English have sent in conyskins and other peltry ware, £8,000. More in white leather, coals, lead and other English commodities for above £6,000. More in foreign commodities to the value of £8,000.

The proceed whereof was wholly returned in the commodities of the eastern countries before named. For bringing home thereof there hath yearly been employed at least 100 sail of English ships, beside the English hath yearly freighted there at least 100 sail of Netherlanders to bring in the gross commodities of that country. But now of late the Netherlanders are fallen into that trade for this country and bring hither all those commodities better cheap than the English can by the reasons aforesaid.

For prevention whereof we are of opinion that his Majesty may for the strengthening and increasing of his decayed navigation by proclamation forbid all strangers whatsoever to bring any gruff goods into these dominions other than in English ships except the native commodities of their countries, so shall the English be encouraged to build shipping and set his Majesty's subjects on work and thereby breed and increase mariners for the general occasion when it shall be needful.

In general.

The Netherlanders beside this trade aforesaid take freight from one foreign part to another and carry commodities, the least their own but of other countries, whereby they do not only weaken all other nations in their shipping but so in exceeding manner they increase their own, which makes them so strong at the seas that they neglect the respect they owe to their neighbour princes and make them bold to offer many insolent wrongs.

And lastly the Netherlanders bring as many foreign commodities as they can, ready wrought. As mainly heretofore flax hath been brought into this land undressed which now they bring ready dressed to the spinner's hand, the dressing whereof hath here in London and in the suburbs maintained above 300 households who did maintain in each household some 6, some 8, and some 10 servants, which now for want of the aforesaid work are fallen into great poverty.

[*Subscribed in another hand*] The consideration of this petition is by his

Majesty referred unto Sir Thomas Smyth, Sir John Wolstenholme, Sir William Russell, Nicholas Leatt and Thomas Stile, who are to report to his Majesty their opinions therein. June 26, 1620.

[*Signed*] G. BUCKINGHAM

(b) *Report of the referees, 1620*[1]

In all humbleness and obedience to your Majesty's pleasure signified unto us upon this petition by the right Honourable the Lord Marquis of Buckingham, we have taken into our consideration and due examination all the several points of this petition and do agree with these petitioners that the Netherlanders by their policy, cheapness of freight, and other advantages have eaten out and consumed the shipping of the eastern cities, and that our trade and shipping for those parts are also at present by the like advantages in a consumption if by your Majesty's wisdom and providence it be not prevented, and this consumption doth plainly appear by the decay of our trade and want of employment of our shipping, for this last year there hath been transported from London little more than one third part of the cloths of former years and little more than one half of the shipping formerly employed by these petitioners. And upon examination we do find that there is employed yearly in the trade of Norway and this of the Sound for England 200 sail of the Netherlands shipping being all ships from 80 and 100 to 300 tons, which may also employ at the least 2,000 of their mariners, the which employment of shipping and mariners if it were made by your Majesty's subjects it would greatly diminish their shipping and greatly strengthen the navy of this kingdom. The freight of their shipping may yearly amount unto the sum £30,000, the most part whereof as we conceive is transported in coin and bullion to the great hurt of his Majesty's kingdom, the laws for employment not extending unto moneys received for freight.

The advantages by which they do undermine not only the trade of these petitioners but of all other your Majesty's merchants in general are principally two, the cheapness of freight and the merchandising with moneys. For of late years all moneys are raised to such an exorbitant value beyond the ancient standard and the true worth thereof through all Germany, Prussia, Poland and Muscovia and all those eastern countries as the Netherlanders do advance upon their moneys 30 in the hundred profit, by which excessive gain upon their moneys they are able to lose 20 in the hundred in their returns of eastern commodities and be yet great gainers in their adventures, whereby in time it must of necessity follow, that the merchants of this kingdom will be compelled to forsake and give over all those eastern trades and so consequently all the shipping employed by them. How to prevent this great mischief by these enhancing of moneys and to reduce them either to their ancient or some equal standard

[1] SP 14/111/126.

through all Christendom we most humbly refer to your Majesty's great wisdom, being a thing far beyond our capacity.

Under your Majesty's gracious favour, for remedy whereof we in our opinions conceive that there is no other present course to be taken but by your Majesty's royal proclamation to prohibit the importation of any those eastern commodities but in the native shipping of your Majesty's kingdoms except the shipping of those countries where those commodities grow, as your Majesty hath already been graciously pleased to grant unto the Levant company whereof there is already good fruits.

All which we most humbly submit to your Majesty's princely judgment.

[*Signed*] THOMAS SMYTHE, JOHN WOLSTENHOLME, WILLIAM RUSSELL, NICHOLAS LEATT, THOMAS STYLL.

2

TWO PAPERS CONCERNING THE EASTLAND TRADE FROM THE PARLIAMENT OF 1621[1]

(*a*) *Reasons of the Eastland merchants showing the decay of their trade*

1. First although moneys of late are excessively risen in the Eastland parts and in Germany yet the cloth and other native commodities of those countries rise not proportionably to the moneys. By means whereof, moneys being risen upwards of 50 per cent within less than two years last past in those countries, the English are enforced to endeavour the sale of their cloth ratable to the true value of their moneys, which far exceeding the rates of former times (before the rising of moneys) and the prices of cloth now made in those countries, there is by this means far less quantities of English cloth vented than otherwise would be.

2. The Hollanders' excessive gains by merchandising with ready moneys and their means thereby to make three returns in a shorter time than the English can one, together with their free liberty to import into England the native commodities of the eastern parts, having also much cheaper freights and in regard of the profit by exporting their freight in moneys that the ships do make, and paying less custom in the Sound of Denmark than the English, enforce our nation to endeavour to sell their cloth proportionable to their estimation of their moneys and so to raise their charge of maintenance solely for them and their families by the sales of cloth, for that by returns in foreign commodities the exporters of our native commodities are not able to keep market with the stranger merchandising with ready moneys.

3. Whereas formerly by means of the English merchants trading for Eastland have had for the most part the sole importation of Eastland

[1] SP 14/118/138, 139. See above, p. 13.

commodities into England, and thereby raising some benefit were enabled to afford the cloth and other commodities of England at indifferent rates, and consequently in greater quantities: now by means of the Hollanders trading and importing the foreign commodities as aforesaid, as also in regard divers shopkeepers of London send or remit over their moneys to buy East country commodities in Holland, and bring the same into England, the English merchant exporting the manufactury of the land is already in part, and likely to be in short time wholly, discouraged and driven out of trade.

4. The great charge which the English exporting our cloth are of necessity enforced to undergo, whereof the cloth made in foreign countries is wholly freed, the stranger by the cheapness of his being encouraged to increase his cloth making and ours by the great charge depending thereon being endeared, is not the least cause that our cloth is vented in lesser quantities than otherwise it would be.

5. For no cloth is more esteemed in the East parts (the prices and goodness indifferently considered) than our English cloth, and the only means to weary out the stranger from making his cloth and put down his looms, is to afford it at indifferent rates. Whereby the stranger in short time may be forced to surcease making and by that means greater quantities of our cloth vented and at better prices, and the English merchant enabled to give better prices to the encouragement of all the woolgrowers, clothiers and others depending thereon.

6. Amongst the great charges imposed upon cloth exported, the pretermitted customs lately raised is 4s. upon a short stuff ['Suff' = Suffolk is probably intended] cloth dyed and dressed, and for piratage 20d. upon the same, which we find to be so great a burthen to the trade as that the Eastland merchants are not able in regard of the dearness of cloth, by means of this and other accustomed charges amounting together to 30s. sterling at the least upon a cloth under £7 price, either to vent that quantity which otherwise they might or yet to raise so much clear benefit towards their great adventures (as the times now are) as the said late imposed charge of pretermitted customs and piratage do alone amount unto.

Wherefore we humbly pray this most honourable assembly will be pleased to take some course that the merchants may be respited from payment of this pretermitted custom, for the cloth they intend to ship this spring until further order be therein taken.

The relief and reformation whereof and of all other grievances they most humbly submit to this most honourable assembly.

(b) *Collections deduced from the said [merchants trading] into the eastern countries showing in part the cause of the great scarcity of silver in England, and some remedy for the same.*

The King of Poland having by the space of four years last past farmed his mint at Bromberg to certain Hollanders they by degrees have so embased their moneys as that the accustomed silver coins of Poland, Muscovia, Lettow and Prussia, which were wont to be very ordinary and common in payment, are wholly exhausted and changed up by those minters, and base coin by 40, 50, 60 and 70 per cent made thereof, and those base coins current in payment at the same rates the former were.

By which means the rixdollar which 18 months last was worth but 50 Polish groshes are now current at 75 and Spanish royals and silver money of England and other nations are also enhanced ratably, in so much as silver bearing so high a rate there hath been brought into those parts by estimation of English coin £50,000 per annum for these four years space.

The Hollanders finding the great profit arising by moneys, coined in their own countries certain pieces of coarser silver of 28 and 30 stivers the piece and dollars, by which coins they gained from 30 to 50 per cent according to the rising of moneys in the eastern parts, and with the said coins bought the commodities of those places, many of them making three returns and more in one year, which made such plenty of Hollands dollars, 30 stiver pieces and 28 stiver pieces, that the most part of payments made by merchants at Danzig, Elbing and Königsberg in the last four years was in the said Holland money, which the Jews, Russes, Poles and Armenians changed up in great abundance and carried into other remote countries rather than they would take the King of Poland's base money coined by the said minters.

From these grounds it plainly appeareth that not only the many thousands of dollars in former times brought by the Merchants Adventurers from Hamburg and by the Eastland merchants from Danzig and other parts of Prussia into England are now wanting and not brought at all, but the same species and great quantities of other silver which by all probability must be Spanish royals and English money, is coined by the Hollanders into the several sorts of coin aforesaid and carried by them into Prussia and other eastern parts, and never returned back again, for that all sorts of money go there at far higher rates than they do here, and being thus embased can never be returned hither to yield profit to the merchant.

And further the Hollanders with ready money so coined and carried by them into the East country, do drive the greatest part of that trade and do not only hinder the vent of English cloth in those parts (the Eastland merchants having formerly vented 8,000 cloths yearly from London and cannot now vent 3,000) but in return for that ready money import into this kingdom eastern commodities in great abundance, which they sell here for ready money and export very little of our native commodities or none at all, and consequently they must export money to the consuming the treasure of this land, the overthrow of the Eastland trade (so necessary for this kingdom), the decay of clothing, of navigation and divers manufactures depending thereupon.

Under favour of this most honourable assembly we conceive that it is not the least means to bring money into this kingdom to have free trade in corn. If therefore it might be provided that (after importation of corn from [foreign] parts into this kingdom and payment of custom due to the King's Majesty at landing thereof) it may be lawful and free for the merchants importers or for any other to whom they shall sell the same, at their pleasure without the contradiction, let or hindrance of any magistrate or person, general or private, and without paying any custom or impost for the same, to export the corn so imported.

Then would English merchants be encouraged to furnish Spain, Portugal and Italy with good quantities of corn, for which store of moneys may lawfully be returned into England, those places being now for the most part served with corn by the Hollanders, who fetch all the said corn from the eastern parts and by means of that trade bring home moneys plentifully to their great advantage, and this kingdom's disadvantage.

Whereas were the corn trade free as before remembered the Eastland merchants might be encouraged to barter store of cloth for corn in those parts, which often may be had for cloth, when moneys is not to be gotten. And although corn should be very plentiful in England (as God be thanked now it is) yet it may easily be proved that this kingdom cannot spare a tenth part of that proportion which is yearly sent for those southern parts, neither is our English corn (especially rye) so well liked there nor so fit for transportation.

3

AN ACT OF THE PRIVY COUNCIL, 17 MAY 1622; IN FAVOUR OF THE CLOTHIERS OF SUFFOLK AND ESSEX[1]

Whereas upon a petition lately presented to the Board by the clothiers of the county of Suffolk and Essex complaining that they were disabled from going forward in their trade by reason of the great quantity of cloths lying upon their hands for which they could find no utterance or vent, it was thought meet that if the Eastland merchants did not forthwith buy off their cloths, the clothiers themselves should have free liberty, as was then desired, to ship forth their cloths into foreign parts, so as they carry them to the said markets and places of residence used by the said merchants; it was accordingly this day ordered that in case the Eastland merchants have not bought up the cloths, but that the market is still clogged therewithal to the prejudice and decay of trade, the Lord High Treasurer of England do give order to the officers of the ports to permit the said clothiers to ship and transport their cloth into foreign parts, as aforesaid, without let or interruption.

[1] *A.P.C. 1621–1623*, pp. 223–4. See above, p. 27.

4

TEXT OF THE LEVANT COMPANY'S PROCLAMATION OF 1615[1]
COMPARED WITH THE EASTLAND COMPANY'S PROCLAMATIONS
OF 1622 AND 1630[2]

(*a*)　*The proclamation of 1615 showing the variances of that of 1622*

By the King.

A proclamation, prohibiting the bringing in of any commodities *traded from the Levant* [1622: traded by the Eastland merchants] into this kingdom; as well by subjects as strangers, not free of that company; also containing a publication of certain statutes, for the restraint of all his Majesty's subjects, from shipping any commodities in strangers' bottoms, either into this kingdom, or out of the same.

It is a great part of our princely care, to maintain and increase the trade of our merchants, and the strength of our navy, the one being as the veins whereby wealth is imported into our estate, and the other as principal sinews for the strength and service of our crown and kingdom:

Whereas therefore the society and company *of our merchants trading the Levant seas* [1622: of our Eastland merchants, trading the Baltic seas], have by the space *of thirty years past* [1622: of forty years past], at the least, had a settled, and constant possession of trade in those parts and have had the sole bringing in of the commodities of those countries, *as namely currants, cotton wools, wines of Candy, galls, etc.* [1622: as namely hemp, flax, potashes, soapashes, Polonia wool, cordage, yarn, Eastland linen cloth, pitch, tar and wood] whereby our kingdom hath been much enriched, *our great ships* [1622: our ships] and mariners set on work, and the honour and fame of our nation and kingdom spread and enlarged *in those remote parts* [1622: in those parts]:

And whereas, for their further encouragement, the said company have had, and enjoyed by letters patents under the great seal of England, *as well in the time of the late Queen, as in our own time* [1622: in the time of the late Queen Elizabeth] privilege for the sole bringing in of the said commodities, *with general prohibitions and restraints, as well of natural subjects, being not free of that society, as of all strangers and aliens whatsoever, to bring in any of the said commodities, contrary to the privilege of the said company* [1622: with general prohibitions and restraints of others not licensed and authorised by the said letters patents, to traffic or trade contrary to the tenor of the same letters patents]:

We minding the upholding and continuance of the said trade, and not to suffer that the said society shall sustain any violation or diminution of

---

[1] SP 14/187/40.
[2] Printed by Sellers, *Acts and Ordinances*, pp. 151 ff. Merely verbal differences are not recorded.

their liberties and privileges, have thought good to ratify and publish unto all persons, as well subjects as strangers, the said *privilege* [1622: privileges] and restraints, to the end that none of them presume to attempt anything against the same: and do hereby straitly charge and command all our customers, comptrollers and all other our officers at the ports, and also the farmers of our customs and their deputies and waiters, that they suffer not *any currants, cotton wool, wines of Candy, galls* [1622: any hemp, flax, potashes, soapashes, Polonia wool, cordage, yarn, Eastland linen cloth, pitch, tar or wood] nor any other commodities whatsoever, brought from any the foreign parts or regions, wherein the said company have used to trade, to be landed, except only such as shall be brought in by such as are free of the said company. [1622: Provided always that the importation of corn and grain be left free and without restraint; anything herein contained to the contrary notwithstanding.]

Furthermore, whereas there hath been in ancient time, divers good and politic laws made against the shipping of merchandises in strangers' bottoms, either inward or outward, as namely the statutes of 5 Richard II, 4 Henry VII, 32 Henry VIII etc. which laws have of later years been much neglected, to the great prejudice of the navigation of our kingdom: we do straitly charge and command, that the said laws be from henceforth duly put in execution *upon the great and grievous pains* [1622: upon the pains] therein contained, and upon pain of our high indignation and displeasure towards all our officers and ministers, which shall be found slack and remiss in procuring and assisting the due execution of the said laws:

Given at Whitehall, the seventeenth day of April, in the thirteenth year of our reign of England, France and Ireland, and of Scotland the eight and fortieth. [1622: Given at our Court at Theobalds, the one and twentieth day of July, in the twentieth year of our reign of England, France and Ireland, and of Scotland the five and fiftieth.]

God save the King.

(b) *The proclamation of 1630*

By the King.

A proclamation reviving and enlarging a former proclamation made in the reign of King James prohibiting the bringing in of any commodities traded by the Eastland merchants into this kingdom, as well by subjects as strangers, not free of that company; with a publication of certain statutes for the restraint of all his Majesty's subjects, from shipping any commodities in strangers' bottoms, either into, or out of this kingdom.

It is a great part of our royal care, like as it was of our royal father of blessed memory deceased, to maintain and increase the trade of our merchants and the strength of our navy as principal veins and sinews for the wealth and strength of our kingdom.

Whereas therefore the society and company of our Eastland merchants, trading the Baltic seas, have by the space of fifty years at the least, had a settled and constant possession of trade in those parts and have had both the sole carrying thither of our English commodities, and also the sole bringing in of all the commodities of those countries as namely hemp, yarn, cable-yarn, flax, potashes, soapashes, Polonia wool, cordage, Eastland linen cloth, pitch, tar and wood, whereby our kingdom hath been much enriched, our ships and mariners set on work, and the honour and fame of our nation and kingdom spread and enlarged in those parts:

And whereas for their further encouragement, the said company have had and enjoyed by letters patents under the great seal of England, in the time of the late Queen Elizabeth, privileges, as well for the sole carrying out to those countries of all our English commodities, as also for the sole bringing in of the abovenamed commodities of the said countries, with general prohibitions and restraint of others not licensed and authorised by the said letters patents, to traffic or trade contrary to the tenor of the same letters patents:

We minding the upholding and continuance of the said trade, and not to suffer that the said society shall sustain any violation or diminution of their liberties and privileges, have thought good to ratify and publish unto all persons, as well subjects as strangers, the said privileges and restraints, to the end that none of them presume to attempt anything against the same: and we do hereby straitly charge and command all our customers, comptrollers and all other our officers at the ports, and also the farmers of our customs and their deputies and waiters, that they suffer not any broad cloth, dozens, kerseys, bays, skins or such-like English commodities, to be shipped for exportation to those parts, nor any hemp, flax dressed or undressed, yarn, cable yarn, cordage, potashes, soapashes, Polonia wool, Eastland linen cloth, pitch, tar or wood nor any other commodities whatsoever of those foreign parts and regions, wherein the said company have used to trade, to be landed, except only such as shall be brought in by such as are free of the said company. Provided always that the importation of corn and grain be left free and without restraint; anything herein contained to the contrary notwithstanding.

Furthermore, whereas there hath been in ancient time, divers good and politic laws made against the shipping of merchandises in strangers' bottoms, either inward or outward, as namely the statutes of 5 Richard II, 4 Henry VII, 32 Henry VIII which laws of later years have been much neglected, to the great prejudice of the navigation of our kingdom: we do straitly charge and command, that the laws be from henceforth duly put in execution and that none of the said company, nor any other be permitted to export or import any of the abovementioned commodities in other than English bottoms, upon the pains in the said statutes contained, and upon pain of our high indignation and displeasure towards all our officers and ministers, which shall be found slack and remiss in procuring and assisting the due execution of the said laws.

Given at our Court at Whitehall, the seventh day of March 1629 in the fifth year of our reign of Great Britain, France and Ireland.

God save the King.

5

A PETITION BY THE EASTLAND COMPANY, 30 JANUARY 1624, ABOUT THE SOAP BUSINESS[1]

[*Endorsed*] The Eastland merchants' demands delivered the 30 of January 1623.

January 30, 1623.

The humble answer of the Eastland merchants and their request to his Majesty's commissioners concerning that part of the new soap business which concerneth their trade.

According to direction from your Honours we have considered of Sir John Bourchier's proposition to make soap of the materials of the kingdom, and although concerning the work itself much may be objected wherein we neither are nor may require to be satisfied, assuring ourselves that his Majesty and the state will take sufficient care that the commonwealth be not wronged under a fair show of benefit, yet concerning our trade we humbly show our opinions.

First, whereas a great quantity of ashes are now on the company's hands, the rumour of this alteration hath caused a great stand in them, of which we are already too sensible, the soapboilers refraining to buy more than serves their present use, fearing they shall shortly meet with some alteration in their trade.

Secondly, if ashes (now about a fourth part of our returns) be taken away, we are sure to be exceedingly straitened in our returns for the time to come, which will hinder the exportation of cloth and impair the navigation of the kingdom, if some course be not taken to supply the want of ashes. Yet if this new way of making soap be found upon due trial so beneficial to the commonwealth as to us it is propounded, we must submit to the wisdom of the state and, as well-willers to a public good, propound what for the present we conceive may help our trade in the want of ashes.

First, we humbly desire that some speedy course may be settled for the taking of those ashes which are now on our hands at a reasonable and convenient price, that we may be the better able to buy cloth this spring,

[1] SP 14/158/63. See above, p. 44.

because many men's stock now lying dead in ashes by means of this new business, they are altogether disabled to proceed in their trade as formerly they have done, and must be forced to petition his Majesty for relief, that either the soapboilers or some others may ease them of that burthen which this business hath cast too heavily upon them.

Secondly, whereas his Majesty hath graciously provided for us by his late proclamation that we should have the sole importation of East country commodities, there seems to be some defect in the penning of the same, but certainly there is much more abuse in the execution; some would interpret his Majesty's meaning to be, that no man shall fetch such commodities in the East country, but if he find them elsewhere he may bring them in, as if the words had reference to the places where we are privileged and not to the commodities of that country growth; but the principal abuse is that the customers take all entries which are brought unto them, especially in the remote parts and ports of this kingdom: wherefore we humbly desire that the true sense and meaning of his Majesty's grant may be published and confirmed that hereafter our privileges be not infringed.

Thirdly, whereas it is conceived that each country may bring in the commodities of its own growth, we find that divers abuses pass under that colour, the Hollanders bringing in much flax and hemp of the East country growth, having only altered their properties by dressing the flax and hemp, and sometimes spinning the flax into thread and turning the hemp into cable yarn and cordage, and they pretend it is of their own country growth, whereby they do not only hinder us in our returns but (as probably may be gathered) deceive his Majesty of a great part of his custom and carry out money for a great part of what they bring in, but certainly they by this means hinder the employment of a great number of his Majesty's subjects who formerly have lived well with their families by dressing flax and hemp and making thread; wherefore if it please his Majesty to forbid the bringing in of dressed flax, dressed hemp, tow, linen yarn black brown and white, brown coloured thread, cable yarn and cordage, to any but the Eastland merchants and Muscovy company in their several privileges, it will be some help to us in our returns, but a far greater benefit to the commonwealth in settling many thousand of the poor on work.[1]

Fourthly, whereas if ashes be taken away from us, for want of other commodities we shall be forced either to carry out less cloth or to bring some money, which we cannot do without great loss, the common coin minted in those parts being base and nowhere else current, and dollars

---

[1] The two preceding paragraphs are the gist of a rough undated paper, SP 14/135/60, which, however, has a slight addition concerning those who have brought in Eastland goods from places outside the Eastland company's privileges: 'Merchant Adventurers and others have brought in divers Eastland commodities from Hamburg and the Low Countries, supposing that having found them in their own privileges they might bring them in notwithstanding the proclamation.'

and ducats lately risen to more than double their old value; wherefore if it please his Majesty to order (according to a proposition which hath been made unto us) that ten in the hundred be allowed unto us yearly towards the loss of such moneys as (in lieu of ashes) we shall bring in, being to the value of £30,000 a year or after that rate for so much thereof as we shall yearly bring in, we may the better (as we conceive) forbear ashes, till either moneys there grow scarcer or be forbidden to be exported.

Lastly, whereas divers from several parts of the land do daily infringe our privileges, both carrying out cloth at a less charge than we can and bringing back the commodities of that country contrary to our charter, all which particulars we cannot prosecute, and when we do begin with any the offenders plead law for themselves, as at present the clothiers do, against whom we have a suit depending in his Majesty's Court of Exchequer; we humbly desire that his Majesty will be pleased to pass an Act of Parliament for confirmation of our charter and privileges, that interlopers being restrained we may have better encouragement to go on in our trade.

6

INTERROGATORIES ADMINISTERED TO WITNESSES IN THE CASE BETWEEN THE GOVERNOR, ASSISTANTS AND SOCIETY OF EAST-LAND MERCHANTS COMPLAINANTS AND MR GEORGE ACTON, THOMAS HALES AND JOHN GOODWYN DEFENDANTS, IN THE COURT OF EXCHEQUER, 1629[1]

(a) *Interrogatories...on the part and behalf of the Governor Assistants and Fellowship of Eastland merchants....*

1. *Imprimis*, do you know the said defendants? How long have you known them, or any of them? Are they or any of them free of the Eastland company? Declare your whole knowledge herein.

2. *Item*, were the defendants and every of them clothiers? Did they exercise the trade of clothing, how long have they exercised that trade, and do they still continue the same?

3. *Item*, do the clothiers of Suffolk and Essex in the vent of their cloths depend only upon the Eastland merchants? Do they not also sell and put off their cloths to the East India company, the Muscovy company, the Turkey merchants, merchants of Barbary, and others? Declare your knowledge herein.

4. *Item*, did not the Eastland merchants proceed in their trade of buying and shipping cloth in the years of our Lord one thousand six hundred and twenty-six and one thousand six hundred and twenty-seven? And what

---

[1] E134/5 Chas. I, Easter 1. The witnesses' depositions (not printed here) are attached to the interrogatories. See above, p. 74.

quantity of cloth did they then buy and ship for and in those two years? Declare your knowledge herein and what you have heard concerning the same.

5. *Item,* did the defendants or any of them make offer of their cloths unto the Eastland merchants at reasonable prices as other clothiers then sold? Or did they not hold them at dearer rates than the market would bear, resolving (as their practice sheweth) to turn merchants and to ship their cloths themselves? And have they not given out speeches in contempt of the company's charter and privileges? Declare your knowledge herein and what you have heard concerning the same.

6. *Item,* did not the defendants about two years since at two shippings ship out one hundred thirty and odd cloths for the East country, deceitfully entering part of them for Amsterdam and part for Rochelle?

7. *Item,* wherein did the defendants make home their returns for the foresaid cloths? Did they not import hemp, flax and potashes, commodities of the East country growth and expressly mentioned and forbidden by proclamation to be imported by any but by the Eastland merchants, of which proclamation the defendants in their answer do confess they took notice? Declare your whole knowledge herein.

(*b*) *Interrogatories...on the part and behalf of George Acton, Thomas Hales, Henry Rowninge and John Goodwyn....*

1. *Imprimis,* do you know the Governor and company of Eastland merchants complainants and the said defendants or either of them, and how long have you known them?

2. *Item,* whether do you know believe or have credibly heard that divers of the clothiers in Suffolk and Essex and namely these defendants or any of them have had at several times for the space of those six or seven years now last past divers broad cloths lying at several times upon their hands, which they could not put off to any of the said company of Eastland merchants the complainants at such rates and prices as have been and was usual and reasonable then and heretofore and since to do? And was not the work and livelihood of a multitude of the poor people by the want of the venting of such their cloths and other men's cloths in Essex and Suffolk much decayed thereby? Declare your knowledge herein and whether do you know or have heard that divers clothiers this last year past had many cloths lying upon their hands which they could not sell, and would have made more if they had had utterance for those which were upon their hands.

3. *Item,* do you know believe or have credibly heard that they these defendants together with other clothiers in Suffolk and Essex had lost before the order made by the lords of the council, namely the seventeenth day of May 1622, the sum of one hundred thousand pounds or thereabouts, and that thereby the trade of clothiers was at a stand and much

decayed both with these defendants and other clothiers both in Essex and Suffolk, and the poor people whose work and livelihood dependeth upon clothing brought into great want and beggary and likely to mutiny thereupon?

4. *Item*, whether do you know believe or have credibly heard that the now defendants together with other clothiers in Suffolk and Essex did about six years since prefer their petition unto the right honourable the lords of the privy council, complaining that they were disabled for going forward in their said trade of clothing by reason of the great quantity of cloths that were upon their hands for which they could find no utterance, and did not the said lords of the privy council declare their opinion that if the Eastland merchants did not then forthwith buy all the cloths which then were upon the hands of these defendants and other of the said county of Essex and Suffolk that then these defendants and other the clothiers of Essex and Suffolk should have free liberty to ship forth their cloth into foreign parts and trade there? And is not this order shewed unto you the council's order? And whether did the said Eastland merchants buy of their said cloths according to the said order or not? Declare your knowledge.

5. *Item*, were not the cloth markets in England at the time of the said petition and at all times since clogged with cloths to the great prejudice and decay of the said trade of clothing, and were not bought out of the hands of these defendants or any other clothiers both in Suffolk and Essex neither by the now complainants nor any of their company nor any other Eastland merchants whatsoever, but the market remained continually clogged, albeit they these defendants and other clothiers of Suffolk and Essex did often offer to divers of them of the said company to sell them their cloths far better cheap than they formerly had usually sold? Declare your knowledge herein.

6. *Item*, was there not, as you know believe or have credibly heard, at all times when these defendants or any of them did transport or send any cloths into the East parts, sufficient and present utterance and sale of the same and for many more if they had been then there, and was not such their sending and transporting their said cloths much beneficial to the late King's Majesty and to his Majesty that now is and the increase of his and their customs and duties, and did not they these defendants pay double custom for the cloths by them so shipped and transported into those parts and did they not utter their cloths at the same market that the said company usually doth?

7. *Item*, whether do you know believe or have credibly heard that the said company of Eastland merchants or any of them did about the time of the said petition and since publish and give out that because that the times were troublesome that they did and would forbear to venture into the East country, and did also publish that the company was dissolved because in those times of war in those parts they were driven and put from their place of residence, and protested that they thought there would be

no more trading unto those parts for four years after, and what were the names of those merchants that did so protest and publish the same unto you?

8. *Item*, whether do you know believe or have credibly heard that it is an usual course of and practice amongst merchants to enter the customs for one place and to transport their commodities to another as occasion require, and that so to do is not any note or imputation of fraud or practice in any that so do neither is the King any ways defrauded in his customs or duties thereby? Declare your knowledge.

9. *Item*, have not these defendants or some of them or some others by their or some of their request to your knowledge been or as you have heard desired to be admitted free of the said company of Eastland merchants and have tendered such fines and composition as hath been usual in that kind, and have not they the Governor and officers or others of the said company refused to admit them thereunto and to accept of their fines and compositions?

7

PAPERS RELATING TO THE EASTLAND COMPANY'S
PROCLAMATION OF 1630[1]

(a) *An undated petition by the Eastland company*[2]

To the Right Honourable the Lords and others of his Majesty's most Honourable Privy Council.

The humble petition of the Eastland merchants resident at London, Ipswich, York, Hull and Newcastle.

Sheweth,

That the company of late years have laboured under many difficulties and discouragements in their trade, first heavy and insupportable losses at sea, secondly the burdens and dangers of war seated in Prussia, the place of their trade, and lastly (which is not the least grievance) the excessive trade of clothiers and mariners outward, and other interlopers both subjects and strangers who daily import Eastland commodities, not only through the Sound of Denmark, but from Hamburg, Amsterdam and other places, upon such advantages of freight and customs as the company can no way keep markets with them, and the shipping and navigation of the kingdom exceedingly suffers, and is like daily to decay unless present remedy be applied.

The petitioners therefore (hoping the late truce will settle their trade beyond sea) do most humbly entreat the favour of this honourable Board,

[1] See above, p. 76.
[2] SP 16/180/49.

for the settling and confirming of their privileges at home, that clothiers, mariners and all other interlopers both inward and outward being restrained, they may cheerfully proceed in their trade as formerly. And as in duty bound they shall ever pray etc.

(b)   An undated note[1]

The Eastland merchants do most humbly desire, that though the proclamation be penned in general words, yet that the order of the Board may particularly forbid the importation of Eastland commodities whether directly through the Sound of Denmark or from Hamburg, Amsterdam or other places, and to prevent all fraudulent practices, that the customers nor their deputies take any entries inward or outward for or from the East country unless the deputy or treasurer for the company dwelling and residing at the port do first pass and allow the same under his hand and seal, otherwise it will not appear who are brethren of the company and who not, and in case of false and collusive entries outward of clothiers or others and inward by such as to avoid the proclamation enter Holland flax, Muscovia hemp and the like, that upon notice or suspicion of the fraud bond be taken by the customer or the goods stayed as your Honours shall think meet.

(c)   An extract from the Privy Council register, 12 February 1630 (new style)[2]

Whereas a humble petition was this day presented to the Board by the merchants of the Eastland company... [here follows a recital of *(a)* above in so far as it concerns privileges at home] their Lordships upon due consideration had thereof being desirous to give the said merchants all furtherance and good encouragement in their said trade and to maintain and preserve them in their just privileges, have thought fit to refer the petitioners' complaints to the Lord Viscount Dorchester, Mr Vice-Chamberlain and Mr Secretary Coke, praying and requiring them upon due consideration had of the just privileges belonging to the said company to advise of a fit course for the settling and preserving of the same *de futuro* and to make report thereof to the Board.

(d)   An extract from the Privy Council register, 19 February 1630 (new style)[3]

...Forasmuch as upon report this day made to the Board by the said committee it appeared that the particulars aforesaid complained of by the said company were contrary and in violation of their charter, his Majesty's proclamation and several orders of this Board, and that the privileges demanded and insisted on by them were agreeable and warranted by the same, being made for the support and establishment of the said Eastland trade, and that the desire of the said company was only to have the privileges intended them by the said charter, proclamation and orders to be

[1] SP 16/180/50.   [2] PC 2/39/642.   [3] PC 2/39/652–654.

more particularly and clearly expressed and set down, by reason that they found by daily experience and to their great prejudice that the penning of the said proclamation and orders in general words gave the more colour to the said interlopers to make evasion of the same; their Lordships upon mature debate and advice had thereof, being careful (as always) to preserve and maintain companies of merchants in their just privileges and immunities, and well knowing how much the supporting and encouragement of this company in particular imports the service and benefit of his Majesty and the state, did think fit that the proclamation should be renewed with such additions and explanations as they have given in direction to Mr Attorney-General, and did further for the better clearing and understanding of the said orders and proclamation, declare and order as followeth viz. that it be expressly prohibited and forbidden unto all persons that are not members of the said company to import any Eastland commodities into this kingdom either directly through the Sound of Denmark or from Hamburg, Amsterdam or any other places. And for the preventing of all fraudulent practices of the said interlopers it is likewise ordered that the officers of the customs of the several ports of this kingdom, their deputies and clerk, be hereby required not to take any entries or suffer any good to be shipped or laden inwards or outwards from or for the East country by any persons whether members of the said company or others but only such as are first passed and allowed of by the deputy or treasurer of the said company residing in the said port under his hand and seal; and in case of suspicion or discovery of any false or collusive entries, either outward by clothiers or others or inward by such as to avoid the proclamation enter Eastland commodities under the title of Holland flax, Muscovia hemp, and the like for cable yarn and other goods, that they either stay the goods themselves or take sufficient bond of the parties to the just value to be answerable for their contempts; whereof the Lord Treasurer is hereby prayed and requested to take knowledge and to give speedy and effectual directions to the officers of the customs of the several ports of this kingdom, for the due observance and execution thereof accordingly as they and every of them will answer the contrary at their perils.

8

AN UNDATED COPY OF A PETITION BY THE EASTLAND COMPANY
ABOUT SOAP (1632)[1]

Sheweth,

That whereas a new way of making soaps out of the materials of the kingdom hath been many years in agitation and his Majesty by proclama-

---

[1] SP 16/279/70. Probably 1632, the proclamation referred to in the first paragraph being presumably Charles I's first proclamation about soap, dated 28 June 1632. See above, p. 45.

tion [hath] now published his royal purpose not only to redress abuses in the making of soap but that the manufacture of potashes and soap shall become the work of his own people; and at present authoriseth the new company of soapmakers and the deputies to search and mark all potashes of what nature soever and further [doth] covenant with them that when they shall declare themselves ready his Majesty will restrain the importation of all foreign ashes;

The petitioners in all humility offer the state of their trade in these following considerations to your Lordships' honourable and judicious view.

The Eastland company both from London and Ipswich export dyed and dressed cloth fully manufactured and fit for the garment, in which respect their trade concerneth not themselves alone but many thousands of his Majesty's subjects from the woolgrower to the poor workmen employed in making and finishing of cloth.

Money being scarce in the East Country, the greatest part mixed and base, and no exchange from thence, their returns lie wholly in commodities, of which potashes are a principal part.

When the company cannot sell cloth for money nor exchange it for other commodities they often barter for potashes, which makes their cloth trade more large and quick than otherwise it could possibly be.

Potashes are not of equal goodness in their first burning, and being subject to receive damage by air or water, the strength doth often in part decay after they are burnt; yet then they are not accessory to the ill smell that is in some soap. Weak and decayed ashes make less quantity of soap but make not soap the less sweet.

In the Eastland trade exportation and importation stand in such relation that the one prospers not without the other; if the importation or use of potashes (a fourth part of the company's returns) be restrained, the vent of a fourth part of the manufactured cloth exported then will be hindered.

His Majesty's customs will be much impaired by this restraint not in potashes alone but in dyeing stuff and cloth exported, and the employment of 1,000 or 1,500 ton of English shipping now set on work for importation of potashes will be hindered.

Lastly much woollen cloth being made in Prussia and Poland the clothmakers of those countries have long looked with an evil eye upon English cloth and have divers ways attempted to discourage the company in that trade. First they set prices upon English cloth since they have brought it under the bondage of Danzig seal, wherein the company in all humble thankfulness acknowledge his Majesty's royal favour and assistance to break that chain, though the success be yet doubtful; and now they are about to forbid all strained English cloth. Several pretences they have for each of these, but certainly their purpose and plot is to abate and consume the trade of English cloth, that more of their own looms might be set up;

if therefore his Majesty forbid the importation or use of potashes, a commodity belonging to the King, nobility and gentry of Poland, they may take occasion from thence to forbid the sale or wearing of English cloth, in which case the Eastland trade hitherto cherished as necessary and of great consequence to this kingdom shall not only be hindered but utterly overthrown.

The petitioners therefore most humbly entreat their Lordships' favour and mediation to his Majesty in their behalf, that since the search and marking of potashes doth nothing advance his Majesty's end for sweet soap, the Eastland company may not be subject to this new corporation in a commodity not at all used in their way; and that the liberty both for importation and use of foreign ashes may still be preserved as in former times.

And as in duty bound your petitioners shall daily pray etc.

9

TWO REPRESENTATIONS[1] BY THE EASTLAND COMPANY DESIRING
RESTORATION OF PRIVILEGE (? 1649 AND 1656)

(a) [Endorsed] *Representation of the Governor, Assistants and Fellowship of Eastland merchants. [In another hand] Presented 10th December, to be considered 17th December [? 1649].*

To the Right Honourable the Great Council of State, the humble representation of the Governor, Assistants and Fellowship of Eastland merchants.

Being, upon our late humble petition to this Great Council, commanded to present in writing the condition of our trade, together with the obstructions therein and the remedies proper to be applied thereto; we do, in pursuance thereof, humbly show....[2]

(b) [Endorsed] *Eastland company's petition and representation 1655. Referred 1 June 1656. [In another hand] This petition and representation with his Highness' reference to the Committee for Trade was presented the 4 January 1655.*

To his Highness Oliver, Lord Protector of the Commonwealth of England, Scotland and Ireland.

---

[1] (a) SP 18/205/41; undated, attributable to 1649. See above, p. 86.
(b) SP 18/123/16, 1. See above, p. 125.
[2] For the continuation of (a) see below.

Sheweth.[1]

That our predecessors were, about 300 years past, at their great charge and hazard, the first discoverers of the trade into the Baltic seas; *whereupon Queen Elizabeth did, in the 21 year of her reign, incorporate them into one body; granting to them a charter* [1656: in which the English had notwithstanding no great interest until it pleased Queen Elizabeth, in the 21 year of her reign, to incorporate them into one body; granting to them a charter under the Great Seal] not only for their encouragement, but also that they might be able (under a well regulated government) to vindicate the trade out of the usurped power of strangers (who then wholly possessed it), to advance it in the hands of skilful and native merchants, and to relieve and protect it abroad from foreign injuries. And with what success of honour and benefit to this nation the same hath been pursued, the precedents of former times do abundantly testify. *Yet for the clearer satisfaction of your Honours with the notable advantages which this commonwealth hath enjoyed by this trade under an orderly government,* [1656: Yet for clearer manifestation of the notable advantages which an orderly government hath formerly produced,] we shall particularly declare some of the effects thereof, which have fallen within the compass of our own memory and experience.

1. We have, not many years past, exported yearly 14,000 broad cloths dyed and dressed and fully manufactured, besides kerseys, northern dozens, perpetuanas and other commodities of wool to the like value, and skinnery ware of all sorts, as by the custom house books may appear. Notwithstanding which great quantities exported by us, our care hath still been, not to debase the commodity by under selling the same at any mean price; but rather in case of too full a market, to preserve it in magazines beyond the sea till an opportunity of better sale; by which means the credit of our English manufactures hath been so upheld in foreign parts, that our main profit hath been raised upon the same out of the purse of the stranger, and not upon our returns here sold to the English, as now it is.

2. Having made this advantage by our English commodities abroad, we were thereby enabled to make plentiful returns in hemp, flax, pitch, tar, potashes, tallow, masts, oars, deals, pipestaves, and trunnels, clapboard, wainscot, oaken boards, and fir timber for building, linen cloth and yarn, and all sorts of canvas, saltpetre, wool for hats, wax, sturgeon, bed-ticking, buckram, goat- and kidskins, copper, iron, steel, and other commodities; most of them being of absolute necessity for the strength and service *of this common wealth* [1656: of this land] and for employment of the poor. With all which this land was furnished at reasonable rates (and oft times cheaper than the same had been bought beyond sea) besides an overplus in gold

---

[1] From this point the texts are similar, with only a few important differences. What follows is the text of 1649, noticing all the material additions and variations made in 1656.

and silver, which we have frequently imported in great quantities, to the augmentation of the general stock of this nation. And of these commodities we also kept a magazine in England, not only for a constant supply of the markets here, but sufficient to furnish other foreign places; and that at easier prices than since the government of the company hath desisted; as may easily be demonstrated.

3. By this vast trade out and home we have employed about 200 sail of English ships yearly, all of great burthen, and fit upon any occasion for the defence and service of the common wealth; and by this means this company (whilst under government) hath proved a singular nursery of seamen; for whose breeding and maintenance we have by good computation disbursed in the way of freight £60,000 per annum; it being also our constant care to enjoin our members to the employment and use of English ships only, if [*1656 omits this clause*] such were to be had, and none others.

4. Nor is this all the benefit that hath accrued to this nation by virtue of our government: for whilst we have been looked upon as an united society, we have been known to be able to make or divert a trade [1656: as indeed we were by settling our residence where we found most advantage], and consequently to oblige cities, to procure right, and sometimes to prevent public misunderstandings; and thereby have been rendered far more considerable instruments to serve and honour our own country in several occasions, especially in trade; in reference to which we have obtained such immunities in foreign parts, as have equalled if not exceeded those of their natives; as in particular a freedom from taxes and sundry burthens which the natives themselves undergo; a liberty to buy and sell not only with the citizens where we trade, but with strangers also; a power to preserve the estate of any Englishman dying in [1656: Prussia and] Poland, which by the law of that country is confiscated to the prince; a power to end all differences between the English before our own officers, without being exposed to the snares and rigour of foreign laws; and if any injury were done by strangers to any particular factor, the same was resented as done against the whole body, and accordingly reparation procured by them with more facility and less expense; and also we were thereby in a better capacity to mitigate the customs and burthens apt to be laid upon trade by foreign princes; it being well known with what vast expense and pains this company hath laboured in several negotiations to the King of Denmark, having some years past, by God's blessing on their endeavours, removed those sad misunderstandings whereby the trade through the Sound was for a time obstructed, and ships and goods confiscated; and have not only recovered satisfaction from that king in some measure, but also opened the trade again for the future, reduced the excessive customs to those paid by other nations, and obtained an abolition of the hundredth penny, *wherewith the trade was long burthened* [1656: a tax wherewith we (and no other nation) have long been burthened]; and all this at the sole

charge of this company [1656: by which means having contracted a great debt, which is now required by our creditors, we are altogether unable to give satisfaction, for want of power to levy moneys, as we were wont to do for so public and necessary occasions]; which services were not to be effected by single persons, who are not able to make so vigorous resistance against oppressions, nor can expect that respect abroad which an united company may enjoy.

Decay of trade.

And indeed the benefits of such a well ordered association will be more visible upon consideration of the sad effects which the late suspension thereof hath produced in our trade, although we confess there want not other foreign causes; all of which, though we shall not now enumerate, yet we shall humbly lay open the great decay of this ample trade, together with the reasons of it and our fears of a total loss thereof, unless effectually and speedily prevented.

1. Our English manufactures are of late incredibly debased in the foreign places of our trade, occasioned by the loose trading of unskilful persons, who taking advantage of this liberty and our want of power to restrain them, carry over what their stock and credit will amount unto, and being there necessitated to take the present market, though to loss, do in a manner give away our native commodity; but being shopkeepers or retailers make the amends therein by their returns, which by their retail they advance far above that the merchant can make; but in the meantime the merchant is defrauded of his privileges, the native commodity brought into base repute, and the general stock of this land wasted; it being a great mistake to suppose that a licentious trade, disorderly carried on by a throng of inconsiderate and unskilful men, can augment or benefit commerce, either in the exportation of our own commodities outwards (since it cannot be imagined that any foreign nation will digest a greater proportion than they have occasion for, or the place is capable of, a glut of the market being rather a surfeit oppressing the stomach than satisfying hunger) or by affording foreign commodities cheaper here, since the contrary most evidently appears in most commodities far dearer now, when all sorts of men trade, than when solely in the company's hands; hemp and flax being dearer 20 per cent, tar 40 per cent, potashes (the prime material for soap) at five times the former value, masts, deals and other commodities much dearer than formerly [*1656 omits all after* 'company's hands']; so that whereas we have been wont to make our profit upon the stranger beyond the seas, by keeping our native commodity at an indifferent value, and thereby afforded the foreign commodity cheaper here, the contrary is now practised, to the great impoverishing of this land; we being unable to make a benefit on our English commodity abroad now that the same is so debased by unexpert persons; and therefore must necessarily advance our profit on the commodity imported. And we desire it may be seriously

considered what a diminution it is to the stock of this common wealth, to sell cheap native commodities for foreign dear, although [*1656 omits this clause*] a gain be afterwards made by the particular shopkeeper.

2. As an effect of this irregular trading and embasing of the English manufactures abroad, [*1656*: the employment of our English shipping is not only greatly diminished but] our cloth and other native commodities vented in the East parts is now contracted to a small proportion in respect of the former quantities there sold by us; especially if we take a calculation thereof out of the custom house books [*1656*: compared also with the quantities landed abroad], wherein so small a proportion is registered that we may confidently conclude that a great part of the cloth now carried into those parts pays no custom here.

3. [*1656 omits*] We are very sensible of a notable decay and almost a total disuse of our English ships, whereof scarce twenty have been this year employed in that trade; and if this loose trading continue, we have sufficient grounds to conclude that they will be the next year wholly laid aside; the stranger and interloper aiming only at their present gain, and finding the advantage of an easier freight paid in Flemish bottoms, which go at half the charge of our English ships. And whereas our special care, whilst we had power, was to prohibit under strict penalties any of the traders to use strangers' shipping, unless we were assured by authentic certificates that no English ships were to be had, the brethren of our own company are now unwillingly necessitated to make use of strangers' bottoms also; being otherwise unable to hold market with the stranger and interloper.

4. [*1656 omits*] And this general employment of Flemish bottoms gives also a greater advantage unto the Hollander to enter upon our trade, as well as to destroy our shipping; for the States being themselves merchants and deeply interested in this very trade, and it being so absolutely necessary to the subsistence of their commonwealth that they can neither eat nor drink without it, they are more intent upon the regulating of this trade than of any other; using all their interest and correspondency with foreign princes and applying all their power and endeavour to engross the same into their own hands; wherein they have already made a large progress through their politic associations, their advantages of sailing in slight vessels, ill manned and cheap freighted, yet secured by convoys at the public charge of the state; by which means they can import those foreign commodities at one half of the charge that we must pay in English ships, being well manned and fitted for defence and service; and they keeping also at Amsterdam a magazine of Eastland goods (as we were wont to have here) they are ready from thence to take the rise of all markets here; and so intercept us in the vent of our returns, making their gain by the public loss of this nation. By all which advantages taken from our confusion here, they will not be easily hindered from eating us out of the trade; which when they have totally gained, they may then set what prices

they please upon those foreign commodities, so necessary for this land (as they have already done in the spice trade of India), and (which is as bad) we shall not be able then, to set out a ship to sea, but at their pleasure.

And as an earnest of their intentions towards us upon such an opportunity it may not be unnecessary to mention the great trouble we find by the Hollanders vying with us in the East, upon our buying of any foreign commodity whereof they know there is a want here; for the sale of which having the freedom of our market here, as well as their own, they occasion an enhancement of the price of sundry useful commodities, some to double the rates heretofore paid, as tar, and others to five times the value, as potashes.

And if a restraint of the Hollander from this trade, and settling it wholly upon the English, may seem to reflect with inconveniency upon that state, it is answered that they have ever been (in the time of our government) wholly excluded from importing Eastland commodities hither; so that it is now a novelty to them to enjoy that freedom.

5. [*1656 omits*] The discredit of our manufactures abroad and diminution of that trade occasioneth the exportation of gold and silver out of this land, which is the customary practice of the stranger, as these late times do remarkably testify; and this enlargement of their trade will much more occasion that evil.

6. [1656: 3]. Great hath been of late the industry of strangers in Poland and Prussia to advance their manufacture of cloth, by procuring English workmen and stealing fuller's earth by Hollanders' means into those parts; and as great hath been the care of our company to prevent such unlawful conveyances; whereas an open trade will be much more help, and confirm them in these designs, to the destruction of our native commodities. And we dare boldly affirm that nothing hath more hindered the cloth-making beyond the seas, than government of companies here.

7. *We have great cause to fear that our want of government here will deprive us of those special immunities in foreign parts which our forefathers have with much pains obtained, and we at our great charge maintained to this day; of which we are in a great measure already sensible; for whereas our estate was wont to be secure in any town where our trade lay, we now find the contrary, the Danzigers taking opportunity from the discontinuance of our government to seize upon our warehouses and goods upon pretended quarrels and slight occasions. And we are in much fear of losing that special privilege which as a society we have long enjoyed, of preserving the estate of any of our nation dying in Poland, which by their law is confiscated to the king, and is at present strongly endeavoured to be put in practice there, to the ruin of many principals and merchants that have their estates in that country, unless prevented.*

[1656: 4.] Whereas we were able (whilst under government) to support ourselves and maintain our privileges wheresoever we resided, with honour and credit, the same are now even totally lost, as by woeful experience we find. For whereas our estates were wont to be secure in any town where our trade lay, it is now otherwise, the Danzigers taking opportunity from the discontinuance of our government to seize upon our warehouses and goods upon pretended quarrels and slight occasions. And that privilege is now also lost, which as a society we have long enjoyed, of preserving the estate of any of our nation dying in Prussia; which (or a great part thereof) is confiscated by a law of that country called the Caduct; which law is at present vigorously endeavoured to be put in practice, to the ruin of many principals and merchants that have their estates there, unless prevented. And a fresh instance of this kind appears by a late severe edict published by the senate at Danzig against the inhabiting of any Englishman in a house of his own within their jurisdiction; whereby (although there were no other cause) we are like to be excluded from that trade. And so are we not only deprived of our wonted privileges abroad, but subjected to these and other unusual burthens, now revived and imposed on us, when we are not in a capacity to repel them.]

Remedy.
And thus have we plainly laid open the state of our trade, with the advantage this nation hath received by an orderly and regular management thereof; and the present declining condition of it, together with the prime causes of such a change; *by all which this Great Council will doubtless quickly discern* [1656: by all which may easily be discerned the difference] between the benefits of government, and the ill consequences of what is called a free trade. And however we may be thought partial to ourselves in our advice, yet our conscience and duty to the common wealth enforceth us humbly to deliver this our opinion, that there will be no effectual way of remedying all or most of these diseases in this trade, but by renewing or confirming the incorporation of the traders, *under such a government and such power as they have formerly had*; [1656: under an orderly government as they have formerly had, or as your Highness in your great wisdom may think fit. (*The rest of the paragraph is omitted.*)] the sum of which hath been lately tendered to this Great Council, and copies of the whole are ready to be presented, upon your command to that purpose.
Nor can the carrying on of this trade under a regulated government be any way esteemed a monopoly, more than the incorporation of any city or town in England, or of any other society of merchants trading beyond the seas; especially since by the customs and orders of our company, any that are qualified for trading [1656: any merchant] may come in upon a *mean and inconsiderable fine of £20* [1656: mean and inconsiderable sum of money, usually paid at admittance, towards necessary charges]; every one of whom is afterwards left free to his own occasions, without the least limitation in commodities exported or imported, either for quantity or price, as in joint stock is usual. And as no merchant, so no port town of

this land is excluded from the benefit of this trade, which is not appropriated to the merchants of London only (as in most societies besides) but hath been freely communicated to York, Hull, Newcastle, Ipswich, Lynn, [1656: Exeter,] Plymouth, Bristol etc., that under a good government they might not only, at their pleasure, export their own native commodities, but also more directly furnish all parts with Eastland returns.

And our government being thus established, we shall not doubt but by degrees, and with time and patience, and the *further assistance of this State upon occasion* [1656: further assistance of your Highness],

To rescue this trade out of the hands of strangers,

To hinder the making of foreign draperies and advance the reputation of our own,

To prevent foreign shipping, and promote the English navigation,

To furnish this land with a constant supply *of corn* [1656: of naval] and other needful commodities of the East, at reasonable rates,

To renew our wonted custom of importing of coin, and prevent the exportation of it by strangers,

And to preserve the estate of factors dying abroad; with those other foreign privileges, not easily to be recovered, if once lost. [1656: To recover and preserve the estates of factors dying abroad; with those other foreign privileges, now lost,

And to raise moneys upon ourselves for payment of our debts, and defraying the needful charges of our trade, and for preserving the same for the public and future advantage of this nation.]

All which is humbly referred to the consideration and judgement of this Great Council. [1656: All which is humbly submitted to your Highness' great judgement.]

[1656, *at the foot in another hand*: His Highness is pleased to refer this petition and representation to the Committee of Trade, conceiving it a business very fit for and worthy of their consideration. 4 January 1655. John Thurloe.]

10

A PAPER SUBMITTED BY THE EASTLAND COMPANY TO A COUNCIL OF TRADE ON PRIVILEGE AT HOME[1] (? 1660)

Further reasons, humbly offered to the Right Honourable the Council for Trade, for support of the Company of Eastland merchants.

The trade of the Baltic seas, was above 300 years past, discovered by our predecessors at great charge and hazard; in which notwithstanding the

---

[1] It is taken from the papers of Thomas Papillon and is here reprinted from A. F. W. Papillon's *Memoirs of Thomas Papillon* (Reading, 1887), pp. 61 ff. A. F. W. Papillon seems to have attributed it to 1668 or 1669, but a more likely date is October 1660. Thomas Papillon was a member of a Council of Trade at both dates. Above, p. 138.

English had no great interest until it pleased Queen Elizabeth (21 Regni) to incorporate them by a charter; which was granted, not only for their encouragement, but also to enable them under a well ordered government to rescue the trade from the hands of other nations, who then almost wholly enjoyed it; and to advance it in the hands of skilful and native merchants; to protect it abroad from foreign injuries and oppressions. And with what success of honour and benefit to this kingdom the same hath been pursued, the precedents of former times do clearly testify, and may appear by the following instances, which have fallen within the compass of our own memory and experience.

1. We have in former years exported annually 14,000 broad cloths, fully manufactured, besides kerseys, perpetuanas, northern dozens, and other commodities of wool to the like value. Notwithstanding which great quantities exported by us, our constant care was, not to debase the commodity, by selling the same at mean rates; but rather, in the case of too full a market, to preserve it in magazines abroad till an opportunity of better sale; by which means the credit of our English manufactures hath been so upheld in foreign parts, that our main profit hath been raised upon the same, out of the purse of the stranger; and not upon our returns here sold to the English, as now it is.

2. Having made this advantage by our English commodities abroad, we were thereby enabled to make plentiful returns in hemp, flax, pitch, tar, potash, tallow, masts, oars, deals, copper, iron, steel, corn, and other commodities, being of absolute necessity for the strength and service of this land, and for employment of the poor: with all which this kingdom was furnished at reasonable rates (sometimes cheaper than the cost) besides an overplus in gold and silver, which we have frequently imported in great quantities, to the increase of the general stock of the nation: and of these foreign commodities we also kept a magazine in England; not only for a constant supply of the markets here, but sufficient to furnish other foreign places, and that at easier rates than since the time our government hath desisted.

3. In this large trade, out and home, we have employed about 200 English ships yearly, all of good burthen and fit for defence and service; by which means this company proved a singular nursery of seamen; having by computation disbursed in way of freight £60,000 per annum; it being also their constant endeavour and care, to use English ships only (if such were to be had) and no other; thereby performing the intent of the Act of Navigation before it was in being; and that with more advantage to the public interest of that trade, than is now produced by the Act.

4. Being looked upon abroad as an united society, we have been understood as able to make or divert a trade; and consequently to oblige cities, to procure justice, and to serve and honour his Majesty and his kingdoms, on several occasions; having obtained such immunities in foreign parts as

have equalled, if not exceeded, those of the natives; as particularly, a freedom from taxes, and several burthens which the natives themselves bore; a liberty to buy and sell, not only with the citizens where we traded, but with strangers also; a power to preserve the estate of any Englishman dying in Poland, which by the laws of that country is confiscated to the prince; a power to end differences of the English amongst themselves, without being exposed to the snares and rigour of foreign laws; and if any injury were done by strangers to any particular factor, the same was resented as done against the whole body, and reparation gained by them with more facility and less charge: which services, with many others, were not to be effected by single persons, who are not so able to resist injuries, nor can expect that respect abroad, which an united society may enjoy.

And that these advantages are to be accounted to a well regulated association may further appear by considering what contrary and sad effects have been produced since the government of this company hath been intermitted for these many years past, viz., since the beginning of the late unhappy troubles, for

1. Our native commodities are incredibly debased in the foreign places of our trade; which hath happened by the confused and uncontrolled trading of interlopers and unskilful persons of late years, and the continued trading of strangers now; by whose practices we being disabled to make profit of our English manufactures abroad, are necessitated to advance the same upon the foreign commodities imported; which we confess must prove a great diminution to the stock of this kingdom.

2. As an effect of this irregular trading and debasing the English manufactures abroad, our cloth and other commodities vented in the East parts, is contracted to a small proportion of the former quantities there sold by us: and of 200 English ships formerly employed in this trade, scarce — are now used in a year.

3. The discredit of our manufactures abroad, and the lessening of that trade occasion the exportation of gold and silver, which is the customary practice of the stranger, as these late times have abundantly testified: and the permission and enlargement of the trade of strangers will much more occasion that evil.

4. Great hath been the industry of strangers in Poland and Prussia of late years, to advance their manufactures of cloth, by procuring English workmen and stealing fullers' earth in those parts; and as great hath been the care of our company to prevent such conveyances; whereas an open trade will much more help and confirm them in those designs, to the destruction of our native commodities: and we dare boldly affirm, that nothing hath more promoted foreign clothing than the want of encouragement to corporations of merchants in these late times.

5. It is evident that through the want of government here we are already in great measure, and shall in a short time be totally deprived of what foreign privileges we have formerly had, and might still enjoy; and

instead thereof be exposed to unusual burdens, when we shall be wholly unable to expel them.

By all which may easily be discerned the benefits of government, and the ill consequences attending the want thereof: most of which mischiefs we humbly conceive will not be effectually remedied otherwise than by encouraging the traders with such privileges and power as they formerly had, and in particular with a continuance of the proclamation first granted by King James, and afterwards by his late Majesty, and since ordered to be renewed by his now Majesty. The sole question in this case seeming to be, whether the carrying on of this trade (so considerable in many respects) should be in the hands of his Majesty's subjects, or of strangers.

All which is humbly submitted.

II

A REPRESENTATION BY THE EASTLAND COMPANY TO THE
COUNCIL OF TRADE, 1660, ON TROUBLES ABROAD[1]

Presented 13th November 1660.

To the Right Honourable the Council for Trade.

The humble representation and petition of the Governor Assistants and Fellowship of the Merchants of Eastland.

Sheweth

That upon intimation received of the pleasure of this honourable council to this purpose we do with all alacrity and thankfulness both to his sacred Majesty and to your Honours humbly present the state of the trade into the Baltic Sea, Sweden, Denmark and Norway together with such grievances as are incumbent on the same.

1. And in the first place we cannot but remember the more than ordinary regard which this company (incorporated the 21 of Q. Elizabeth) hath from time to time received from his Majesty's royal progenitors in respect of the public advantages accruing to this nation, both by their great exportation of great quantities of cloth and all sorts of woollen commodities fully manufactured, and by importing coin and foreign commodities of absolute necessity for the strength and service of this kingdom and for furnishing the navy and employment of the poor (as hemp, flax, masts, pitch, tar etc.) besides the notable advantage of English shipping thereby, so we cannot but remain the more sensible of the discouragement we have for these last twenty years lain under for want of countenance and support in the due observance of our charter which hath produced sad effects, and almost a total loss of this important trade by the

[1] From a copy in the Council's records (B.M. Add. MS. 25115/23–30, 103). Above, p. 139–140.

intrusion and irregular and unrestrained trade of foreigners and interlopers, and by their debasing our English manufactures, and consequently
diminishing its vent abroad and augmenting the price of foreign commodities both there and here, losing sundry privileges obtained and settled
by us with great trouble and charge and exposing us to scorn and infamy
in the places of our trade, all which and more, hath happened by this
violation and breach made upon our government and charter, which as
it hath been the ruin of several traders (especially such as gave us the
interruption) having a main influence both upon our home and foreign
distempers.

2. In the Sound of Denmark to the ancient and sole duty of a rose
noble paid time out of mind by every ship passing to or fro, as an acknow-
ledgment for beacons and buoys kept all along that passage, there was in
1566 an exaction added called last gelt being a duty by the last or poundage
which continued uncertain and arbitrary till 1645 but so high that we were
then necessitated at a vast expense, and not without contracting a great
debt to employ commissioners into Denmark, by whose means not only
an ancient tax upon the English trade through the Sound called the hundred
penny was totally abolished; but likewise this other duty of last gelt was
reduced to a certain and more moderate rate not exceeding one per cent.
Yet the imposition though thus mitigated, may be judged unreasonable,
because the English have only a passage through the Sound, and proceed
for trade to other countries.

3. In Sweden the customs are exorbitantly high and arbitrary,
amounting in some goods to 20, 25 or 30 per cent if imported in English
ships, whereas a moderate custom is paid on their own vessels, which also
pay no duties in the Sound [and] do by consequence manage almost the
whole trade of Sweden.

And besides this burthen in customs the English even after payment
thereof are not masters of their own goods, which are opened and viewed
and then carried by their officers to a packhouse of their appointing, and
their detained, not without much injury to the merchants.

4. The English carrying salt to any ports of the Swedes in Livland, and
not being able to sell it without loss, are denied liberty to land there till
a fitter opportunity of sale which is a great discouragement to merchants
when they must either sell at a loss or bring their goods back again.

5. At Danzig a duty called toolag or excise which in reason and even
by their own law is payable by their natives, is notwithstanding laid as
a burthen upon the English.

6. And a greater burden lies on us also at that place for the citizens of
Danzig have long since for their own ends obtained a privilege from the
King of Poland, that no cloth should (on penalty of confiscation) be
vended in any part of his dominion, where the only vent thereof is, unless
the same were first stamped with the seal of that city, by which means we
are enforced to confine ourselves to that place as the staple of our trade,

although upon hard and worse terms than we might elsewhere enjoy, and under colour hereof that seal is set to base cloth made at Danzig and other adjacent places to the great disparagement of ours, and the increase of their own manufactures.

For remedy whereof it is humbly desired

1. That as his Majesty hath been graciously pleased upon our late humble petition to give order and put us into a way for confirmation of our charter, so it will please this honourable council to add some further-ance and expedition thereto, and since we cannot but hope that the parlia-ment upon experience of the late great defection, and apparent decay of trade for want of government, will in time think meet to add their approbation, we will humbly presume that your Honours will also see cause to become instrumental therein, and in promoting a trade so advantageous and necessary to this kingdom.

2. That if the imposition of last gelt paid in the Sound of Denmark may not be taken off yet certain provision may be made that the present rates thereof may not be raised either there or in Norway and that if the Hollander or any other nation without the Sound shall at any time pay less, the English may be at least equal with them, and that all the particulars in the late treaties with Denmark in 1645 and 1646 may be explained and ratified.

3. That the customs in Sweden paid by English may be reduced to a reasonable rate, and English men have the command and custody of their own goods, with liberty to sell them to the most advantage.

4. That in case of want of a market for any English merchants' goods in any Swedish port the proprietor may have leave to lay up his goods in safe custody, and under his own command, till an opportunity of sale as is used in other parts of the Baltic Sea.

5. That the English having paid their customs be not liable to disburse any other municipal duties particularly toolag or anlag at Danzig since it ought to be paid by the citizen, and not by strangers.

6. That some effectual course may be taken either with the Senate of Danzig, or King of Poland or both, for abolishing that custom and monopoly of sealing our cloth, whereby the great inconveniencies depending thereupon as is before mentioned may be prevented and the traders released from so great a bondage.

7. That upon occasion of treaty with Danzig or any other place within the Baltic Sea this company may be further heard touching the concern-ments of their trade at those places which they shall be ready to do when-soever this honourable council shall judge it reasonable.

8. That for the better collection of such duties as we lay upon ourselves for defraying the necessary charge of our government, and paying our debts, your Honours will be pleased to grant, or to procure order to the commissioners of the customs, not to pass entries to or from the parts of our privileges without our company's seal, or the hand of such officer as

we shall appoint, as hath been heretofore in use by this company, and is now practised by others.

9. That in your own due time, your Honours will be pleased to take into consideration the regulating of our English manufactures and restraining the exportation of wool, woolfells and fuller's earth.

All which is humbly submitted to the great judgement of this Honourable Council.

. . . .

At the Council of Trade the 24th of January 1660.[1]

To the Right Honourable his Majesty's Council for Trade.

The humble petition of the Governor Assistants and Fellowship of Merchants of the Eastland.

Sheweth

That besides several grievances whereof they lately presumed to tender a list to your Honours, the petitioners are sensible of one very considerable in this trade to Sweden, namely a monopoly of pitch and tar which by virtue of a patent hath been for several years past bought up and engrossed by some few persons of that country unto whom alone the first owners are necessitated to sell the same commodities which although they buy at low rates of 16 dollars the last yet they vent it to your petitioners and others at 24, 26 and 28 dollars the last or otherwise at their pleasure, besides an engagement they lay upon the buyers to carry the same to such ports only as those Swedish engrossers please, which restraints upon so material and useful commodities with other obstructions are no mean discouragement to the trade.

And therefore they humbly pray that it will please this Honourable Council to admit of this particular as an addition to the other complaints of the petitioners formerly made and tendered and to put the same into such a way of redress as to your Honours shall seem convenient.

And they shall pray etc.

By order of the Eastland company,
Mr Evans, Secretary.

12

A COPY OF A PETITION BY THE EASTLAND COMPANY READ
IN PRIVY COUNCIL ON 18 SEPTEMBER 1668[2]

To the King's most excellent Majesty.

The humble petition of the Governor Assistants and Fellowship of Eastland Merchants.

---

[1] Or later, but before 14 February 1660 (old style).
[2] SP 29/289/124 III. PC 2/61/16–17. Above, p. 148. The copy was made in 1671.

Sheweth

That Queen Elizabeth by her letters patents bearing date the 17 August 21 regni did for better government of this company and advantage of the trade of this nation, and for the honour and service of this kingdom, and other weighty considerations, incorporate the said company; with several powers to them and prohibitions to all others to intermeddle in this trade. But the said letters patents not directly and in express terms forbidding the trade of strangers, the same was so greatly increased, that the English shipping decayed, and the vent of English manufactures abated from 17,000 cloths usually exported from London annually, to 2,500.

That in 1622, for the reasons above mentioned, and for support of a trade of such consequence, the Lords of the Council moving to that end, it pleased your royal grandfather King James to grant his proclamation in their behalf; which in 1629 was renewed by his late Majesty of blessed memory, publishing to all persons, as well subjects as strangers, the company's privilege for the bringing in of Eastland commodities.

After which the exportation of English cloths was again raised to the former quantity, and more.

That the said proclamation producing so good effects, was so firmly observed, that several strangers importing Eastland commodities were enforced either to carry out the same again, or else compound with the company; as by particular instances in a list hereto annexed may appear.[1] That your most excellent Majesty since your happy restoration hath not only by your letters patents dated 20 February 1660 confirmed the said company's charter, but also given way that a proclamation should be passed, in way of revival of those before mentioned; having by your royal command the 29 August 1661 appointed your Majesty's counsel at law to prepare a bill to that end for your royal signature; which was accordingly done, but is not as yet passed your Majesty's Privy Council, in respect of the late obstructing calamities of the pestilence, fire and war.

That for want of this additional power, the greatest part of this trade to the Eastland is fallen into the hands of aliens, and is like in short time to be totally lost: forasmuch as the burghers of Danzig unto whom your petitioners formerly sold their English draperies, and in return thereof imported their foreign commodities into England, are now providing ships of their own, and setting up a company to manage that trade themselves both out and home, and to exclude your Majesty's subjects. Whereto they have manifold encouragements, by their freedom to buy and sell to whom and how they please; whereas we are restrained to that sole place (where we never enjoyed any privileges at all) and therein to their burghers only. Besides their ships and seamen being exceedingly cheaper than ours, their freight will be proportionably less, and ours laid aside; and these advantages are in no measure balanced by their payment of

[1] See summary of the annexure at the end of the petition.

strangers' custom here; which being but $\frac{1}{4}$ part more than is paid by your Majesty's subjects, is so insignificant, as that it now invites the English to manage their trade in strangers' names, and to use strangers' vessels, as being the easiest way of charge. And of what consequence this may prove, by the destruction of English shipping and trade, unless some timely remedy be applied, the petitioners humbly refer to your royal wisdom.

Most humbly praying your Majesty to be graciously pleased to perfect your royal intentions to your petitioners and their trade, by commanding the said proclamation to be renewed and published.

SUMMARY OF THE ANNEXURE[1]

27 December 1625. Hans Smith, alien, was ordered to transport potashes imported contrary to the proclamation.[2]

17 September 1628. Dirick Garrett, alien, was ordered to transport 14 lasts of flax, or to compound with the company.[3]

28 January 1631 [new style]. 'The Lords command the coal owners and all others strictly to observe the proclamation; not suffering any strangers whatsoever (excepting Danes and in their own ships) to import wood or Eastland commodities.'[4]

1630. George Gorden, importing tar and iron from Sweden, contrary to the second proclamation, was referred to the Eastland company and paid them a fine.[5]

1632. Jacob Druken submitted to the company for 20 bags of Polonia wool.

1634. Conrad Streitholt, a merchant stranger of the Stillyard, submitted to the company for five bags of Polonia wool.

13 January 1663 [new style]. John Baptista Vanderhoven was ordered to attend the company, 'who are desired to deal moderately with him in his fine'.[6]

---

[1] From the copy made in 1671, (SP 29/289/124 IV).
[2] According to SP 29/67/152, which has a similar list, Hans Smith was a Danziger.
[3] PC 2/38/459; see p. 77 n., above.
[4] PC 2/39/778; see p. 77 above.
[5] PC 2/40/235; he was a Scot and pleaded ignorance of the proclamation.
[6] PC 2/56/164, 172; see p. 141 above.

Appendix B

THE ADVOCATE AND *FREE PORTS*[1]

THE ADVOCATE

London, Printed by William Du-Gard, Printer to the Council of State; and are to bee sold by Nicolas Bourn in Cornhil, at the Corner shop, at the entrance into the Exchange. 1652.

To the Right Honorable the Council of State
Right Honorable!

I Am often in very great doubt (if I may so speak), that the Goodness & Wisdom of God, & *his thoughts of these*, are very rarely met with, in the Paths, which the scantling of Man's Reason and Judgment walk in; And as I dare not but own the Belief of the Coming of his Appearance, and the breaking forth, very shortly, of his Glorie: So I believ likewise, this will bee a sight very strange, and very unexspected to men; and not onely greatly above, but in som measure even contrarie (and perhaps, very unwelcom) unto the most enlarged and raised thoughts wee have yet prepared our selvs with, to receiv it.

The *sign* of which Coming, will bee the Detection, by little and little, of all *Imposture*, and the laying of all things low, naked, and mean before him; the stripping men of that Honor, Credit, and Repute, that they had by several means been gaining with themselvs, (and by themselvs) with others, either through a Not-knowledg, or through an artificial concealing of themselvs.

In *these very things* (if well observed) lying, and within *these* indeed, beeing spent and consumed, the whole Indeavors, Practice, Studie and Wisdom (if not Religion) of *All* States, Ages, Nations and Men, *viz.*

Either in devising shifts (by acquisition of such and such Power, Habits, or otherwise) not to appear uncomly to themselvs, but to beget rather a greatness, esteem and satisfaction in themselvs, and others of themselvs;

Or, in Concealing and keeping close (by several Glosses) the Imperfections, weaknesses, and uncomlinesses, (known to themselvs) from the sight and apprehensions of others;

The more exquisite Wit exceeding the more inferior only in this, that the former is able to finde out more tight and exquisite textures for it self then the other; And the most fortunate man in this world, having the

---

[1] Reprinted from copies in the British Museum. This is the second edition of *The Advocate.* See above, pp. 89 ff.

Advantage of the more unfortunate, but after the same manner also, *viz.* that the covering of this fall's off a little sooner, and the other wrap's himself up in it a while longer.

For thus all Lusts whatsoever (whether those of Acquisition) in the minde (or others to exterior things) both in their first Issuings forth, and in their utmost Accomplishments, are still but either to give countenance unto, or further to heap up a kinde of greatness, Repute and Esteem in us for us. The Assumption (on the other side) of a Repute and Esteemence to our selvs, is, That which after give's a kinde of lawfulness, boldness, and currancy (during it) to all Lusts. (These two, observing tune, and holding time each to the measures and motions of the other) and within this Circle therefore is concluded *whole Humane Nature*, with all the Parts, and the most perfect Actions of it.

Upon these thoughts (*Right Honorable!*) I finding none not very ready to have asscribed to himself the name of beeing (in som measure) wise, *becaus it is estimable*, finde none that can endure the Manifestation (in any kinde) of their Follie; or that can bee willing to have this their Wisdom and Glorie to bee flatly and plainly called a Pageantrie, Mumming, or playing at bo-peep with themselvs and others; and yet (it really beeing no honester) if wee cannot bear the judgments thus one of another, how shall wee abide the Trial, or bee able to stand before the Judgment of God, which seeth us, (and will shortly search us) with more pure and uncorrupt Eies? And how miserably then are the Imaginations of almost all men muffled up here in their own dressings? when the Truth most certainly is in our Beeings, at their best (natural, or acquir'd) Appearances, are yet such feign'd Things, and Propp'd up with such Lyes and fundamental mistakes of themselvs, that they would (*Belshazzer* like,) moulder and shatter themselves to pieces, should they bee taken quite asunder from the disguises and patchings they have put upon themselvs, bare-facedly and undeceivedly to see themselvs but one small part of an hour.

Beeing convinced, by these, therefore (*Right Honorable!*) of the low Condition wee are herein, I not knowing what the Councils of God intend to bring forth for the settlement of this Nation; Nor how hee hath resolved in his Wisdom to dispose of it, (as to its outward Condition,) whether Hee intend's wee shall bee oppressed by other Nations about us, that hee may the more manifest his Power and Protection over us: Or that wee shall bee advanced in Prosperitie above others, that so hee may perhaps shew us our vanitie (the casting of the Scale either way in appearance much depending upon the present Councils) I say, not knowing this, I can as little judge what means Providence will pleas to use in order to the bringing to pass these his purposes, whether hee will chuse This, or reject That.

But in this Case, notwithstanding remembering the advice of *Solomon*, and knowing nothing (for I do affirm it but as to mine own understanding) that hath presented it self in this Commonwealth, of more Import to bee looked after, or to bee very heedfully taken into Consideration, then Matters of *Trade*, (if wee shall either regard the *Safetie, Unanimitie*, or *Defence* of this Nation) Nor any other waie possible but This, to preserv and maintein this Countrie: calling also to minde, how many times I have heard it urged, That there is no other means to quiet or keep up the spirits of the poorer sort of people: No other to give them Imploiment, or to finde a vent and Incouragement for their Labors (when they have wrought) and consequently no other to provide against the wants and distempers of them, and of the Generalitie, but solely by *Trade*, and by a due Order and Regulation of it. All these things making up a very strong Affection in mee, I judged it my dutie (*Right Honorable!*), and what necessarily became the faithfulness I owe to the Commonwealth's service, to indevor the representing of this Truth (for your *Honor's* fuller Information) with the clearest Grounds and demonstration I could, which beeing a matter that did much depend upon Experience, I knew not how to bring this more home, then by propounding a President for it in our Neighbors the *Hollanders*; and such an one, as is still in sight, which may at once witness, The Advantage of *Trade, By themselves, and the benefit they have found by it*; The Disadvantage of neglecting it, *By what they have brought upon us*; And the clear waie of Governing it, *By the Courses they Actually took, and have practised to effect both these.*

All which Conceptions, nevertheless, are with all humbleness submitted By

Your Honor's servant

Febr. 11. 165½.

Φιλοπατρις

THE

ADVOCATE:

OR,

A NARRATIVE

Of the state and condition of things between the *English* and *Dutch* Nation, in relation to TRADE, and the consequences depending thereupon, to either Common-wealth; as it was presented in *August* 1651.

It hath been a thing for many years generally received, That the Design of *Spain* (and which, to this daie, hee still in his Councils carrie's on) is, to get the Universal Monarchie of Christendom. Nor is it a thing less true (how little soever observed) that our Neighbors [the *Dutch*] (after they had settled their Libertie, and been a while encouraged by Prosperitie) have, likewise, for som years, aimed to laie a foundation to themselvs for ingrossing the Universal Trade not onely of Christendom, but indeed, of the greater part of the known world; that so they might poiz the Affairs of any other State about them, and make their own Considerable, if not by the Largeness of their Countrie; yet, however, by the Greatness of their Wealth; and by their potencie at Sea, in strength and multitude of Shipping.

For the clear and certain carrying on of which, there beeing none (that was) like to bee so great a Bar to them, in this their Aim, as the *English* Nation; nor any that laie so conveniently to keep up a Proportion of Trade with them: It concerned them, therefore, by all means and waies possible to discourage and beat out the *English* in all places of Trade, as far (at least) as was discreet for them, without too much Alaruming them; of having too early or hastie a Breach with them.

Their particular Practices to which purpose in the *East-Indies*, at *Guiny*, *Greenland*, *Russia*, with the several unfair Carriages (of som among them) to us, in those places; and even in our own Seas, is not intended to bee here mentioned: It sufficeth, that these following Advantages they had clearly gotten above us:

1. In the great Trade they did drive to *East-land*, and to the *Baltick* Sea; for Masts, Timber, Hemp, Pitch, Tar, Copper, Iron, Salt-peter, all sorts of Grain, Pot-ashes, &c. the like most necessarie Commodities.

2. In their Herring-fishing; imploying yearly upon the Coast of this Land onely, above 2000 Sail of great Vessels, or Shipping.

3. In the preserving and advancing their Manufactures; their Cloathing Trade of late arising and increasing (as it is judged) to above 60000 Cloths yearly.

4. In their *East-India* Trade; and by it, Monopolizing three sorts of Spices almost to the whole world; as, Cloves, Nuts, and Mace, and lately much Cinnamon.

The means whereby they have pursued and upheld these Advantages, were

By the great number of Shipping they have constantly built; and by the manner of managing their Trade and Shipping, in a conformitie and direction to their Grand End:

For,

1. Few Merchant's Ships among the *Hollanders* were ships of much Defence, unless these going to *India*; and so they were neither at so great a charge of Guns in building them; nor did carrie a proportion of men, or victual (in setting them out) near, or answerable to *English* Shipping of the same Burthen.

2. Several Trades they did drive in Fleets, with great Flutes, or Vessels, having never a Gun at all in them, nor more men then would possibly sail them, as most of their *East-land* Trade, their Herring-Buss Trade, and their Salt Trade, which were driven after this manner.

3. Those their Fleets were, and have been alwaies carefully and constantly attended with a Convoy at the Publick charge; and which was alway ready beforehand, and had their directions given them not from

the State, but from the several Admiralties; whereby they were held to their Dutie, and strictly tied up to that service.

4. Much of the Trade which they did drive to the south-ward (not in Fleets, nor with Convoy, but in single shipping) they would often ensure in *England*; so that when loss came, it was wee somtimes that bare it, and our stock that was lessened and diminished by it.

By all which means,

1. They did engross the whole Trade of all Bulkie Commodities (to themselves singly), as Timber, Clap-board, Masts, Grain, Salt, &c.

2. And were, in som Commodities, able to go as cheap again for Freight, as wee: in som, half as cheap; and near in all, a full third penie cheaper then wee.

Which Cheapness of Freight produced again other great Advantages to themselvs;   For

1. In som Commodities it was above 20 in the Hundred gain; in som 15; in others 10; and near 4 or 5 *per Cent.* in most; (which was a years Interest with them)   And by which,

2. They were sure to get the preference of the Market of us in other Countries, and if occasion were, to under-sel us also as much *per Cent.* in all places, and upon all Trades; yea, somtimes in our own Commodities: And this together with an easie pretence of the unsafetie of our *English* shipping through our late Troubles.

3. Compelled our Nation (that wee might maintein a Stock going with them) to hire and freight the *Holland* shipping, without which, indeed, wee could not well have held up a Trade here with them, either out or home: Which beeing once begun by som, was immediately (by reason of the Advantage of it) followed by as many others as could: But This (though a good and beneficial expedient for the particular Merchant) begat notwithstanding several very great mischiefs to this Nation in general:

      For,

1. By this wee encouraged the building more and more of our Neighbors Shipping, and discouraged our own; which hereupon were laid up by the walls in great numbers.

2. Wee encreased (by this) their great Trade for the *Baltick* Sea, and *East-land*, and gave them still the greater opportunitie to make themselvs the Mart and Masters over us, of all Commodities belonging to the building or furnishing of Shipping, whereby their Trade still came home in a Circle; they (like wise men) laying such a Cours, as one part of it strengthened another.

3. Wee dis-obliged and discontented our own people and sea-men, and insensibly weakned the strength and defence of this Nation: For by this cours, wee must at length have been reduced to have hired their Marriners,

when wee come to set out our Men of War: nor was it possible (had it held) to have prevented it.

4. They, by this means, carried away much unnecessarie Treasure out of this Nation, taken for Freights; and so insensibly impoverished also this Countrie; our monie occasioning a Luxe to their people, while our own Seamen starved at home for meer want, and through lack of imploiment.

5. And as the Cheapness of their Freight enabled them to under-sell us abroad, in many Commodities carried to forreign Markets by them, & by us, to sell: So it enabled them equally to over-bid us abroad for the Forreign Commodities, which they and wee bought, and to rais the price of them upon us, which while they had libertie to bring in hither, they either prevented our Merchant of the first of the Market, and then made us paie Sauce for them: or, if not, they carried them into their Countrie: or here watched the opportunitie of another seasonable vent of them. And thus they served us, as for all our *Norwey*, *East-land*, and *Russia* Commodities; so also lately in our Wines, Fruits, Oils, Currans, &c. which were the Commodities of *Spain*, *Canaries*, and the *Streights*: By both these means (*viz.* by discouraging and beating us down abroad in the selling of som Commodities; and by raising and enhaunsing us abroad in the price, or buying up of others) concluding with themselvs, to wearie us out at length from all Trade, and to have the sole buying and selling of all Commodities for us.

For this method and manner of managing their affairs, daily adding to *their* stock, and answerably diminishing the Stock and Treasure of *this* Nation: and by laying it so, as it *run* thus in a Circle, each part of it (as wee said) strengthning another part: it would unavoidably have tended to a greater and greater disenabling us to hold anie Trade with them: and to have made themselvs, for Wealth and Shipping, the Masters over us: A sufficient testimonie of which (over and above what wee have said also) wee might further see in the actual progress that they had gained upon us in our Shipping.

For,

1. In our Trade of *East-land*, whereas wee did use formerly to send thither 200 Sail of Shipping in a year, wee now did not send 16 Sail: The *Hollanders* in the mean time employing not less then 600 Sail thither; and whereby (had not a good Providence crossed or hindered a strict Alliance and Conjunction between som of those Eastern States and them) wee must soon have given them their Price, and been at their disposing for all Commodities belonging to Shipping: and then it had been too great an hazard for us (by anie Law made here) to have recovered our Trade from them.

2. In our Plantations they had three, if not four Sail of Ships, for our one: whereas they never suffered us so much as to Trade at all in any place or Plantation settled by them.

3. In *India* they have 20 Sail, and above, for our one.

4. At *Spain*, *Canaries*, *Zant*, with several other places in the *Streights*, where they formerly rarely laded hither one ship of Goods; they now lately laded hither more then wee.

And thus, in the waie and manner of the managing the Trade in their shipping, laie much of their vigilancie to gain their advantage and design upon us.

A *second* Cours (therefore) whereby they do and have upheld their advantages above us, is, The greatness of the Stock they emploie, which (as wee now intimated) was more and more increased by the wisdom of this their Method in Shipping: And which, on the other side, as it did encreas and grow great, did enable them the more to give the Laws of Trade to us, both in the Government of the Exchange, and of the Markets abroad for Foreign Commodities.

A *third* Cours for the gaining and upholding their Advantages of us, was, The singular and prudent care they took in preserving the Credit of most of those Commodities which are their own proper Manufactures; By which they keep up the Repute and Sale of them abroad; taking hereby a very great advantage of the contrarie Neglect in us; and by this means, likewise, very much damnifying and spoiling us.

Which that wee may clearly see of what Import this one thing alone is to us, wee shall here set down certain general *Canons* or *Rules*, belonging to Manufactures.

1. That although Divine Providence, in the greatness of his Wisdom, hath placed natural commodities, som here, som there; yet no Manufacture or artificial commoditie, but may possibly bee had or transplanted into anie Countrie.

2. That all Manufactures (especially such as are of Necessitie) if they are of a certain goodness, They are (like Coin) of a certain value and price also; and so on the contrarie. If of an uncertain goodness, They, &c.

3. That two persons selling or making commodities of a like goodness, hee shall have the preference of the Market, that will sell them the cheapest. *And so two Nations likewise.*

4. That the cheapness of Manufactures, and artificial commodities, doth altogether depend upon the plentie and cheapness of the matter, and upon the like cheapness of price, for Handie-labor.

And these (though few) beeing unalterable Laws in all Manufactures, it cannot but bee acknowledged, that it is through our want of the like Care, as our Neighbors, and onely through that, that the *Hollander* hath anie kinde of Woollen Manufacture:

For,

1. The matter of no Woollen Manufacture groweth in his Countrie at all; but hee is forced to fetch it from other places; whereas wee have it here, within this Nation, plentie.

2. The price of labor depending much upon the price of victuals, hous-

rent, and other things necessarie, It is certain (especially to any that know both Countries) that all this is much cheaper with us, then with our Neighbors, and are like so to bee.

3. Our Nation, as they were heretofore the onely workmen of these commodities; so none can excel them for Art, Skill, or Goodness, were but encouragement given them, and an Order, Regulation, and Government of the Manufactures settled among them: And therefore

It is not our Neighbor's singular Industrie above us, or a power they have to work cheaper then us; so much·as it is the Carelesness of this Nation, in keeping our Manufactures to their due contents, weight, and goodness. Their Neglect in settling a Regulation, Government, and Superspection over them, and in Inflicting due and just punishments for the fals-making of them. That is (humbly conceived to bee) the Caus of the so great thriving of our Neighbor's Cloathing, and of the so great Ruine and Decaie (on the contrarie) of our own Woollen Manufactures, and of the people depending upon them.

A *fourth* Cours taken by our Neighbors, Is, The Improvements of Trade that they have made by their Treaties or Articles of Confederations with other Princes; *and by making this their Care and Protection of Trade abroad in all places their Interest of State.* Thus taking hold of the Juncture of Circumstances, and making use of the Necessitie of the King of *Denmark*, they have farmed the *Sound* of him: Thus also at the Treatie of *Munster* have they reserved a power of shutting us out of the *Scheld*, and have carefully in that Peace concluded on several other Articles and Provisions in order to the securing and promoting of their Traffick. And thus—&c.

A *fifth* Cours (and not the least means for the upholding and encreasing their Trade) Is, the smalness of their Custom, or Port-duties; also their prudent laying on and taking off Impositions, for the furtherance of their own Manufactures, and for the Incouragement of bringing in som, and Discouragement of bringing in other Commodities; and of which they have given us two ill Instances, The one in laying on a great Tax upon our *English* Cloths and Manufactures; The other in forbidding our Cloths wholly to bee imported, if drest or died in the Cloth; of both which wee have had som caus to complain long, as beeing plainly an Inhibition of Commerce, and if not strictly against the Laws of Nations; yet at least against the Cours of Amitie, Alliance, and Friendship.

A *sixt* way hath been, The Constant Reward and Incouragement given to persons bringing in Inventions; making of new Discoveries, and propounding things profitable for publick and common interest: which (how little a thing soever it may seem to som), yet it hath ever been, and is constantly, a very great spur to Industrie.

And these are humbly asserted to bee the principal Causes of their so much greatness and flourishing in Trade above us.

Other Causes that have been less principal and accessarie to these, are,

1. The Easiness or Lowness of Interest in that Countrie.

2. The great facilitating of their Trade by a Bank.

3. And last of all (the onely thing proper to them) the dearness and scarcitie of Land: and the dividing their Estates equally to their children: whereby Trade is (as it were) continued in a Line without Interruption; the contrarie beeing customarie with us.

Animadversion

All which Discours beeing onely an Evidence given in from matter of known fact; It will (as is humbly conceived) manifest it self.

I

That our Neighbors have no such extraordinarie advantage in matter of Trade, either through their Countrie, its Situation, or otherwise, as is proper or peculiar to them only, beyond all other Nations, (as hath been long the opinion of som) but it is the manner of their Care, and of the Government that is among them, and the meer vigilancie over Trade, that is observed by them:
    For,
If the Nature of those Courses, which they have taken and pursued for the Incouragement of Trade, bee looked into and considered (as they are obvious to any other that will pleas to heed them) it cannot bee imagined but they shall make any people great, rich and flourishing in Trade, that useth them; and therefore that they will do the like in anie other place as well as in *Holland*, if put in execution, especially, if it bee a place, as this of ours is, seated for Trade, and the people of the Countrie apt for it.

II

It is presumed, That our Neighbors would not think it just, if wee should condemn them, meerly for the taking these good Courses for themselvs; or becaus they have given all Incouragements that were requisite to their Trade in their own Countrie: Much less then would they exspect, that wee should actually impute these things as Crimes to them, or ground hence anie occasion to Estrange our selvs, or make a Breach with them: Nor will our neighbors therefore (as it is hoped) take it more ill from us, if wee (having now likewise recovered our Liberties) see the Necessitie of providing for the Defence of this Common-wealth by Shipping (as beeing *Islanders*); or if wee take up som of the like Courses as They, for the Incouragement of Trade among us: Without which, indeed, Shipping can neither bee had, or mainteined; which now also to neglect, were a very great Carelesness, and would, indeed, bee rather a Reproach to us then otherwise; having been so well taught, even by their own Example and Practice,   That
    1. It is by Trade, and the due ordering and governing of it, and by no other means, that Wealth and Shipping can either bee encreased, or

upheld; and consequently by no other, that the power of any Nation can bee susteined by Land, or by Sea: It beeing not possible (as is humblie thought) according to the Cours of humane affairs, for anie Nation (having no Mines to supplie it self) to make it self powerful in either of these (that is, either Monie, or Shipping) without Trade, or a thorow Inspection into Trade, and the Cours of it.

2. That it is by a Knowledge of Trade and Commerce, and the Cours of it, that one Nation or State know's perfectly how to straighten and pinch another, and to compel a Compliance from them, which may bee, either

By debarring or deriving the Cours of som necessarie Commodities from them; as for War, for Shipping, for Food, &c.   Or

By obstructing the Sale or Vent of the Native Commodities belonging to them: Or

By weakening them in their Shipping, and dreyning them by degrees of their Treasure and Coin.

By any of which Courses, if not spied, or (when spied, if) not able to bee prevented, a People or Nation must at length bee straightned and subjected: And every one of which Inconveniencies wee were very manifestly liable unto (as appear's by the foregoing Narrative) through the Advantages our Neighbors had over us, and through the Wisdom of those Courses they had laid in their Trade with us: We beeing so near pinched, that it had been very hard, fairly to have wrested our selvs out of the Nets of our Neighbors, had *Sweden* been as much shut to us, as *Denmark*; and that the King of *Poland* likewise could have exercised his Arbitrarie Power on us at *Dantzick*: And had not (at length) that Cours about our Shipping and Navigation been so happily and timely established by the Parlament; which, as the Necessitie of it could not suddenly bee so well judged of by those that had not considered or been acquainted with the substance of the foregoing Relation: So certainly, beeing laid upon so equal and Necessarie Grounds, if continued to bee exercised, It will bee a means, in som measure, to recover us.

For, besides what wee said of the Constraint, that for the foregoing causes, laie upon us, It must even, from the Primitive grounds of Reason, bee acknowledged, That a Common-wealth cannot bee enriched, nor the People thereof provided for, by any other means, then by reducing those very Courses into general Practice, which are used by Private men to that purpose. And Therefore as Private men, that buie and sell to sute the Conveniencies of others, as well as themselvs, do Constantly observ these, or the like Rules:

1. To buie at the first or best hand, or there, where they may have the Commoditie cheapest.

Answerable to which, Is,

To fetch Commodities at the immediate places of their Production or Growth, or as near as conveniently may bee.

2. To carrie Commodities to places where they are most needed.

Answerable to which, Is

To send all Commodities Native or other to their farthest, or utmost Market, where they are probable to yield the greatest price, and have the quickest sale.

So these Canons and Rules must bee as inviolably observed also by any Nation who will pretend an Interest, hope, or benefit from Trade: otherwise they may justly bee reproved of less Care and Knowledg, then common or ordinarie Shop-keepers. Which Rules, notwithstanding, are not to bee pursued by any State, nor can bee imitated by any Commonwealth, without giving all the possible Indulgence and Incouragement, that may bee, to their Shipping.

And this whole state of things, and these reasons that have been produced, beeing therefore all of them duly and equally considered, It is hoped, little will remain of Dis-satisfaction (or Objection upon us) about the PARLAMENT's late Act for the Incouragement, and Increas of our Navigation; Which was, indeed, the Thing principally propounded to bee here Argued, and the Censure of which is therefore freely Submitted.

FINIS

FREE PORTS

The Nature and Necessitie of them stated

London, Printed by William Du-Gard, Printer to the Council of State; and are to bee sold by Nicolas Bourn in Cornhil, at the Corner shop, at the entrance into the Exchange. 1652.

Upon this certain and clear ground, that som Countries can best spare their Commodities at som seasons of the year; and that other Countries have not at the same time alike urgencie or occasion for them, doth arise the wisdom of som Nations in fetching Commodities from the places of their Growth at that fit and seasonable time, and storing them up till the Necessitie of other Nations do call for them.

At which time, those Countries that have this Necessitie, beeing furnished from those Magazines or Stores, both the Shipping of the said Countries are by this means prevented of their emploiment, and the Price, as much as the Market will bear, is raised upon them.

As

First, all Countries, whose commodities are Annual, such as are Wines, Fruits, Grain, Fish, Oils, Tobacco, Sugars, Galls, Cottons, Silks, Indico, and many other Drugs, as many of the Commodities of *Spain*, *France*, most part of the Commodities of the East and West *Indies*, *Canaries*, *Streights*, &c. All these have their Seasons, and Harvest for those Commodities, at which time, they are most cheap, and easiest to bee had.

Secondly, All Countries who are subject to Mounsons, or Trade-windes, to extremities of seasons for heat or cold, or to deluges of Rain, among which wee may reckon many Ports of the *East-Indies*, many of *Guiny*, and *Africa*, som Coasts on the *West-Indies*, with all the more Northerly Regions of *Greenland*, *Russia*, *Poland*, *Norwey*, *Sweden*, *Denmark*, *Prussia*, &c. all those do likewise oblige a Commerce to them, at som times of the Year onely.

Countries therefore, who have no immediate Traffique with these places named, or that do neglect the going thither with ships of their own, at those fit Seasons; As such Countries as are either not well seated for Trade to those Parts, or as have not Convenient Ports, and number of Shipping to manage the Trade; or who are not expert in matters of Traffique, and Navigation; or such as are at feud or war with those other Nations; All these Countries, it is certain, when they stand in need of the Commodities of any of the aforesaid places, must bee beholding to the said Stores, or Magazines for them; and must bee content to abide the Prices or Rates set upon them.

Those Nations on the other side, who lie advantageously upon the Sea, and abound with good Harbors, Rivers, and Shipping; whose People also are well experienced in the managing of affairs of Traffique, and Navigation; and go generally secure from danger; These have likewise this Advantage further, of beeing able, at their own pleasure, to make themselvs such a rich and general Magazine or Store as wee speak of for other Nations:

Which design scarce any People hath ever pursued with such studied Industrie, or made proof of the vast benefits and advantage which come's thereby, to so high a degree, as hath *Holland*.

They fetching the Commodities of *Russia*, *Norwey*, *Poland*, *Prussia*, *Sweden*, *Denmark*, &c. and bringing them into their own Countries, do laie them up there at pleasure, till by advice weekly from all other parts, they are directed where to finde a Market for them; And accordingly carrie them into *England*, *Ireland*, *Scotland*, *France*, *Portugal*, *Streights*, or other places Southward: They on the other side go at fit Seasons to the *Streights*, *Portugal*, *France*, *Spain*, *West* and *East-Indies*; and fetching the Commodities of those Southern countries, do usually dispers them again back, into the more Northerly Regions; both into those that belong unto this Common-wealth, and to those others also that wee speak of, placing their whole Interest in the encouragement and sagacious Managerie of this Cours and Circle of Traffique.

*Arguments tendred to move this Nation to under-
take the like general Mart, as hath the*
HOLLANDER;
Drawn,

First, From Expectation of like benefit to us, that our Neighbors have upon this Accompt certainly gained to themselvs, seeing this kinde of Trade would effectually conduce

*Both to the increasing, and to the better distributing Riches to this Nation,
then by that wee now have; That is,*

If Ports for Landing and Storing up forreign commodities; and exporting them again upon such easie Duties, as wee may hold the Market in all other countries with our Neighbors the *Hollanders,* may in all the fittest places of this Common-wealth bee opened.

Secondly, It would tend as much also to the encreasing the Power and Strength of this Nation, both by Land and by Sea: as well in Guarding and plentifully planting and peopling those Maritime or Frontier-Towns, and the Countries thereabouts, which shall bee appointed and allowed for free Ports; as in multiplying the Shipping of our Countrie. A proof of which wee have alreadie had in *Dover,* which, after the Composition-Trade was settled there (that made it in som kind a free Port) did within Ten years time arise from nothing to have neer two hundred sail of prettie great Shipping; with an Increas of Stock, Houses, and all things answerable, although, having lost it now but neer as long, it is quite decaied in all again.

More particularly, Opening of Free Ports, will conduce to the Quickning of Trade; to the Imploiment of the poor throughout the whole Common-wealth: to the making of all Forreign Commodities more cheap, and more plentiful; seeing every man will bring in, when hee know's hee may (if hee finde no market here) freely carrie it out again. It will likewise serv to the preventing of Famine, and scarcitie of Corn; to the raising the Exchange, and bringing in of Bullion: to the augmenting of the Revenue of the State: and to the making other Nations more dependent upon this.

As a further Inducement to all which, is offered to Consideration the many Advantages that this Commonwealth hath above our Neighbors, the *Hollanders,* (how much soever they have raised themselvs by this Art) for the putting in Practice such an universal intercours of Traffique as is desired.

As

First, From the Largeness of this Common-wealth's Dominions, and number of our Ports and Harbors, above those of our Neighbors.

Secondly, From the plentie of commoditie wee have from within our selvs, and from our own Plantations: which alone beeing now restrained to our own Shipping, will afford a Stock very great to begin with.

Thirdly, From the Freedom and Independencie that our Shipping have upon the Ports of any other State, or Nation; and the Soveraigntie wee keep and maintein in our own Channel. Whereas it is well known that our Neighbors the *Hollander's* ships, have not onely a great, but a necessarie Relying upon the Ports and Protection of this Common-wealth: Great Fleets of their shipping continually beeing forced to put in, and for the most part to Winter in our Harbors, wee in the mean time very seldom or rarely bearing into any forreign Port for shelter.

Fourthly, From the Privileges many of our Ports have for beeing fitter Out-lets on any windes, then those of our Neighbors, and better situated for most Trades, either Southerly or Northerly.

Lastly, From the Boldness of our Coasts safe and excellent Road-steads; And for beeing at all seasons free from beeing frozen in and stopped; Whereas our Neighbors have on the other side a flat and dangerous Coast, barr'd and inconvenient Harbors; and such as are by reason of Ice, shut up and useless for almost a third or fourth part of the year; which singular Conveniencies or Privileges coming to this Nation so immediately from Providence, are not altogether to bee neglected.

The third Consideration (although in som regard most principal to bee weighed) is, the Inconveniencies wee at present lie under from the Trade wee have; and the Damages that will unavoidably grow upon us, if this Trade onely continue;

For,

First, The trade wee now drive tend's, or is onely for Consumption; it beeing very little of forrein commodities that is re-transported upon the present encouragement or settled rate of half Custom.

For, though it may bee objected, that look what Tonnage, Subsidie, or Custom is paid upon foreign goods inwards, which are spent in the Nation, is onely disbursed for a while by the Merchant, and at length really accompted for to the immediate Buyer or Spender; and that therefore this Custom inwards, though it should bee great, cannot destroie the Merchant: Yet the case is however very different, and altogether otherwise in a Tax or Rate of half that custom set upon all the same unconsumed Goods when carried outwards, specially if there was an Over-valuing (as in many there is) of those Goods inwards.

Seeing although it bee said the other was paid by the Nation (that is the custom inwards), upon all Goods here spent; yet this custom outwards is solely taken from the purs of the Merchant, and cannot bee re-imbursed to him again in other countries, especially when another forreign Merchant shall carrie the same commoditie thither, and by paying less custom shall afford it cheaper; for then this Tax outward must eat our Merchant up by little and little, and put a discouragement upon him.

For Example

The *Hollander* and wee deal for spice, for Wines, for Sugar, Indico, Silk, Cotton, and for the Manufacture of Spanish Wool: all which (with other Commodities) wee fetch from the places of their Growth, or first Production, in the respective shipping of each Nation; for som of which Commodities our Merchants at coming in pay in Custom, in Impost, and by over-rating the commoditie 10.15. and in som things neer 20 per *Cent.* which if those Goods were sold here, and spent in the Commonwealth, the Merchant perhaps could not so much feel it (unless in a perishable and uncertain commoditie, where hee oft suffer's) for hee then rate's his Goods accordingly when hee sell's them.

But if hee shall desire to transport again those Goods into the East-Lands, into the Streights, or into any other places or countries where hee know's they are wanted: Though of this great custom hee do receiv the one half back again;

Yet if the *Hollanders* shall upon the same Goods paie but 2 *per Cent.* Custom, they have the Advantage by this means before our Merchant of 5. 6. or 8. *per Cent.* in their Market (beyond Sea) beeing clean so much loss as to our Merchant, so to the Nation, and to the emploiment of its Shipping; this kinde of outward Trade beeing by this means at length wholly left off and deserted.

These two wholly differing in kinde one from another; For a Nation to deal or traffique in Wares and Merchandizes for its own expence and consumption, as countrie Gentlemen, or ordinarie Trades-men; And for a Nation to make its self a shop, and to buy and sell for the furnishing and provision of other Nations; as a man that keep's a Ware-hous, or Store-hous; which latter Trade is that wee speak of;

In regard that a Nation that onely buie's and trade's to furnish it self, is confined to a Stock, and such a Stock, as must not exceed its own expence or Consumption: And the Emploiment of Shipping and Returns of forreign Goods must bee still as confined, and limited answerably; and neither Trade, nor Shipping, nor Stock are at utmost able to exceed the value of our Native Commoditie exported: For if the Libertie here of the Merchant and People for Trading and buying of Foreign Commoditie, should exceed our Exportation, or the value thereof, and not rather bee less then otherwise, it doth but tend more and more to the Loss of our Wealth, and to our Decay and Ruine.

Wherefore all Consultations whatsoever about Trade, if *Free Ports* bee not opened, and this Whole-sale or general Trade bee not incouraged, do still but terminate in som Advice or other about Regulating our Consumption; and have no other good at farthest, but preventional, *that our Ballance of Import exceed not our Export:* which to confine our selvs to alone, is, on the other side, a Cours so short, as it will neither serv to rais the Strength of this Nation in Shipping, or to Govern the Exchange abroad; nor yet to avoid the Damage and Mischief the Subtiltie of the forreign Merchant will hereby bring upon us.

Whereas if *Free Ports* bee opened, and Exportation of forreign Goods encouraged; not onely the Mischief of the Consumption and carrying out of our Treasure; and of Lowness of Exchange, will most effectually bee prevented, but both our Stock and Shipping will bee indefinitely or proportionably increased.

Lastly, A great Part of the Revenue of the State is for want of this general Trade clearly lost; for supposing *Free Ports* to bee opened, wee must grant there will bee an Access of wealth to the Nation, and an Increas to this Common-wealth by Strangers.

And consequently, Our Consumption of forreign Commodities will not bee at all less, but more; and therefore the Incom or Custom paid upon it. Over and above which, the State may have a Custom or Dutie in a very short time of one *per Cent.* upon the value of som Millions of Goods yearly, which now (by Reason of the Discouragements aforesaid) are carried into other Parts, and for which they yet receiv not one Farthing.

B.W.

FINIS

Appendix C

SOME MEMBERS OF THE EASTLAND COMPANY[1]

I

EXPORTERS OF BROADCLOTH IN COMPANY SHIPS: FROM
LONDON (L) IN 1620,[2] 1632 AND 1640; FROM IPSWICH (I)
IN 1624, 1625 AND 1636[3]

Abbott, Toby   I. 1624, 1625
Bank, Richard   L. 1632
Barker, William   L. 1640
Beale, James   I. 1624, L. 1640
Blake, Edmund   L. 1640
Blithe, John   I. 1624, 1625, 1636
Brinley, John   L. 1632
Brownrigg, I. 1625
Brunskell, William   L. 1632, 1640
Burnell, John   L. 1620
Burnell, Thomas   L. 1620, 1632
Burningham, John   L. 1620
Chambers, George   L. 1620
Champion, Richard   I. 1636
Cheney, William   L. 1640
Clark, Thomas   L. 1632
Clebourne, Thomas   L. 1640
Clinch, Edmund   I. 1636
Clinch, John   I. 1624, 1625, 1636
Clitherow, Christopher   L. 1620
Cockayne, William, Junior   L. 1620
Cootes, Mary, widow   L. 1620
Cradock, Matthew   L. 1620, I. 1624,
   1625, L. 1632, I. 1636, L. 1640
Crew, Randolph   L. 1620, I. 1624, 1625,
   1636
Cross, John   I. 1636, L. 1640
Cutler, Benjamin   I. 1624, 1625
Cutler, Robert   I. 1624, 1625
Cutler, Roger   I. 1624, 1625
Cutler, Samuel   I. 1624, 1625
Daniel, Edward   L. 1640
Eaton, Theophilus   L. 1620, 1632
English, John   L. 1620
Fenwick, Martin   L. 1632

Filmer, Reynold   L. 1632
Franklin, Richard   L. 1632
Freshwater, John   I. 1624
Garrard, John   L. 1620
Gerrard, Robert   L. 1620
Gibbs (Gippis), Robert   I. 1624
Goldwell, John   I. 1624, L. 1632, I. 1636
Goodyear, Michael   I. 1624, 1625
Gore, John, Alderman   L. 1620
Gorsuch, Daniel   L. 1620, 1632
Gough, James   L. 1640
Green, Elizabeth   L. 1620
Grimwade, William   I. 1624, L. 1632
Haines, Thomas   L. 1620, I. 1624
Harris, Edward   L. 1640
Harrison, Benjamin   L. 1640
Harrison, Thomas   L. 1640
Haveland, Anthony   I. 1625
Hawks, Thomas   L. 1632
Hayward, Henry   L. 1620
Hemings (Hening), Roger   L. 1620,
   1632
Highlord, Zachary   I. 1624, 1625
Hobson, John   L. 1640
Hodges, Henry   L. 1620
Hodges, William   L. 1632
Hoop, John   L. 1640
Humphreys, Pharoah   L. 1640
Jackson, Randolph   L. 1640
James, Edward   L. 1620
Jordan, Thomas   L. 1640
Inglethorpe, William   I. 1624, 1625
Kent, Roger   L. 1640
King, George   I. 1624, 1625
Knapp, Robert   I. 1624, 1625, 1636

---

[1] Some of these names are doubtful and require further collation. Some tentative
variants are offered in parentheses. Specially suspect readings are marked (?).
[2] From notes courteously placed at my disposal by Mr B. E. Supple.
[3] From port books, E 190/23/3, 36/5, 43/1, 602/6, 7, 604/6.

Knapp, Thomas   I. 1636
Leatt, Nicholas   L. 1620
Lewis, Edward   L. 1640
Lewis, Thomas   I. 1625
Long, George   L. 1620
Lovell, Samuel   I. 1625
Lymber, Robert   I. 1624, 1625
Maddison, Ralph   L. 1632
Mantell, Richard   L. 1620, I. 1624, 1625,
   L. 1632, I. 1636
Master, Robert   L. 1640
Merrill, Walter   I. 1636
Moore, John   L. 1620, 1632
Noor, Ralph   I. 1624, 1636
Pain, Ambrose   I. 1624, 1625, 1636
Pain, George   L. 1632
Patrickson, John   L. 1640
Paul, Daniel   I. 1625
Price, George   L. 1632, 1640
Rand, John   I. 1624, 1625
Read, Lawrence   L. 1632
Read, Samuel   L. 1640
Revett (Rivet?), John   L. 1620
Samon, William   L. 1640
Sanderson, Francis   L. 1640
Seely, Thomas   I. 1624, 1625, 1636
Sewter, Henry   L. 1620, I. 1624, 1625

Shaw, Robert   I. 1625
Silvester, Thomas   L. 1640
Smith, Simon   L. 1640
Smith, Thomas   L. 1640
Smith, William   I. 1625
Smither, John   I. 1624, 1625, 1636
Snelling, Robert   I. 1624, 1625
Spicer, Nicholas   L. 1620
Stiles (Still), Thomas   L. 1620, I. 1624,
   1625
Stratford, Henry   I. 1625
Taylor, Abraham   L. 1632
Thompson, Samuel   L. 1640
Travell, John   L. 1620, 1632
Trimmel (?), John   L. 1632
Vanderputt,   L. 1640
Vaughan, Robert   L. 1632, 1640
Vincent, Christopher   L. 1620
Wadloe, Francis   L. 1620
Wasse, Richard   I. 1624
Webb, Robert   I. 1624, 1625
Whitlock, Richard   L. 1620, 1632, 1640
Wightman, Humphrey   L. 1640
Williams, Robert   L. 1640
Woodgate, Thomas   L. 1632, I. 1636,
   L. 1640
Young, James   L. 1620, 1632, I. 1636

2

SIGNATORIES TO B.M. ADD. MS. 22546/164, JANUARY 1654,
AT LONDON[1]

21   Alens (?), Akens (?), Robert
24   Asty, Francis
2   Barker, William
17   Bilton, Edward
4   Boldero, John
12   Brooke, Robert
16   Brunskell, William
14   Burnell, Thomas
1   Chiverton, Richard
11   Coles, Benjamin
5   Dering, Charles
9   Eccleston, Richard
26   Freeman, John, Junior
13   Goldwell, John

22   Gore, William
20   Gould, John
18   Jordan, Thomas
19   Lewes, Edward
15   Price, George
25   Rivet, John
10   Rivet, William
23   Searles, Robert
3   Travell, John
27   Travers, Philip
6   Wescombe, Edward
7   Whitlock, Robert
8   Young, James

[1] These may well be the names of the governor, deputy, treasurer, and twenty-four assistants; I have therefore indicated the order in which they signed. See above, p. 123.

3

(*a*) RESIDENTS AT DANZIG IN 1651[1] AND IN 1656[2]

Acton, Gamaliel 1651, 1656	Lloyd, Owen 1656
Ayloff, Benjamin 1656	Lockwood, Willis 1651
Barker, Thomas 1656	Lorymer, Nevill 1656
Bautry, Thomas 1651	Maister (Master?), Henry 1656
Benson, Thomas 1656	Markham, William 1656
Bilton, Edward 1651	Nichols, Nicholas 1651
Brown, Robert 1656	Pease (Pierce?), Thomas 1651
Clifford, George 1656	Pierce, Michael 1651
Cock, George 1656	Sanderson, Francis 1651, 1656
Collins, John 1651	Sayer, John 1656
Daniel, Edward 1651, 1656	Spencer, Nathaniel 1656
Fisher, John 1656	Travell, Samuel, Senior 1656
Green, William 1651	Wallis, Richard 1651, 1656
Grimwade, Robert 1656	Whitlock, Richard 1651, 1656
Haswell, Henry 1656	Williamson, William 1651

(*b*) THE COMMITTEE AT DANZIG IN 1664 AND 1669; AND SIGNATORIES OF AN OFFICIAL LETTER FROM KÖNIGSBERG IN 1685[3]

Barker, Thomas 1664, 1669	Kerby, Christopher 1669
Beauchamp, Richard 1669	Mathews, John 1664, 1669
Bilton, Edward 1669	Sanderson, Francis 1664, 1669
Broadhead, Daniel 1669	Scarlett, John 1685
Collam (Kellam?), Thomas 1685	Stoles (Stote, Stiles?), Thomas 1685
Collins, Daniel 1685	Taylor, Thomas 1685
Collins, Edward 1685	Travell, Samuel 1664, 1669
Harwell (Haswell), Edward 1664	Warren, Thomas 1664
Heathcote, John 1685	Wyniffe, Thomas 1669

4

ADMISSIONS TO THE EASTLAND COMPANY 1660–1700[4]

1661	
	Haswell, Henry p or s
Chester r	Hammond, John r
Harrison, John r	Rayne, William p or s
Saramore r	Fisher, David r
Grace, Edward r	Doggett, John r
Dering, Charles p or s	Mann, Richard r
Collins, Daniel p or s	Johnson, Thomas, of Hull r

[1] SP 18/15/95, 16/36.
[2] *Thurloe Papers*, IV, 370, V, 88, 107.
[3] Sellers, *Acts and Ordinances*, 87, 90, 119.
[4] Extracted from their treasurer's book; p=by patrimony, s=by service, r=by redemption.

Papillon, Thomas   r
Smith, William   r
Philp, Anthony   r
Kent, Griffith (*paid by Edward Smith*)   r
Hillary, Robert (*paid by Thomas Boatry [Bautry?]*)   r
Kirk, Richard   s
Willson, John   s
Gold (Gould?), Bernard   s
Bonfoy, Thomas   r
Jenkinson, James (*paid by Henry Haswell*)   r

1662

Johnson, Timothy, of Hull   r
Allott, Colonel William   r
Clench, William ⎱
Clench, Edmund ⎬ (*by Mr Deputy Nore of Ipswich*)   p *or* s
Moody, John ⎰
28 persons (*By Mr Deputy Horner of York*)   p *or* s
18 persons (*by Mr Deputy Dobson of Hull*)   p *or* s
60 persons (*by Mr White for Mr Deputy Gray of Newcastle*)   p *or* s
Moody, John, of Ipswich (*paid by George Boldero*)   r
Moody, Henry   r
Foxwell, Henry   r
Westland, Oliver   r
Harrison, Benjamin   r
Copin, Robert, of Ipswich   r
2 persons at Lynn (*by Mr Deputy Symms*)   r
Lile, Henry   r
Sherman, Edward   r
Purplett, Richard, of Yarmouth   p *or* s
Lockwood, Richard   r
Burkin, Captain   r
Wassall, Abraham   r
Watkinson, Christopher, of Leeds (*paid by Henry Haswell*)   r

1663

Cankery, Thomas   r
Watson, George (*paid by John Doggett*)   r
Purplett, Thomas   p *or* s
Seagood, William   p *or* s
Spurstoe, Henry   p *or* s
Davis, Thomas   p *or* s
Child, John   r
Horsfall, Hillary   r
Ayloff, Benjamin   p *or* s
Ferry, John   r
Watson, Peter   p *or* s
Watson, George   p *or* s

Butler, Henry   r
Bowyer, William   p *or* s

1664

5 persons at York (*by Mr Bryan Dawson*)   p *or* s
Gower, Richard   r
Walker, Robert   r
Cawston, John   r
Cadogan, Thomas   r
Lloyd, Owen   s
Smith, Thomas   s
Wyniffe, Thomas   s
Pottenger, Henry   s
Popple, Israel   r
Shorter, Charles   r
Moody, George   r
Cooke, James   r
Calvert, George   p *or* s
Bilton, William   p *or* s
Beauchamp, Richard   p *or* s
Deake, John   p *or* s
Orme, Robert   p *or* s

1665

Brewster, Thomas   p *or* s
Spalding, George   p *or* s
Tygh, Robert (*paid by Colonel Allott*)   r

1666

Lyell (Lile?), Adam   r
Daniel, Richard   p *or* s

1667

Cawston, Peter   r
Scott   p *or* s

1668

Newton, Edward   p *or* s
Taylor, William   p *or* s
Milford, John   p *or* s

1669

Feake (?), Samuel   p *or* s
Smith, William   p *or* s
Lyell (Lile?), James   r
Short, William   p *or* s
Bilton, Edward   p *or* s
Philp, Thomas   r
Sowton (?), Samuel   r

1670

Smith, Andrew   p *or* s
Philp, Arthur   p *or* s
Winyere, Robert   r

Strangh, William   r
Morrice, Humphrey   r

1671

Halford, Edward   r
Butcher, John} (*by service to Mr Sherley*
Sayer, Roger } *and Mr Gould*)
Lumsdale, William   r
Callender, Edward   r
Hartby, John (*by service to Alderman
    Doggett*)

1672

How, Richard, Esquire   r
Clark, Captain John   r
Shuttleworth, George   p *or* s
Birkhead, William   p *or* s
Kent, Thomas   p *or* s
Martin, Joseph   p *or* s
Sclater, Edward   p *or* s

1673

Batchellor, Matthias   r

1674

Burren, Anthony   s
Rivet, John   s
Archer, John   s

1675

Stote, Sir Richard   p *or* s
Sayers, John   p *or* s

1676

Westland, Nathaniel   p *or* s
Wilmer, John   r
Norwich, Erasmus   p *or* s
Cooke, George   r
Kett, Thomas   r
Linch, William   r
Hosea, Alexander   r
Wessell, Leonard   p *or* s
Arthur, John   r
Nightingale, Jeffery   r
Tichbourne, William   r
Tichbourne, John   r
Barkell, Robert   r
Mason, Nathaniel   r
Vanhowsen, Garat   r
Jacobson, Theodore   r
Fisher, John   r
Bellamy, William   r
Goodfellow, Matthias   r
Shipherd, Thomas   r
Smith, William   r
Boynton, Francis   r

Bodington, George   r
Washington, James   r

1677

Wiggett, John   r
Mayne, John   r
Harrison, John   r
Allen, Daniel   r
Smith, John   r
Bilton, Henry   s
Taylor, John   s
Asty, Ambrose   s
Cook, John   r
Scarlet, William   r
Norwich, Simon   r
Dering, Edward   r
Collins, Edward   r

1678

Hamilton, Chrisostom   r
Urrey, Richard   r
Vansistart, Peter   r
Woodhouse, John   s
Lydell, Robert   r
Hunt, Francis   r
Godbolt, William   r
Shaw, William   r
Glover, William   r
Kemp, Francis   r
Woodroke, Thomas   r
Booth, Edward, Esquire   r

1679

Storey, Samuel   r
Lloyd, John   r
Carew, Thomas   r
Lodwick, Ralph   r
Travell, Samuel, Junior   p *or* s
Hall, Urban   p *or* s
Rolfe, Abraham   p *or* s
Benson, Thomas   p *or* s

1680

Randall, Edward   r
Dawson, William (*by service to Mr Kett*)
Godfrey, Michael   r
Scisson, John   s
Kerrington, Nicholas   r
Bilton, Robert   r

1681

Lodwick, Simon   r
Davis, William   r
Strode, Hugh   r
Gore, William   r

1682

Asty, Francis   p *or* s
Shepherd, Dormer   r
Hawes, Thomas   r
Benson, William   r
Tippett, Robert   r
Heathcote, Samuel   p *or* s
David, Jacob   r
Watts, Edward   r
Rayner, Christopher (?)   r

1683

Joy, Peter   r
Hayes, William   r
Coulson, Moses   r
Middlethwaite, Nathaniel   r

1684

Preston, John   r
Lambert, Anthony   r
Woodhouse, Jonathan   r
Coniers, Gera' (?)   r
Bond, David   r
Sykes, Joseph   r
Cooke, John   r
Willson, Thomas   r
Willson, Richard   r
Thearsby, Ralph   r
Harrinson, William   r
Heathcote, Caleb   s
Carleton, Edward   r
Kitchingman, Joseph   r
Lodwick, Charles   r
Clark, Samuel   r
Sanders, George   r

1685

Glover, John   r
Smith, James   r
Goddard, Thomas   r
Heathcote, Josiah   p *or* s
Phill (Philp?), Henry   p *or* s
Heathcote, William   r
Whitehall, Edmund   p *or* s
Chitty, Matthew   r
Valentine, John   r
Cary, John   r
Carleton, Dudley   r
Snell, Lawrence   r
Chitty, Abraham   r
Manwood, George   r
Denham, Joseph   r
Von der Stegen, Dirrick   r
Brown, Joseph   r
Young, James, Junior   r

1686

Nisbet, Philip p *or* s
Gould, Nathaniel   r
Cottham, John   r
Cornelison, William Henry   r

1687

Pigou, John   r
Micklethwaite (Middlethwaite?),
    Nathaniel   r
Vernon, Thomas   r
Snelling, William   r
Taylor, James   r
Adderly, Henry,   r
Whichcote, Benjamin   r
Collins, Edward, Junior   r
Lane, John   r
Beckhoff, Cornelis   r
Schroder, John   r
De Grave, John   r

1688

Young, John   p
Young, Paul   s
Swallow, Richard   r
Booth, John   r
Woolf, Joseph   s
Disher, William   r
Bawds, Captain Thomas   r
Carleton, Matthew   r
Kellam, Edward   r
Tomlinson, John   r
Fisher, Thomas   r
Lloyd, John, Junior   r
Meaux, Thomas   s
Dawson, Lemuel   r

1689

Monkley, ?   r
Justice, Emanuel   r
Masters, Robert   r
Foot, Samuel   r
Brailsford, Thomas   r
Cutler, Nicholas   r
Dunston, John   r
Beers, Charles   r

1690

Collins, Edward   r
Micklethwaite, Jonathan (*by service to*
    John Archer)
Jefferies, Jeffery   r

1691

Mr Jacobson's man (*paid by Mr Jacobson*)
  r
Dodd, r
South, r
Kemp, r
Mr Delachamber and two others r
Stratford, Francis r
Lodwick, George, 'Gent' (?) r
Kugelman, Henry Philip r

1692

Newcastle, William Carr *or* ⎫
  Carr, William, of Newcastle⎭ p
Sewter, John r
Michell, Robert r
Caulier, John r
White, John r
Horne, Joseph r
Goodfellow, Matthias r
Nisbet, Thomas r

1693

Jackson, Robert r
Blackham, Richard r
Van Hythusen, Garrard r
Meade, Samuel r
Lyell, Henry p
Dumwell, Michael r
Lorymer, Alexander r
Berenbery (?), John Henry r
Leiter, Myer r
Hoyle, Henry r
Stevens, Edward r

1694

Malthus p *or* s
Attwood r
Godfrey, Peter p *or* s
Gills, Leonard p *or* s
Wight, Samuel r
Utgar, John r

1695

Mr Archer's man s
Mr Benson's man of York r
Davy, Henry r
Renew, Peter r
Dutry, Dennis r

1696

Armiger, r
Bloome, Robert r
Cary, Thomas r
Crisp, Edmund r
Moor, Thomas r
Benthall, Walter r
Brain, Benjamin r
Ormstone, Joshua r
Hatley, George r

1697

Preston, John r
Bottomley, Anthony r
Geling, Isaac r

1698

Nelthorpe, George r
Brown, Benjamin r
Utgar, Daniel r
Lenton (?), Henetage (?) ?

1699

Palmer, Thomas r
Dodson, John r
Fernely, Joseph, at Hull r

1700

Brown, William r
Mallabar, George r
Dumatre, John r
Springell, Daniel r
Walker, Richard r
Davis, Giles r
Collett, Joseph r
Walter, Thomas r

Appendix D

SOME FIGURES OF BALTIC TRADE, 1591–1700

Column (*a*) gives annual average wheat prices in England, in shillings per quarter, for years ending in September, from Thorold Rogers's *History of Agriculture and Prices* (Oxford, 1866–1902), v, 268–71.

Columns (*b*) and (*c*) concern ships employed in the English import trade from the Baltic.

Column (*b*) gives the number of English ships passing through the Sound westward. As a rule nearly all were laden; exceptional years are footnoted. It is thought that few, if any, were bound elsewhere than for England until the latter part of the period.

From 1669, when shipmasters were first required to declare their destinations, is given also the number, laden, for Dutch and southern ports. Some few bound for Norway and Germany are ignored on the assumption that they came to England afterwards. Sound Tables *1497–1660*, vol. 1, and *1661–1783*, vol. 1.

Column (*c*) gives the number of Baltic and Scandinavian ships eastward bound at the Sound from England, to serve as an indication of the number westward bound to England.

From 1669 is given also the true number westward bound for England, laden. The greater part were free ships of Sweden or the Swedish dominions. These are taken from the Sound Tables *1661–1783*, vol. 2 i. Otherwise the source is as for column (*b*).

Column (*d*) gives the number of Dutch (United Provinces) ships eastward bound at the Sound from England, again as an indication—though obviously a poor one—of the number westward bound to England.

From 1669 is given also the true number westward bound for England. The sources as for column (*b*).

These three columns support remarks in the text about the import trade. They illustrate short-term fluctuations in its volume, and alterations in the proportion of English, Eastland and Dutch shipping. A few ships of Hamburg, Bremen, Scotland and other western places have been ignored.

Columns (*e*) and (*f*) concern the cloth trade from England.

Column (*e*) gives to the nearest thousand the number of pieces of cloth, of all kinds and value, registered at the Sound in all ships from England. Sound Tables *1497–1660*, vol. 2 A, and *1661–1783*, vol. 2 i. The Sound toll registers are less reliable for cargoes than for ships. Also they do not record the cargoes of toll-free ships: many toll-free Swedish ships sailed from England after 1660. But in 1676–9, when there were no Swedish ships, the cloth figures do not deviate from the general trend. Also to be noted is the reorganisation of the system of toll-collection in 1618 which resulted in a stricter registration of cargoes, and raised the figures especially of cheap cloth.

Column (*f*) gives to the nearest hundred cloth recorded at the Sound as 'kleide': i.e. broadcloth, in this case principally short Suffolks. (But towards the end of the century it perhaps also includes some Spanish cloths.) The series is in two parts: up to 1660 it gives figures for cloth in English ships only, following the scheme adopted in Sound Tables *1497–1660*; from 1661 it gives cloth in all ships from England (except free ships), compiled from Sound Tables *1661–1783*. The discontinuity is probably more technical than real. It is also to be noted that 1618 made less difference in the registration of dear cloth than of cheap. Columns (*e*) and (*f*), taken together, to some extent correct each other's deficiencies.

Columns (*g*) and (*h*) concern the Dutch Baltic trade.

Column (*g*) gives the number of Dutch ships passing through the Sound westward, from Sound Tables *1497–1660*, vol. 1, and *1661–1783*, vol. 1. It is intended for comparison with column (*b*) for English ships.

Column (*h*) gives to the nearest thousand the number of pieces of cloth of all kinds in all ships from the Netherlands, from Sound Tables *1497–1660*, vol. 2 A, and *1661–1783*, vol. 2 i. It is intended for comparison with column (*e*) for English cloth. The pronounced rise in 1619 must be to some extent artificial and indicates that before 1618 Dutch cargoes were less accurately registered than English.

A little additional information is given in footnotes.

	(a)	(b)		(c)		(d)		(e) 000's	(f) 000's	(g)	(h) 000's
1591	25	72	—	16	—	8	—	24	6·2	1362	1
1592	18	61	—	20	—	3	—	16	6·0	1556	0
1593	21	82	—	31	—	1	—	16	7·2	1773	2
1594	25	91	—	29	—	2	—	18	8·7	1797	0
1595	38	123[1]	—	59[1]	—	20[1]	—	21	9·9	1851	1
1596	41	73	—	41	—	12	—	20	10·5	1568	1
1597	57	150	—	83	—	25	—	37	21·5	1945	4
1598	52	110	—	52	—	14	—	47	14·7	1678	6
1599	31	74	—	11	—	13	—	47	13·6	1403	7
1600	30	77	—	13	—	4	—	41	12·1	1160	6
1601	35	100	—	18	—	14	—	37	11·2	1299	4
1602	24	70	—	11	—	3	—	30	8·4	1083	1
1603	27	64	—	10	—	7	—	29	8·4	1282	3
1604	27	70	—	9	—	9	—	30	12·4	1065	4
1605	30	70[2]	—	28[2]	—	9[2]	—	28	9·8	1084	4
1606	28	104	—	16	—	11	—	34	10·2	1269	7

[1] 1595. Westward. English ships carrying foreign-owned goods, 0; Eastland ships carrying English-owned goods, 55; Dutch ships carrying English-owned goods, 83.

[2] 1605. Westward. English ships carrying foreign-owned goods, 2; Eastland ships carrying English-owned goods, 24; Dutch ships carrying English-owned goods, 23.

	(a)	(b)		(c)		(d)		(e) 000's	(f) 000's	(g)	(h) 000's
1607	32	105	—	13	—	14	—	26	7·8	1572	10
1608	38	148	—	18	—	24	—	39	10·4	2165	11
1609	53	119	—	13	—	30	—	39	14·2	1406	13
1610	35	87	—	12	—	18	—	28	8·3	1279	10
1611	33	77	—	9	—	30	—	27	8·8	1325	9
1612	37	108	—	11	—	39	—	31	9·1	1719	14
1613	42	75	—	8	—	20	—	27	7·9	1292	7
1614	45	95	—	27	—	61	—	39	9·4	1904	8
1615	35	133[1]	—	13[1]	—	49[1]	—	34	7·6	1654	5
1616	34	135	—	10	—	37	—	27	8·4	1602	6
1617	43	97	—	11	—	28	—	21	6·9	1522	6
1618	45	93	—	10	—	61	—	37	10·3	2146	29
1619	33	78	—	14	—	49	—	43	7·5	1915	35
1620	26	54	—	2	—	12	—	26	4·4	1907	23
1621	25	71	—	3	—	13	—	19	4·2	1761	20
1622	41	112	—	22	—	33	—	34	5·1	1242	30
1623	51	159	—	8	—	19	—	60	11·1	1450	55
1624	38	92	—	4	—	15	—	57	10·4	1217	53
1625	43	81[2]	—	11[2]	—	8[2]	—	47	7·5	849	32
1626	48	61	—	13	—	9	—	34	5·6	987	29
1627	33	46	—	6	—	5	—	12	3·4	965	21
1628	26	39	—	11	—	6	—	19	3·3	678	20
1629	32	51	—	10	—	10	—	9	3·0	882	17
1630	42	46	—	12	—	10	—	24	7·0	728	34
1631	65	105[3]	—	14	—	4	—	17	6·9	1108	37
1632	41	—	—	—	—	—	—	—	—	—	—
1633	47	115	—	21	—	3	—	27	13·3	1035	34
1634	44	—	—	—	—	—	—	—	—	—	—
1635	42	117[4]	—	25[4]	—	3[4]	—	33	6·0	1211	35
1636	45	142	—	47	—	1	—	55	5·9	1055	71
1637	43	145	—	53	—	3	—	45	5·8	916	43
1638	48	132	—	66	—	1	—	31	4·7	978	38
1639	39	106	—	46	—	0	—	35	7·3	935	35
1640	35	157	—	57	—	1	—	28	9·1	897	26
1641	44	170	—	72	—	1	—	33	7·9	1118	45
1642	36	145	—	53	—	0	—	42	8·1	1015	40
1643	35	52	—	19	—	0	—	8	2·3	1157	48
1644	34	24	—	15	—	0	—	5	1·2	1031	42
1645	35	62	—	31	—	1	—	22	7·3	—	—
1646	35	89[5]	—	28[5]	—	0[5]	—	24	6·8	1039	44
1647	52	130	—	53	—	0	—	20	5·4	1045	43

[1] 1615. Westward. English ships carrying foreign-owned goods, 0; Eastland ships carrying English-owned goods, 14; Dutch ships carrying English-owned goods, 88.

[2] 1625. Westward. English ships carrying foreign-owned goods, 2; Eastland ships carrying English-owned goods, 6; Dutch ships carrying English-owned goods, 3.

[3] 1631. Including 25 'in ballast'.

[4] 1635. Westward. English ships carrying foreign-owned goods, 4; Eastland ships carrying English-owned goods, 24; Dutch ships carrying English-owned goods, 0.

[5] 1646. Westward. English ships carrying foreign-owned goods, 1; Eastland ships carrying English-owned goods, 17; Dutch ships carrying English-owned goods, 3.

	(a)	(b)		(c)		(d)		(e) 000's	(f) 000's	(g)	(h) 000's
1648	63	93	—	63	—	4	—	20	4·3	1126	34
1649	68	64	—	86	—	19	—	15	1·9	1542	33
1650	66	46	—	42	—	32	—	18	4·5	1527	?
1651	55	22	—	28	—	22	—	11	3·8	1243	?
1652	49	26	—	29	—	3	—	15	3·8	848	?
1653	34	0	—	23	—	3	—	4	0	622	?
1654	25	69[1]	—	44	—	4	—	26	5·2	970	35
1655	22	53[2]	—	44[2]	—	2[2]	—	11	2·5	997	13
1656	33	37	—	40	—	2	—	8	2·0	821	11
1657	37	34	—	40	—	16	—	12	0·9	653	22
1658	47	—	—	—	—	—	—	—	—	—	—
1659	58	—	—	—	—	—	—	—	—	—	—
1660	52	—	—	—	—	—	—	—	—	—	—
1661	52	92[3]	—	11	—	4	—	19	3·0	614	24
1662	71	90	—	31	—	3	—	22	4·5	704	23
1663	46	89[4]	—	18[4]	—	0[4]	—	23	4·2	745	25
1664	47	104	—	39	—	0	—	18	2·2	670	14
1665	39	16	—	22	—	0	—	4	0·2	165	1
1666	36	4	—	35	—	1	—	3	0·2	438	7
1667	28	5	—	36	—	0	—	9	1·9	505	19
1668	31	72	—	42	—	2	—	18	3·1	974	28
1669	38	95	1	55	83	1	1	21	3·5	996	33
1670	33	102	1	75	102	1	7	13	0·9	904	24
1671	36	104	1	48	69	1	1	11	1·4	816	21
1672	34	10	1	53	88	0	0	5	1·1	195	2
1673	36	5	0	72	129	0	1	2	0·5	256	3
1674	55	116	6	72	116	0	0	16	1·8	696	14
1675	52	356	32	19	26	0	2	16	2·0	432	17
1676	36	403	46	7	13	0	0	18	1·8	445	32
1677	31	358	24	10	14	0	0	24	2·1	600	34
1678	47	311	9	2	7	0	0	25	1·9	619	31
1679	53	308	22	4	6	5	1	24	1·6	864	39
1680	39	227	9	9	12	0	2	22	1·8	884	33
1681	40	279	12	26	40	0	1	24	1·5	962	32
1682	36	284	6	38	57	1	2	21	1·7	988	28
1683	35	337	6	25	28	0	0	20	2·1	1102	35
1684	37	250	8	23	32	1	1	22	3·0	1080	37
1685	46	274	8	25	56	0	1	22	2·7	998	49
1686	28	266	1	50	71	0	2	20	1·9	989	41
1687	32	267	4	60	91	0	2	23	2·0	1009	60
1688	27	258	2	44	68	0	0	22	2·5	1012	63
1689	27	156	1	35	48	0	1	20	1·6	748	42
1690	30	80	3	64	124	0	1	15	0·7	567	35
1691	29	109	0	84	142	0	1	13	1·9	430	13
1692	38	106	1	74	115	0	0	21	1·7	517	7
1693	50	100	3	76	124	8	1	6	1·8	714	24

[1] 1654. Including 12 'in ballast'.
[2] 1655. Westward. English ships carrying foreign-owned goods, 10; Eastland ships carrying English-owned goods, 3; Dutch ships carrying English-owned goods, 0.
[3] 1661. Including 10 'in ballast'.
[4] 1663. Including 9 'in ballast'.

	(a)	(b)		(c)		(d)		(e) 000's	(f) 000's	(g)	(h) 000's
1694	63	99	5	50	115	0	1	18	2·2	547	28
1695	37	86	0	47	98	1	1	28	4·4	562	27
1696	50	94	0	60	137	4	1	13	2·5	336	15
1697	51	58	0	67	65	5	1	11	1·1	373	15
1698	62	171	2	70	96	4	3	21	2·1	758	39
1699	57	236	2	57	84	2	12	25	2·3	861	40
1700	45	272	2	10	25	2	2	24	2·1	615	32

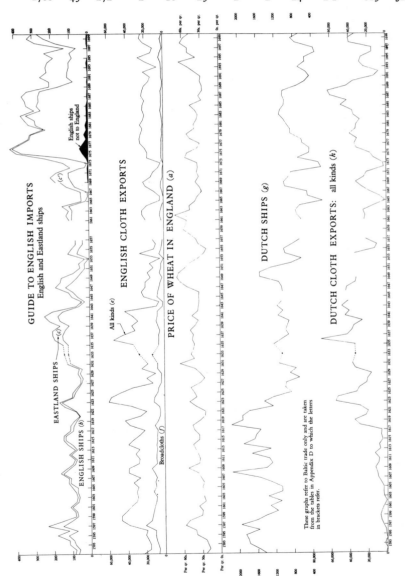

Index